SIX SIGMA
for LEADERSHIP

Seven Principles of Problem-Solving Technology[SM]
To Achieve Significant Financial Results

Greg Brue

Creative Designs, Inc.
Albuquerque, New Mexico

Six Sigma for Leadership

Seven Principles of Problem-Solving Technology^{SM}
To Achieve Significant Financial Results

Exec. Editor: Jonathan Morningstar
Assoc. Editors   Maurissa Morningstar
                 Lynn Grasberg
                 Robert L. Vauthier
                 Max Gordon

The terms Champion, Master Black Belt, Black Belt, and Green Belt are service marks of Six Sigma Academy and used with permission as a licensee of Six Sigma Academy. Seven Principles of Problem-Solving Technology is a service mark of Six Sigma Consultants, Inc.

Library of Congress Catalogue Card Number 00-132352

ISBN 1-880047-80-2

Printed in the United States of America

Dedicated

To my wife, Kelly, who has been by my side through the Six Sigma journey and has experienced my challenges and success.

Acknowledgment

To Mikel J. Harry, CEO of Six Sigma Academy and Richard Schroeder, President of Six Sigma Academy for introducing me to Six Sigma and for initiating the domino effect in the business community. Thank you for your continued support.

Special Thanks

To all of the Companies, Champions, Black Belts, Master Black Belts, Green Belts, and their teams for doing the real work of Six Sigma and achieving incredible bottom line results.

About the Author

Greg Brue, Senior Master Black Belt and CEO of Six Sigma Consultants, has been at work in corporate America implementing Six Sigma since 1994. He worked directly for executives at AT&T Bell Labs, Compaq Computer, and Dell Computer, focusing on key business issues and problems. Greg was Co-President, CEO, and one of the original founders of Six Sigma International. He works with Six Sigma Academy (SSA) and Mikel Harry, the pioneer of Six Sigma, and is a licensee of the Academy.

Greg Brue

Greg is responsible for ensuring the success of Six Sigma implementation in the corporate world by maintaining direct contact with many Black Belts, Master Black Belts, Champions, and senior managers during the Six Sigma implementation process. He and his team provide on-site support and training for company's implementing Six Sigma worldwide. Greg has successfully applied the Six Sigma methodology to over 1,000 business and manufacturing processes. Greg developed the **Seven Principles of Problem-Solving Technology**[sm] from years of in-the-trenches experience as a way to easily communicate the vision of Six Sigma.

Greg spends the majority of his time training Corporate Champions and mentoring CEO's, senior level executives and directors of corporations. He is a guest speaker for major business events and quality conferences, and conducts Six Sigma seminars, and Executive Boot Camps on a monthly basis. He has helped change the mindset and the infrastructure of some of today's corporations to focus on achieving Six Sigma quality for financial results. He and Six Sigma Consultants (www.dosixsigma.com) offer the corporate world Vision, Velocity and Quantum Gains as an experienced Six Sigma partner.

Author's Personal Message

I have been in the trenches called Implementing Six Sigma within major corporations since 1994. I offer this book to share the technology of Six Sigma as a way to shift a company's culture from complacency to one of incredible accomplishments.

This book is designed for business leaders who want to know the data and reality about Six Sigma and who are ready for major breakthroughs to improve their company's bottom line profits. This book will teach you how Six Sigma identifies and eliminates waste in all your business processes. Waste, once identified and eliminated, becomes your investment currency for growth.

The Six Sigma methodology was developed, tested and proven at Motorola in the early 1980s. After the methods became widely recognized and accepted as tools for success at Motorola, AlliedSignal embraced Six Sigma and the dominos started to fall. General Electric was the next company to adopt Six Sigma.

As Jack Welch, CEO of General Electric tells it in the recent book, *The GE Way Fieldbook*, only one person hated quality programs more than he did – Larry Bossidy, CEO of AlliedSignal. Larry called Jack one day and said "I've been to Motorola. I've got to eat crow. It's fabulous what their quality program is doing. You've got to take a look at it." Jack did, and GE bought into the program. I worked with both AlliedSignal and GE and participated in that domino effect, and have continued on the Six Sigma journey with other corporations.

I have written this book to share my experience from the beginning of the wave of Six Sigma building through the next several years. This book presents not only the facts about Six Sigma, but also a brief history of what it means to Do Six Sigma for companies who are dedicated to enhanced growth and increased profits. I will show you their decisions, their experiences, and how Six Sigma has improved their bottom line profits. In addition, I have translated those experiences into the **Seven Principles of Problem-Solving Technology.** The principles are the key drivers within each organization that must be in place for Six Sigma to be successful.

I have seen it all when it comes to the mistakes and errors of implementing Six Sigma. I am not a statistician. I am a practitioner with a lot of war stories and real-life examples of how-to and how-NOT-to deploy this method. I am frustrated by some of the so called implementers, whom I have never met during this war against wasteful variation. These self-proclaimed implementers have really only been spectators in this sport. These people are selling Six Sigma short, creating a bad reputation for a method which, when implemented with integrity and discipline, will profoundly impact every aspect of a company, specifically financial results and growth.

The beauty of business is simple — we have no "right" to exist. The world can go on without us. If business were easy we would all be multi-millionaires. Therefore, the overriding purpose of this book is to confront and engage you as a leader. Confront you with the complacency we all can fall prey to and engage you in the "buzz" of achievement.

Six Sigma is the game plan. All game plans keep score and have clear, measurable goals. Six Sigma ups the ante and delivers.

Good Luck!

Greg Brue
Senior Master Black Belt,
Founder and CEO, Six Sigma Consultants

A Licensee of Six Sigma Academy

Foreword by
Mikel J. Harry, Ph.D.

CEO, Six Sigma Academy

Over the last decade, it has been my distinct privilege to serve as Greg Brue's Six Sigma mentor. I have astutely watched him extend and perfect his base of knowledge during the 90s, as evidenced by the increasing depth and scope of his many Black Belt projects. Owing to this solid technical foundation, others began to seek his advice and leadership.

During the early 90s, Greg focused his pursuit of Six Sigma by leveraging his leadership skills on the issues surrounding implementation and deployment during his tenure at the Six Sigma Academy. Moving into the 21st century, Greg has rightfully positioned himself as a true global leader on the playing field of Six Sigma. Today, he is forging new and original ideas from the solid ore mined from his past, as evidenced by this book.

Mikel J. Harry, Ph.D.
Founder and CEO
Six Sigma Academy

Preface

It was 1994 when I first engaged in the implementation of Six Sigma. AlliedSignal was the first large-scale deployment, and since then I have been privileged to see the transformation of some of the largest corporations in the world, including General Electric, Siebe, Crane, Navistar, Bombardier, Nokia, GenCorp and others. The Six Sigma methodology allowed them to lower costs, increase production, produce efficient customer service, achieve outstanding financial results and return on investment, and experience major growth.

This book, and the **Seven Principles of Problem-Solving Technology**^{SM} it presents, will serve as a guide for corporate leaders who are willing to step forward to strive for profound company growth and extraordinary customer service. The purpose of this book is to stimulate, train, and focus you on the first needed steps for your relentless Six Sigma journey.

The philosophy of Six Sigma is that there is a measurable and direct relationship between product defects and customer dissatisfaction. Implementing Six Sigma provides the means to achieve product and service excellence. At the level of Six Sigma, products and services are designed to be nearly perfect. Most companies today are at Four Sigma, a level which tolerates 6,210 defects per million opportunities. Companies operating at Six Sigma create an almost defect-free environment, allowing for only 3.4 defects per million opportunities.

Most companies are aware that defects which reach the customer are a significant problem. What businesses often do not recognize is that defects that are corrected prior to shipment still represent unnecessary expense in lost time and materials. In working with many excellent companies, I and other Six Sigma practitioners have compiled data which demonstrates that the cost of defects at the Four Sigma level represents as much as 25 percent of total sales.

Six Sigma's beginnings at Motorola in the 1980s is grounded in this discovery. In 1983, Motorola engineer Bill Smith presented a paper concluding that if a product were found defective and corrected during the production process, other defects were bound to be missed and found later by the customer during the early use of the product. However, if the product were assembled error free, the product rarely failed during early use by the consumer.

Motorola also found that best-in-class manufacturers were making products that required no repair or rework during the manufacturing process. Six Sigma naturally began in the electronics industry because a computer chip contains millions of transistors, so the defect requirement has to be very low for the chip to operate at all. For a truck or car manufacturer, you can hammer a part into place and the vehicle will still run, even with a defect or two.

While working at Motorola, Mikel J. Harry, Ph.D., focused on quality issues, and was a conceptual originator of the Six Sigma methodology. After Motorola attained a Five Sigma level, Dr. Harry founded the Six Sigma Research Institute and continued to work on the tools needed for this advancing application for corporate America. He also worked with other companies that are now top in their fields. Dr. Harry now heads the Six Sigma Academy (SSA), which deploys Six Sigma for Fortune 100 companies. I was part of Dr. Harry's original SSA team, and I am a licensee of the Academy.

This journey is about human "assets" being armed with problem-solving techniques for huge cash results. This book is designed to help you, as a business leader, start implementing a rock-solid Six Sigma strategy in your company, removing confusion by focusing on the *Seven Principles of Problem-Solving Technology.*

This book is for leaders of today and tomorrow. Human beings *want* compelling, focused, and visionary leaders. Six Sigma provides a way to lead your company to greater excellence using the refined methodology that Dr. Harry developed. This methodology works *unfailingly*!

The methodology and philosophy needed to achieve Six Sigma results are all in this book and the accompanying CD for those who are willing to read and digest the information. If you want a "How To Cookbook," this isn't it. "Cookbooks" don't work — they presume that the same resources are available to every company, that the historical experience is the same between companies. Six Sigma is a refined methodology. It will ask the tough questions that require hard data about your processes in order to answer them. The answers provide focus for your efforts to achieve performance excellence.

The methods you have used to attack problems in the past is input data. How you lead your people is input data. These differ from company to company. A start-up company is quite different from one that has been radically down-sized. An Asian company is vastly different from a U.S. company or a Swedish company. These differences in corporate culture exist, and the methodology of Six Sigma is flexible and robust enough to produce results in any company or culture. Unless, of course, there are no waste or defects in your world!

At the end of this book, I will not only wish you good luck, but will also encourage you on how to stay focused on this highly intensive, results-driven goal.

If you are not prepared to stay focused on this goal for 3 to 5 years, please do not waste your time, focus, or money on this book. Do yourself a favor and put this book back on the shelf and walk away.

Implementing the **Seven Principles of Problem-Solving Technology** in a Six Sigma-focused organization will create an environment for change, initiate a new quality-oriented awareness, a culture shift, and generate an infrastructure that can sustain the quality focus. The key questions for business leaders of today and tomorrow to answer are:

What do you really want to accomplish?

What do you want your legacy to be, growth or blame?

I welcome you to this relentless, constant journey.

Greg Brue

"In getting to 5.4 Sigma capability, we have reduced our in-process defect level by 50 times during the five-year period. We have improved the reliability of the products we ship to customers. And, we have saved a significant amount of the cost of manufacturing; $700 million during 1991 and $2.3 billion since the beginning of our Six Sigma thrust."

George Fisher
Former CEO
Motorola

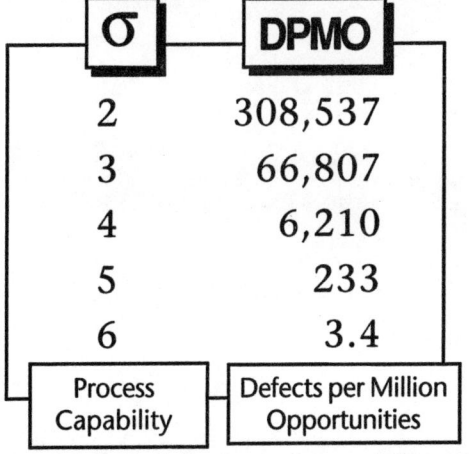

FIGURE 1
Six Sigma as a Goal

σ	DPMO
2	308,537
3	66,807
4	6,210
5	233
6	3.4
Process Capability	Defects per Million Opportunities

Sigma is a statistical measurement that reflects process capability. The sigma scale of measurement is perfectly correlated to such characteristics as defects-per-unit, parts-per-million defective, and the probability of a failure or error.

Adapted from "The Vision of Six Sigma" by Mikel Harry, Ph.D.
©1994 Sigma Publishing Co

Table of Contents

List of Figures

List of Figures

List of Figures

Applying the
Seven Principles of
Problem-Solving Technology^{SM}
will significantly improve your
company's financial results.

1) Compelling Leaders
The Vision to Do Six Sigma

2) Embracing Customers
Delivering and Anticipating
What the Customer Wants

3) Discovering the "$tealth" Factory
The Real Cost of Doing It Wrong

4) Exposing the "Vital Few"
$$Y = f(x_1...x_n)$$

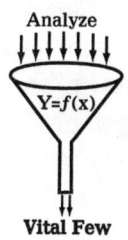

5) Empowering People
The "Best of the Best"

6) Harnessing the Magic of Data
The Method (MA¢IC) Without
the "G" for Guesswork

7) Relentless, Constant Journey
"The Will"

6σ

Six Sigma Defined

The term Six Sigma defines an optimum measurement of quality: 3.4 defects per million opportunities. The Greek letter σ (SIGMA) is a mathematical term that simply represents a measure of variation, the distribution or spread around the mean or average of any process or procedure in manufacturing, engineering, services or transactions. The sigma value, or standard deviation, indicates how well any process is performing. The higher the value, the fewer defects per million opportunities.

Six Sigma is the disciplined application of statistical problem-solving tools that show you where wasteful costs are and points you toward the precise steps for improvement. These tools apply a refined methodology of measurement and discovery to gain a comprehensive understanding of performance and key variables affecting the quality of a company's products and services. A level of Six Sigma represents the peak of quality – the virtual elimination of defects from every product and process within an organization. As sigma increases, customer satisfaction goes up while at the same time cycle time goes down and costs plummet.

Introduction

The industrial revolution profoundly affected the way the world produced goods. It was a system of management and production that was based on *quantity*, requiring brawn and obedience from workers. Most of the time, management could see the whole process — all the parts — and dictated how things were done.

Today companies are extremely complex. Only a few people can see the whole process and not everything takes place in one location. *Quality* of products is now more important than *quantity* — a paradigm shift brought about by W. Edwards Deming in Japan in the 1950s and adopted by US companies in the 1980s.

Moving from the *quantity* focus of mass production to the *quality* focus of W. Edwards Deming's Total Quality Management (TQM) is the most important change in production since the industrial revolution. Deming's 14 Points of Total Quality Management are the foundation for further efforts to improve quality, just like the Six Sigma *Seven Principles of Problem-Solving Technology* which are presented in this book. Deming's points (see Appendix A) promoted the idea that everything is a process and continuous improvement could lead to higher quality and lower cost, as proven by Japanese industry after World War II — Deming's most famous "client."

If Deming was known as the "Father of Total Quality Management," Dr. Mikel Harry has led the "next generation" in perfecting the application of statistical tools to the quality improvement process. Dr. Harry's introduction of Six Sigma quality processes is beginning to revolutionize the business world again.

The aim of the Deming system is to deliver improved products and services at reduced cost. However, Six Sigma is more focused, using business metrics to identify and measure the *"Vital Few"* processes that contribute the most to product and service costs and quality. Six Sigma focuses your efforts on finding "the money." It doesn't focus on quality just for quality's sake. Six Sigma saves time and delivers measurable financial results quickly. It finally links quality to cost, which makes Six Sigma quality a profit generator.

Why should you take a serious look at Six Sigma as a quality improvement program? I'll let the following people answer that important question.

"In terms of a system that can be deployed across all elements of our business, we found no other system that could accomplish what Six Sigma can. The Six Sigma System extends well beyond traditional quality systems in the areas of comprehensive resource training, methodology tools for execution, focus on financial improvement versus the traditional quality metrics, and the ability to be deployed across all business functions."

Don G. Colton
Executive Vice President, Corporate Quality - Seagate
The Vision of Six Sigma, Winter 1999

"Six Sigma programs simultaneously benefit both the profitability of a company and its sales growth by enabling it to take market share as a preferred supplier in its industry. The benefits of Six Sigma are multifaceted. Six Sigma drives top-line growth, increases operating margins, expands cash flow, reduces working capital requirements and capital spending needs, frees up additional production capacity and enhances growth when the economy is not doing well, by improving a company's prospects of becoming a customer's preferred supplier."

Prudential Securities

The beauty of business is that you have no "right" to exist — you don't *have* to exist. Your company is either a jumble of assets or a revenue-producing, growing company.

Six Sigma is deliberately and profoundly affecting the way we *all* do business. The data shows that the **Seven Principles of Problem-Solving Technology** always bring a company to the heights of perfection, regardless of the size or scope of the business. Six Sigma and the **Seven Principles of Problem-Solving Technology** offers a new perspective to address perfecting company performance.

Inconsistent processes cost you money. Six Sigma allows for correction and control of variation at the earliest possible point. By attacking variation during the design phase of products and processes, a company better ensures that the downstream processes are set-up for success.

The $64 million dollar question is: **Why isn't YOUR company doing Six Sigma?** The question requires an answer grounded in data about your company's performance. Every CEO should be required by their stockholders to create a business case for why they are NOT doing Six Sigma. If you can answer with hard data that you are already getting Six Sigma results in defects per unit, rolled throughput yield, cost of poor quality, etc., then you don't need it. You don't have to "DO SIX SIGMA" to achieve Six Sigma results. At Honda and Toyota they don't have Black Belts and Champions, but they're achieving Six Sigma outcomes. Six Sigma is a defined methodology which you can buy, like a get-fit program, but you have to follow it — DO IT — to get results. Your Six Sigma partner is just a catalyst to achieve Six Sigma performance.

Since few companies can show that they already achieve Six Sigma results, the next question is: **What's stopping you?** Some companies won't do Six Sigma, and that's OK. If a company doesn't want to do Six Sigma, then they may eventually become just the summation of cents on the dollar for tooling, real estate, intellectual property, etc. This becomes even more of a reality if their competition is doing Six Sigma. They'll eventually become a wonderful "BUY" opportunity for a turnaround expert to come in and ferret out the waste and defects that erode their profits. Even if you do go out of business, your customer won't care if you cease to exist — whatever product or service you provide will quickly be replaced in the marketplace.

FIGURE 1

3σ Capability	Historical Standard
4σ Capability	Current Standard
6σ Capability	New Standard

Sigma	Area	Spelling	Money	Time
3σ	Floor space of a small hardware store	1.5 misspelled words per page in a book	$2.7 million indebtedness per $1 Billion in assets	3 1/2 months per century
4σ	Floor space of a typical living room	1 misspelled word per 30 pages in a book	$63,000 indebtedness per $1 Billion in assets	2 1/2 days per century
5σ	Size of the bottom of your telephone	1 misspelled word in a set of encyclopedias	$570 indebtedness per $1 Billion in assets	30 minutes per century
6σ	Size of a typical diamond	1 misspelled word in all the books in a library	$2 indebtedness per $1 Billion in assets	6 seconds per century

What is the difference between Three and Six Sigma? This table shows the magnitude of change between the historical, current, and new standards for quality.

Adapted from: The Vision of Six Sigma: A Roadmap for Breakthrough, Mikel J. Harry, © 1994 Sigma Publishing Co.

THE GE EXPERIENCE:

" A typical process at GE generates about 35,000 defects per million, which sounds like a lot, and is a lot, but it is consistent with the defect levels of most successful companies. That number of defects per million is referred to in the very precise jargon of statistics as about three and one-half sigma. For those of you who flew to Charlottesville, you are sitting here in your seats today because the airlines' record in getting passengers safely from one place to another is even better than six sigma, with less than one-half failure per million. If you think about airlines, they run two operations. They get you from point A to point B at from Seven to Eight Sigma. Your bags get there at Three Sigma."

Jack Welch, CEO, General Electric
1996 Annual Meeting
Letter to Shareholders

Mistakes are expensive! Product defects, inaccurate billing, surplus materials, inefficient production processes and procedures all translate into millions of dollars not going to the bottom line. The name Six Sigma defines an optimum measurement of quality: 3.4 defects per 1,000,000 opportunities (see Figure 1). However, to attain this high quality requires immense commitment from every person involved in a company, starting with the highest level of management.

It is estimated that companies operating at about Four Sigma (today's U.S. average) lose up to 25 percent of their total revenue due to defects. This means if you are a *BILLION DOLLAR BUSINESS*, you are wasting **$250 MILLION** in revenue due to defects. On top of that, what does it cost you to have some of your brightest minds dedicated to just "clean up" projects or fire fighting? Do you measure it?

Most companies today operate at Three to Four Sigma. That makes them only as good as their competition. These companies often are firmly set in their ways and refuse to believe that a higher quality product would actually cost less to produce. This inflexible "mindset" is the flaw of the benchmarking scenario. What I mean by that is, yes, I benchmark and that tells me that I have "the best of the best" product. But it may not be the right "best of the best" to go after. You have to be careful about what you are "best" at doing. You could be first in a pig race!

Don't just be happy because your competitor is doing this and you're doing that. You want to annihilate your competitor and increase the gap between you and your competition. General Electric did not **need** Six Sigma, what they wanted to do was **increase the gap** between them and any nearby competitor. That was their strategy and they're still executing it.

FIGURE 2

Notice the Rate Of Change

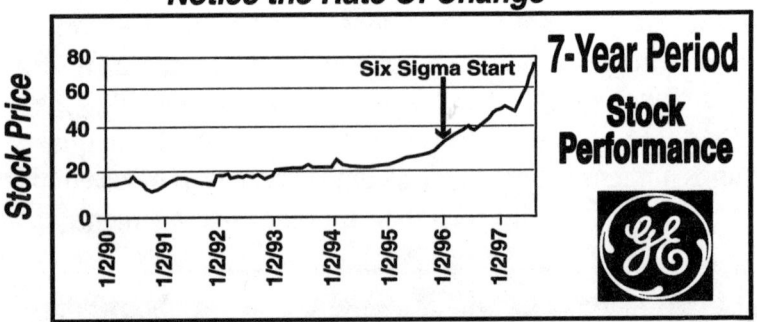

GE stock price performance

The Difference Between a Six Sigma and a Four Sigma Company

History has shown that there are several significant differences in philosophy, policies and procedures, actions, behaviors, and beliefs between companies that are at Four Sigma capability and those that are at Six Sigma.

The biggest single difference between a true Six Sigma company and those companies that are stuck permanently at Four Sigma is the mindset. The underachieving companies are unconcerned, unaware, arrogant, and not able to internalize the idea that they must make massive changes in process quality if they are to achieve and keep an advantage over their competition.

Complacent companies have many things in common:

- As many as one out of four customers is dissatisfied with the company's products or services, and they share their dissatisfaction with others. (Studies suggest only 1 out of 20 customers actually complains to the company.)

- They are experiencing increased competition.

- Their business is expanding and their profits are increasing.

- They have experienced a downturn in the sales price of their product.

- They have a program in place for quality assurance.

- The cost of repairing or reworking defective products before they reach the customer may account for 10 to 25 percent of sales dollars.

- They do not know that identifiable excellent competitors have comparable processes that operate at "zero-defects."

- They are using many more suppliers than necessary.

- They believe their employees are "cost centers," not revenue centers.

- They do not believe that Six Sigma as a goal is possible or affordable.

FIGURE 3
ATTITUDES DIFFER!

Average Company	Six Sigma Company
Status quo maintained	"There's a better way"
"We've always done it this way"	Work smarter, not harder
"It's good enough" Work-arounds are common	Design for Six Sigma quality
No one listens to the clerical or line worker	The "bottom of the pyramid" holds the knowledge
People = Cost	People = Assets
Training = Cost	Training = Assets
"If I save $, my budget will be cut."	Saving $ is rewarded

Many companies - and managers - take refuge in
one or more of the following beliefs:
To err is human.
Excessive quality costs too much, takes too long.
Just beating last year's numbers is good enough.
Soft errors (like paperwork) are more excusable.
We are still better than our competitors.
Fire fighting our way out of a quality emergency
in the nick of time is a badge of honor;
it was even fun.

Robert Galvin, "The Idea of Ideas"
Motorola University Press, 1991

FIGURE 4

THE SIX SIGMA APPROACH

Example of a company with $1 Billion in sales
which implements Six Sigma and
increases bottom line profits
from 3 percent to 12.5 percent

Assumptions:

- Profit margin is between 1 percent and 3 percent, or *$10 to 30 million.*
- The Cost of Poor Quality (COPQ) is 25 percent of total sales, or *$250 million.*

This waste is their investment currency for growth.

- If COPQ is decreased by 50 percent to 12.5 percent —

$125 million is added to the bottom line profit!

OR

$125 million is available to invest for growth.

Calculate Your Potential Bottom Line Increase.

Your Total Sales _____ x

_____ percent (current margin) = _____

(your current profit margin)

Total Sales x 25 percent = _____

(your estimated COPQ)

This is your potential investment currency for growth.

Total COPQ x .25 = _____ savings

x .50 = _____ savings

x .75 = _____ savings

*How much investment currency or
profit do you want? What do you think you can
accomplish in a year?*

THE SIX SIGMA APPROACH IS DIFFERENT

No matter what type of business, industry or activity your company is engaged in, regardless of the size of your organization, decision-making is always part of the routine. Many decisions are made based on intuition or experience. ***The Six Sigma approach is different.***

Six Sigma teaches you to ***quantify*** using statistical tools to define the issues being decided upon. Once the issues are quantified, statistics can be applied to provide probabilities of success and failure. Mistakes such as product defects, incorrect billing, wasted materials, and inefficient production processes cost your company valuable time and money. These mistakes translate into millions or billions of dollars lost.

You will hear things like "I think," "I feel," or "I believe." I don't really care about those statements. I care about the facts. I want to talk about the facts. As Sgt. Joe Friday said on the TV show Dragnet, "Just the facts, ma'am."

You can't get facts without measurement – I can teach you HOW and WHAT to measure, so you can analyze it and uncover problems, improve the process and finally control variation.

The Seven Principles of Problem-Solving Technology facilitate positive, dramatic changes in the way your employees think and perform on the job. Employees can become Six Sigma "Black Belts" – experts leading projects, solving problems, preventing defects long before they occur, and improving quality throughout your organization. Six Sigma is about the transformation of the human beings that go through the process – people actually grow, and they don't look at anything the same way again. Transformed people then begin to transform the company. Six Sigma programs leverage the most under-utilized assets in your company – your people and their knowledge.

However, this transformation can only happen with the **unqualified support** from the leaders of your company. **Six Sigma connects the vision of the leader with the actions of the people on the floor.**

Inherent in the application of the **Seven Principles of Problem-Solving Technology** are the following three elements:

Vision = 100 percent support from leadership;

Velocity = 20-year-old problems can be solved in six months;

Quantum Gains = quality and cost savings.

Velocity means you are moving quickly — it may be scary to move so quickly but you will get results. If you want to move slowly, you can. But it's like buying a Jaguar and never shifting out of second gear — why would you? By applying the techniques presented in this book you are starting the Six Sigma journey.

Implementing Six Sigma will:

- **Demand** that you strive (with measurable results) to reach your company's goal of being the highest-quality provider of products and services in your industry.

- **Enable** your company to become the lowest-cost provider of products and services in your industry.

- **Teach** your management team the meaning of data-driven decision-making.

- **Integrate** a new business metric that will phenomenally increase customer satisfaction levels.

- **Reduce** cycle time per unit of work.

- **Compel** you as a leader and empower your management team to become Champions and Black Belts for extraordinary customer service and quality.

[handwritten note: Needs to be a part of corporate mission statement]

Six Sigma implementation success stories abound as industry searches for new ways to increase profitability. Successful companies include:

Motorola (1987)
Texas Instruments (1988)
Asea Brown Boveri (1993)
AlliedSignal (1994)
General Electric (1995)
GenCorp (1995)
Siebe, PLC (1996)
Navistar (1996)
Nokia (1996)
Polaroid (1996)
Lockheed Martin (1996)
Bombardier (1996)
Crane Co. (1996)
DuPont (1997)
Libbey-Owens-Ford (1997)
Sony (1998)

These companies are beginning to directly tie quality to their bottom line. Even companies adverse to management fads are embracing Six Sigma, believing that it is a method of substance that will increase market share, decrease costs, and grow profit margins. We are no longer pioneers, we have the opportunity to learn from what others have done. *Your objective is to be the next Six Sigma company on this list.*

FIGURE 6

Notice the Rate Of Change

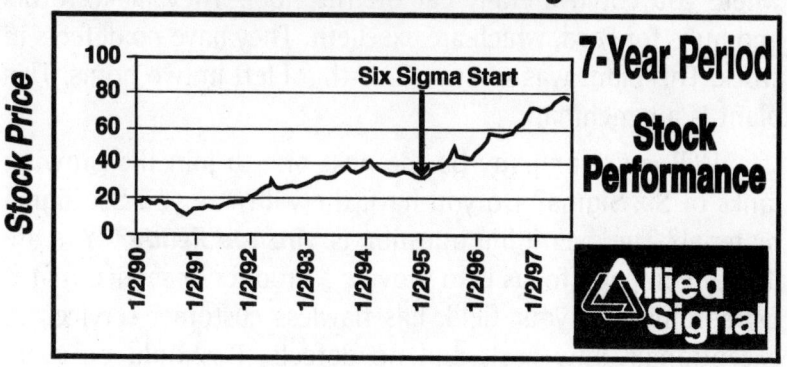

AlliedSignal stock price performance

Who is in charge of the Quality Profit Center for your company? Six Sigma should be part of the "genetic code" of a company once it is started. It should be part of the total makeup. There is a company in Nevada, Missouri that had a safety record of over 900 days without any safety violations. The company makes 20,000 filters per week along with other products. Even though their number of defects were small, they still relentlessly pursued perfection. This company is beautifully run and it is obvious that the genetic code of this company is Six Sigma. They are naturally doing an excellent job.

> *"Six Sigma is quickly becoming a part of the genetic code of our future leadership. Six Sigma training is now an ironclad prerequisite for promotion to any professional or managerial position in the Company — and a requirement for any award of stock options."*
>
> Jack Welch
> CEO and COB
> General Electric

In reality I have only seen three plants that are truly outstanding. I went to an AlliedSignal plant in Frankfurt, Ohio where you could literally eat off the floor. They make rotors and hubs for Ford, which are excellent. They have no defects in stock. This plant was so organized that I left in two hours. This plant is a benchmark.

Will your company be the next one to join the growing ranks of Six Sigma? Do you have the will? Are you Six Sigma material? The overriding question is: **Are You Ready?** You are if your company focus is to provide a product or service that is extraordinary in your field, has flawless customer service, an exceptionally low cost, and no defects. It should be every business leader's goal to lead his or her company into the next millennium with a Six Sigma quality mindset.

Think about it:
The highest-quality provider of goods and services is the lowest-cost provider of goods and services!

"Quality for the sake of quality is no good. TQM was a great thing if you had 30 years to realize the gains from it. Stockholders today are not willing to wait 30 days."
Mikel Harry, Ph.D.
1999 Annual Quality Congress

FREQUENTLY ASKED QUESTIONS:

Why does my company need Six Sigma? What problem does it solve?

Customers today are demanding high-quality products and services for less money. To meet that demand you need to identify areas in all parts of your business that produce waste and defects. Six Sigma teaches you how to find the *vital few* processes that produce the most waste and defects. Waste and defects cost money! The money you save can either add to your overall profitability or allow you to reduce the sales price of your product or service without losing money.

What does it cost to implement?

How much does it cost NOT to do it? Ask yourself, what did our company pay out on average the last five years in warranty costs? What does it cost you to fix what you don't even know is broken until it gets out into the hands of your customer and breaks? Your customer is the final inspection point.

The cost to implement Six Sigma depends on the size of your company and how many Black Belts are needed (typically 10 per 1000 employees). Black Belt training costs from $8,000 to $30,000 per Black Belt (again, depending on the total number trained).

What is the return on investment for Six Sigma? What bottom line financial results can we expect?

You can expect radical net income increases that start to show up shortly after implementation of Six Sigma. Black Belts are trained to focus on high-leverage projects that lead to significant (greater than 50 percent) improvement in the process selected for improvement. Each project saves on average $175,000. Each Black Belt can complete four to six projects per year. Thus you can expect $1 million in bottom line savings per year per Black Belt.

How long does it take to see results?

You can expect to see results immediately. The four-month Black Belt training process requires that the Black Belt applies the techniques to a project that results in significant cost savings. Usually, the initial Black Belt projects more than make up for the cost of training and company-wide Six Sigma implementation.

Who else has done this?

Six Sigma started at Motorola, and it turned their company's performance around in the 1980s. AlliedSignal, General Electric, Asea Brown Boveri, GenCorp, Nokia, Texas Instruments, Sony, Libbey-Owens-Ford, and many others have adopted the Six Sigma methodology in the last decade. Chapter 7 contains case histories that demonstrate the broad applicability of this methodology in design, manufacturing, transaction, and service environments.

Why is this the best method? Is this just a rehash of something we've already done? Why is it any different from other quality programs?

Six Sigma is more focused on linking quality improvement to bottom line cost savings than existing quality initiatives. Six Sigma's benefits are measured in dollars. It is not subjective. It provides absolute, real, quantifiable results. Most quality improvement programs do not deliver documented, tangible increases in shareholder value — Six Sigma does. Six Sigma requires upper management leadership commitment and links quality to growth and profit.

We just completed QS-9000. How does Six Sigma fit in?

Congratulations! QS-9000 is a great place to begin. Now what do you know about your processes in data terms? Every system is creating data every moment — Six Sigma trains your people to capture and interpret the data. QS-9000 describes and documents your processes, resulting in a library of information on how to do the process. Six Sigma asks you to describe those processes in measurement terms.

How does Six Sigma fit into our business?

Six Sigma has been applied to areas of manufacturing, service, delivery, human resources, transactions, administration, and clerical. Any part of your company or business can utilize the Six Sigma methodology to reduce waste and defects.

Will Six Sigma have an impact on shareholder value?

Yes, companies that have implemented Six Sigma have shown an increase in shareholder value. Today's typical company operates at a level of Three to Four Sigma. At that level, the cost of poor quality is about 25 percent of sales revenue. The difference is added to the bottom line profitability of the company. Stock analysts want **predictability** in your financial projections and they love Six Sigma as a tool to achieve predictability. We have presented this information to the major stock analysts so they know about Six Sigma.

The train of Six Sigma is on the tracks and moving fast. Do you want to get on board, or get run over?

FIGURE 7

Notice the Rate Of Change

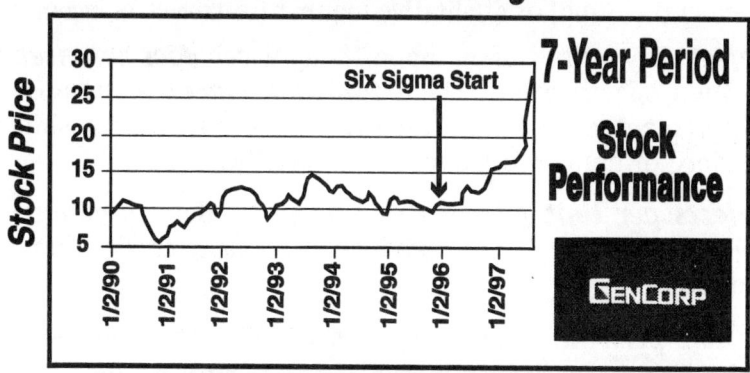

GenCorp stock price performance

Six Sigma Terms Defined

Analysis of Variance (ANOVA) A statistical process that is used to uncover the significant effects in a factorial experiment.

Benchmarking Finding the pinnacle of comprehensive excellence in products, services, processes, procedures, and facilities. Finding out who is the 'best in class' at doing what you want done. Benchmarking requires searching for the best methods, within and without your industry, and adopting or adapting those methods to your particular situation, thus allowing your company to become "the best of the best."

Cost of Poor Quality (COPQ) Also known as the cost of doing it wrong (CODW). Time, material, and resources expended in nonproductive/saleable products and services.

Customer Anyone who receives a product, service or information from an operation or process. The term is frequently used to describe "External" customers — those who purchase the manufactured products or services which are the basis for the existence of the business. However, "Internal" customers are also important. Internal customers receive the intermediate or internal products or services from internal "Suppliers."

Critical to Quality Characteristic (CTQ) A characteristic of a product, service or information which is important to the customer. CTQ's must be measurable in either a "quantitative" manner (i.e. 3 mg) or qualitative manner (i.e. correct or incorrect).

Defect Any *output* of an opportunity which *does not meet* a defined specification; OR a *failure to meet* an imposed requirement on a single quality characteristic or a single instance of nonconformance to the specification.

Defects per Unit (DPU) The number of defects counted, divided by the number of "products" or "characteristics" (units) produced.

Defects per Million Opportunities (DPMO) The number of defects counted, divided by the actual number of opportunities to generate that defect, multiplied by one million.

Design of Experiments (DOE) Methodology for experiments where factor levels are assessed in a fractional factorial experiment or full factorial experiment structure.

Evolutionary Operation (EVOP) An approach for analyzing a situation where process conditions are changed structurally in a manufacturing process in order to determine what changes to make for product improvement.

Expectations and Fulfillment Interaction What the customer wants, needs and expects should determine what actions a company takes to provide products and services. We only add value to a product when we do what our customers need.

F-test A statistical test that uses tabular values from the F-distribution to determine significance.

Failure Mode and Effects Analysis (FMEA) Analytical approach for preventing defects by prioritizing potential problems and their resolution.

Fishbone Chart A cause and effect (C&E) diagram useful in problem-solving where possible causes from various sources are identified as a starting point to begin brainstorming discussions.

Fractional Factorial Experiment A strategy for experimental design that assesses several variables or factors at the same time, where only a fraction of all the possible combinations of factors are tested to identify important factors. More efficient than testing factors one at a time.

Full Factorial Experiment All combinations of factor levels are tested.

Gauge Repeatability and Reproducibility (Gauge R&R) Study A study that evaluates gauges – measuring instruments – to determine if they are capable of giving a precise and repeatable measurement. Gauge repeatability is the variation in measurements considering one part and one operator. Gauge reproducibility is the variation **between** operators measuring one part.

Mean Sample mean is the sum of all responses or measurements divided by the size of the sample. Population mean is the sum of all responses of the population divided by the population size.

Opportunity Any event which generates an output (product, service or information). For a product, opportunity is all the parts on the bill of materials plus all the connection points.

PPM Parts per million.

Pareto Chart A way to display data graphically which quantifies problems from most to least so that the "Vital Few" can be identified. Named after Wufredo Pareto, a European economist.

Pareto Principle The 80/20 rule. 80 percent of the trouble comes from 20 percent of the problems — the basis of the "Vital Few."

Robust Processes Robust processes simply mean that if you do have a glitch or a defect in your process, the customer is not adversely affected so it does not translate into a "cost of poor quality" or a lost customer.

Standard Deviation A mathematical quantity that describes the variability of a response. It is the square root of variance.

Stealth Factory This is the *real* factory — also referred to as the "Hidden Factory." Another way to describe the cost of poor quality, this represents the obvious and less obvious costs of all the defects that exist in a process. Only five to eight percent of COPQ is possibly accounted for. Another 15 to 20 percent is hidden. Most companies identify only one to two percent, but this is not reality.

T-test A statistical test that uses tabular values from the T-distribution to determine whether two population means are different.

Unit A discrete item (lamp, invoice, etc.) which has one or more CTQ factor. "Units" must be considered with regard for the specific CTQ's of concern by a customer and/or for a specific process.

Variation Any deviation from specification limits for a product or process. Defects arise from excess variation and these defects determine customer satisfaction with your product or service.

Xs — INPUT Variables An **independent** material or element, with descriptive characteristic(s), which is either an **object** (going into) or a **parameter** of a process (step) and which has a **significant** effect on the output of the process.

Ys — OUTPUT Variables A **dependent** material or element, with descriptive characteristic(s), which is the **result** of a process (step) which either is, or **significantly affects,** the customer's CTQ.

Y= f (x$_1$-x$_N$) The characteristic of quality in a product you are trying to achieve (Y) is a function of or is controlled by several key process variables, or Xs. The Xs are the "Vital Few". Identify these "key knobs" and control them.

Dorian Shanin (one of the most famous problem-solvers in the world) had an equation which was A = P+R. "A" stands for <u>A</u>ll the variation and is equal to "P" for <u>P</u>art of the variation plus "R" standing for all the <u>R</u>est. We don't want to work on the <u>R</u>est of the variation, which results in no financial benefit.

A Six Sigma Readiness Checklist

If you agree with the following statements and can answer the questions, you may already be on the Six Sigma journey. Here's a worksheet to find out where you are.

1. Customers have critical-to-business expectations.
   - Can you list your customer's top four expectations?

   1._____ 3._____
   2._____ 4._____

2. We are in business to achieve a phenomenal customer satisfaction rate that exceeds critical-to-business expectations.
   - Can you quantify your customer's current level of satisfaction? (Y/N)
   - If yes, on a scale of 1 to 10, what is it ? _____
     How has that changed over the last 5 years? ____ %

3. We strive to produce profitable BOTTOM LINE RE$ULTS. We are in business to make money!!
   - List the last five years of profit your company made.

     Year 1 $_____
     Year 2 $_____
     Year 3 $_____
     Year 4 $_____
     Year 5 $_____

4. We have repetitive processes in our business which create products and services for our customers.
   - List four major repetitive processes in your business.

     Process #1 _____
     Process #2 _____
     Process #3 _____
     Process #4 _____
   - How many times do you do these processes per year? _____

5. In our process the goal is to create knowledge and actions to reduce cycle time, defects, and variations.

- Take process number 1 and 2 above, and list the reduction of cycle time, defects, and variation in those processes.

	Cycle Time	Defects or Yield
Process #1		
Baseline:	_____	_____
Currently:	_____	_____
Process #2		
Baseline:	_____	_____
Currently:	_____	_____

6. We do this by collecting data, stating the problem in statistical terms such as the mean and standard deviation of the process.

- Does your company know the vital statistics of Process #1-4? (Y/N)

7. We validate the data collected through the *Measure* phase of the Six Sigma MAIC Method.

- Is your data validated? Can it be trusted? (Y/N)
- Can you test the data for repeatability and reproducibility by others? (Y/N)
- Is the data accurate and precise? (Y/N)
- If Yes, then what are the results of the test?
  _____ percent R&R (repeatable and reproducible)

8. We then look for the vital few factors that are the root of the problem by *Analyzing* the data to uncover the Vital Few factors that determine quality.

- For Process #1 what are the Vital Few?
  Factor #1: _____
  Factor #2: _____
  Factor #3: _____

9. This moves us into the *Improvement* phase to create a predictable equation or relationship between the process variables (Vital Few) and output of product with a low defect level.

- Can you calculate a result equation for process #1? What is $Y = f(x)$? _____

10. Finally, we *Control* and sustain the reduction in defects while always quantifying our bottom line result.

- If process #1 is in the control phase, what are the controls?
- What is the financial result of the project? $_____

You should know the money benefit!

11. We share our knowledge to ensure that everyone understands and benefits from that knowledge.

- How does your company transfer knowledge?
- What velocity is involved in that knowledge transfer?
- Is there an infrastructure in place? (i.e. intranet or database sharing)

12. We as a company achieve our goals, which results in sustained and satisfied internal and external customers.

- What are the goals that have been met in the last two years?

    Goal #1 _____

    Goal #2 _____

Were you able to understand and answer every question?
(Y/N)

If NO, then your company is an excellent candidate for Doing Six Sigma!

FIGURE 8

CHRONOLOGY OF SIX SIGMA

1983 • Motorola Engineer Bill Smith invents Six Sigma

1984 • Dr. Harry further refines Six Sigma with his "Breakthrough Strategy" at Motorola

1985 • Dr. Harry authors "The Nature of Six Sigma"
• Dr. Harry establishes the Six Sigma Research Institute

1993 • Richard Schroeder leaves Motorola to join Asea Brown Boveri (ABB)

1994 • Dr. Harry leaves Motorola to join ABB
• Dr. Harry and Mr. Schroeder join forces at ABB
• Dr. Harry establishes Six Sigma Academy (SSA)
• Richard Schroeder joins AlliedSignal
• AlliedSignal retains SSA
• Greg Brue joins SSA
• Greg Brue forms Six Sigma Consultants (SSC)

1995 • General Electric retains Six Sigma Academy
• Six Sigma Consultants work as independent consultants with SSA to help implement Six Sigma for General Electric

1996 • Richard Schroeder leaves AlliedSignal and joins SSA

1997 • Dr. Terry Ziemer joins SSA to develop new intellectual property tool called the Navigator™. It is a computer-based learning system and Six Sigma knowledge tool

1998 • SSA forms an alliance with The American Society for Quality (ASQ) and MINITAB software
• Navigator software completed

1999 • SSA forms an alliance with Six Sigma Consultants. SSC provides expertise to implement Six Sigma for clients — an approach that offers *vision, velocity,* and *quantum gains*

"When we start approaching
what we don't know,
that is the beginning
of the Six Sigma journey."

CHAPTER 1

Why Do Six Sigma?

For outstanding financial results — the money!
You don't do Six Sigma for the fun of it,
you do it strictly as a plan for growth and
financial performance.

I know what you are thinking. I've heard from CEO after CEO. "We already **'DO'** quality in our company — we've been doing it since Deming himself taught it to me! Is Six Sigma any more than the latest buzzword or passing fad? What does it provide beyond what I'm already doing?"

I'm always pleased to hear that a company has already adopted a quality mindset. Deming's philosophy of Total Quality Management (TQM) is an excellent foundation for the next step, the quantum leap in quality that Six Sigma provides. The shift to **quality** vs. **quantity** management techniques that took hold in the 1980s was a bigger change than the belief in a flat earth vs. a sphere, bigger than believing the sun revolved around us rather than the other way around. Companies that adopted Deming's TQM approach underwent a major paradigm shift — a corporate transformation — unlearning everything they had been taught and believed, overturning the "sacred cows" of management theory.

Well, get ready for another challenging ride! Six Sigma represents a paradigm shift from TQM — from looking at continuous improvement of **all** processes to discovering the principle of the **"Vital Few"** processes that matter the most. Six

Sigma **Problem-Solving Technology** uses statistical tools that have been perfected in order to identify the **Vital Few.** Six Sigma is a quantum leap beyond where TQM has taken your company. With TQM it was "I feel good, but I didn't make any money!" Six Sigma ties quality improvement directly to the financial result of making money – **substantial** amounts of money!

Standard quality improvement methods have sometimes resulted in companies reaching Four Sigma levels, often after years of continuous improvement and focused effort. That's a great accomplishment compared to the Two Sigma levels represented by the **quantity management** characteristic of the assembly line mindset. However, reaching Six Sigma levels of near zero defects requires more: It requires the **Seven Principles of Problem-Solving Technology** and an experienced guide to train and mentor your employees to become Six Sigma "Black Belts" for quality.

There are multiple reasons to **"DO Six Sigma"**:

For the Money

For Better Decision-Making

For the Knowledge

To Become Faster, Better, and Cheaper than the Competition

To Attain "World Class" Status

To Defeat the Enemy: Variation

To Get Maximum Results in the Shortest Period of Time

And there are a lot of companies doing it, even those whose CEO's are most resistant to the latest management fad. General Electric's Jack Welch, a self-proclaimed cynic when it comes to quality programs, describes Six Sigma as *"the most important initiative GE has ever undertaken."*

FIGURE 1.1

The Seven Principles of Problem-Solving Technology

1) Compelling Leaders
The Vision to Do Six Sigma

2) Embracing Customers
Delivering and Anticipating What the Customer Wants

3) Discovering the "$tealth" Factory
The Real Cost of Doing It Wrong

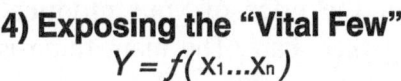

4) Exposing the "Vital Few"
$$Y = f(x_1...x_n)$$

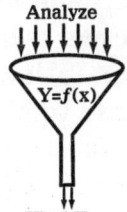

5) Empowering People
The "Best of the Best"

6) Harnessing the Magic of Data
The Method (MAGIC) Without the "G" for Guesswork

7) Relentless, Constant Journey
"The Will"

Do It For The Money

The ultimate goal of implementing the Problem-Solving Technology of Six Sigma is to improve company profitability, enhance stockholder value, and improve customer confidence and satisfaction.

"Show me the money!" the star football player screamed in the movie <u>Jerry Maguire</u>. And show you the money I will. **The Seven Principles of Problem-Solving Technology** will enable you to implement proven ways to reduce operating costs by reducing the cost of goods and services, improving quality, and achieving measurably improved financial performance.

Most companies today are providing products or services in a highly competitive market where the price is determined by that competitive market. If you attack the cost of all the waste, defects and unproductive activity going on in your business processes, then your profit margin will increase. Or you have a choice to lower the price of your product or service and increase your market share. The main thing is that you have some great choices!

FIGURE 1.2

COST-OF-GOODS-SOLD

Computer Example (numbers are assumptions)

Price	$2,000
Cost of Goods Sold (COGS)	95 percent
Profit (5 percent)	$100/unit
Margin-killing COGS cost drivers:	
1. Hard disk failures	$20/unit
2. Interconnector PCB	$15/unit
3. Warranty	$5/unit
4. Assembly Error	$75/unit
5. PCB Assembly functional failure test	$150/unit

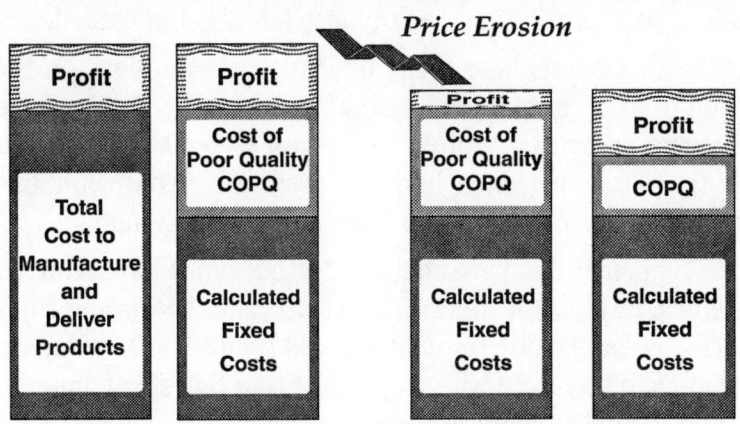

FIGURE 1.3

The Reason to Focus on Cost Of Poor Quality (COPQ)

Price Erosion

If COPQ is NOT decreased, profits will suffer.

In Figure 1.2, the greatest opportunity for saving money is in item #5. If a solution can be created to solve 50 percent of item #5, then the profit would be $75 more per unit. That's an 8.75 percent margin versus 5 percent! The Six Sigma methodology is used to scrutinize the functional failures.

We gather data to create a baseline for measuring Y — the characteristic of the product causing failures. Then we can answer the big question; **What contributes to the functional failures? Y = f (X)** What are the **Vital Few factors** (Xs) that contribute to the failure rate, and which ones should be the focus of improvement and control for long-term success?

"Six Sigma companies typically achieve faster working capital turns, lower capital spending as capacity is freed up, more productive R&D spending, faster new product development, and greater customer satisfaction."
Jennifer Pokrsywinski, Analyst
Morgan Stanley, Dean Witter, Discover and Co.
Quality Progress, May 1998

When you control the cost of poor quality, your fixed costs stay the same but the total cost to manufacture and deliver a product declines. When the marketplace experiences price erosion, your profits stay healthy instead of being eroded.

Stock analysts base their "buy" recommendations on the reliability of a company to predict performance. That's where Six Sigma helps as a tool: It allows you to predict where you will find or experience bad performance. When you can predict bad performance, you understand your system.

Companies that have implemented Six Sigma have achieved incredible results that show up in their balance sheets and stock prices. General Electric estimates it will spend $500 million on Six Sigma in 1999 and will gain at least four times that amount, or more than $2 billion in savings.

YES, WE WANT THE MONEY!

On one of my many assessment trips, I was at an automobile manufacturing facility in the southeastern United States presenting Six Sigma. During the plant tour, I witnessed the fitting of dashboards in some of the automobiles. All dashboards did not fit perfectly and some were installed with the help of a two-by-four and a sledge hammer! I used this "reworking" procedure as an example of where significant money could be saved. This procedure represented only a small portion of the potential costly defects in this car. When I asked the US Division President if his company really wanted to save money at this facility, he stood up and slammed his fist on the table, declaring, "Yes, we want the money!" Yet in follow-up contacts, the President was always unavailable and word got back to me that he was satisfied with his division's profit margins. Contrary to his emphatic YES, it appears that **he did not really want to exert the effort to make the money.**

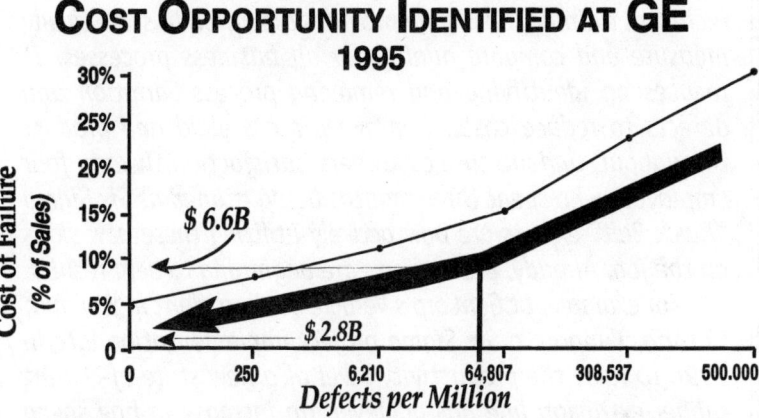

FIGURE 1.4

GE WANTED THE MONEY!

COST OPPORTUNITY IDENTIFIED AT GE
1995

*GE found $4 Billion cost savings opportunity with Six Sigma,
and their stock price responded accordingly.*

FIGURE 1.5

Notice the Rate Of Change

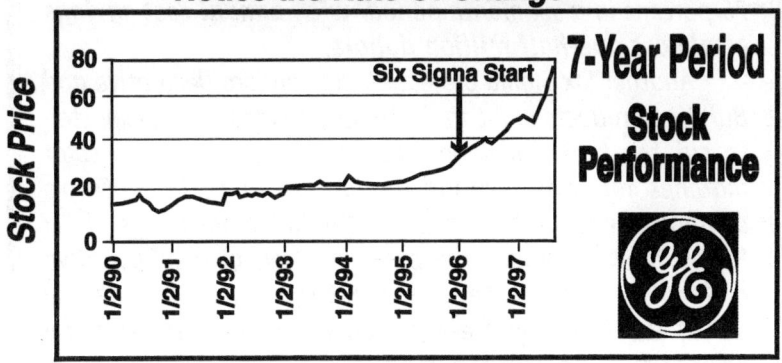

GE stock price performance

GenCorp Improves Quality with Six Sigma

Major strides were made in 1996 to build process and quality improvement capability through extensive Six Sigma technical training. Six Sigma provides a method to statistically measure and compare quality for all business processes. It focuses on identifying and removing process variation and defects to reduce costs, improve process yield and product throughput, and increase customers' satisfaction. Twenty-four employees who spent three months being trained as Six Sigma "Black Belt" experts are now actively utilizing these new skills on the job. Already, their efforts are beginning to bear results.

For example, at GenCorp's Vehicle Sealing plant in Welland, Ontario, Canada, a Six Sigma project implementation late in 1996 to raise the productivity level of a new state-of-the-art rubber extrusion line has achieved an increase in line speed of 50 percent, reduced product scrap by 50 percent, and led to other critical quality characteristic improvements. Significant savings are projected for this single extrusion line project.

*Six Sigma-based statistical investigation and problem-solving is also being utilized at the GenCorp Specialty Polymers Mogadore, Ohio, plant to ultimately eliminate the costly method of filtration to remove residue from latex used for carpet backing. By applying the disciplines of Six Sigma, the level of residue in this particular latex has been reduced by 70 percent in a six-month period, **with annual cost savings of almost one-half million dollars.***

Another Six Sigma project at the GenCorp Decorative and Building Products plant in Columbus, Mississippi, is expected to cut the time and labor costs required to prepare color matches for wall covering production in half. GenCorp's corporate headquarters office is also taking advantage of Six Sigma tools to reduce the costs involved in administrative and transactional services. Similar Six Sigma projects underway across the Company are expected to provide very material savings over the next few years.

GenCorp
1996 Annual Report

Achieving Six Sigma capability results in processes which yield 3.4 defects per million opportunities. Ultimately, Six Sigma results include:

- Reduced Cost of Poor Quality
- Increased Profit Margins
- Increased Market Share
- Reduced Cycle Times
- Lower Inventory Levels
- Increased Product Reliability

The Bathtub Curve

Motorola engineer Bill Smith demonstrated in 1983 that if you find and fix defects before a product gets to the customer, other defects are bound to have been missed, only to show up later. The "fixed" or reworked product was much less reliable in the field and resulted in higher warranty costs to the company.

The "Bathtub Curve" is a classic representation of the reliability of a product over its life cycle. Like the human life cycle, it describes pre-birth and infancy, including infant mortality, useful life, and old age. How is that related to producing a product? Prior to shipping the product we identify a defect rate or failure rate. When the product leaves the company, it goes out to the customer base, and is in the *infant mortality curve.* The curve flattens out in the *useful life phase* or warranty phase. Then the curve goes up in the wear-out period, or *old age.* The infant mortality is a function of the product's defect rate, and is an indication of how good or bad a company is doing inside its world.

For example, refrigerators have a welded fitting for holding the refrigerant. The moment one leaks and has to be reworked, it has a higher infant mortality rate because it has been reworked. This is a predictor of what is likely to happen in the useful life period. If the refrigerator went through the production process clean, with no defects, it will have a longer useful life; *there is a statistical difference.* The more rework

1.6 Bathtub Curve

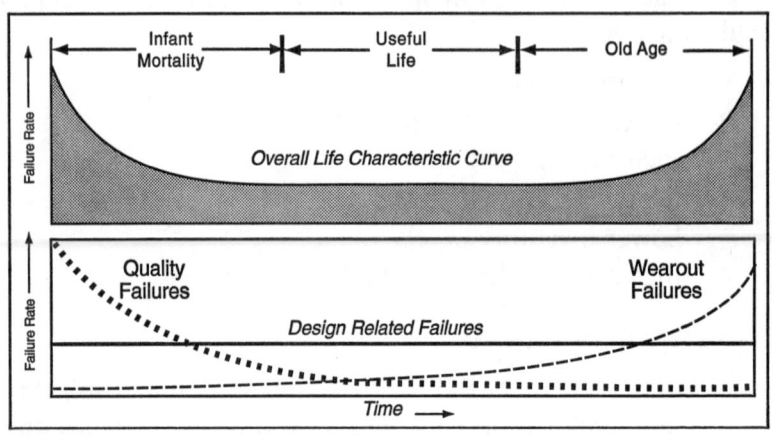

Adapted from: Six Sigma Producibility Analysis and Process Characterization by Mikel J. Harry and J. Ronald Lawson, © 1992 by Motorola Inc.

you have in your production processes, the more it will cost. If you have a high infant mortality rate, there is less useful life. So the lower you can get the "infant mortality" of a product, the faster you can get to a useful life and the more money you can make.

The cost of doing business (i.e. warranty costs) is killing business in the infant mortality phase. The goal is to get beyond the warranty period without having to repair the product. The fewer repairs in the field, the more money you make. There is a relationship between the actual infant mortality, what happens inside your world of production, and your costs. The higher the failure rate, the more money it costs. Ask your finance department how much money they put aside for reserves to meet warranty costs. How much of this is excess because of high failure rates?

Do It For Better Decision-Making

In every type of business, industry, or activity, decision-making is always part of the routine, and the approach to many

decisions is very often based solely on intuition and/or experience; the so-called gut reaction or shooting from the hip.

Six Sigma removes that personal element by quantifying the issues and by using statistics to provide a way to determine the probability of success and failure. The application of this methodology eliminates the use of opinion – "I think," "I feel," and "I believe" – and drives the organization to a more scientific means of decision-making. Questions are critical to this process.

Questions lead, answers follow. If you keep asking the same questions, you keep getting the same answers and the same results. *You need new questions!*

SIX SIGMA GENERATES BIG SAVINGS

With $2.5 billion in estimated savings already achieved, Six Sigma is one of the most ambitious projects we have ever undertaken. It's been a major factor in the company's improved performance, because it's changed our people's mindset about their daily work. By providing them with unique training and new tools to effect change, it's expanded their thinking about our capacity for improvement.

When our Six Sigma defect-reduction program began in 1992, AlliedSignal was an average-quality manufacturer. Today, we're substantially above average, and getting better.

Six Sigma productivity efforts have also significantly increased the capacity of our plants without the need to expend capital on brick and mortar. By reducing defects which lead to wasted labor and materials, existing factories and machinery can produce more products.

Six Sigma productivity efforts are especially valuable in reducing turnaround times on our repair and overhaul services. For example, it now takes us 29 days to overhaul an auxiliary power unit, down from 45 days in 1995. Shorter turnarounds have led to more satisfied customers and more business, illustrating the interdependence of productivity and growth.

Larry Bossidy, Chairman and CEO
AlliedSignal, 1997 Annual Report on Six Sigma

DO IT FOR THE KNOWLEDGE

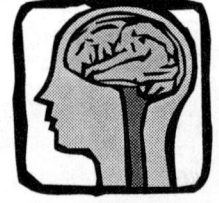

For any process or product, excess variation is the main reason for poor performance capability, resulting in costly rework. The key focus of Six Sigma's **Seven Principles** is to "seek to understand" what is going on, then take action to correct the problem. Defects arise from variation rooted in process, material, or design inadequacies. A defect results when a characteristic does not conform to a specification. The Six Sigma focus is to reduce the variation by understanding the **Vital Few** key factors that account for most of the variation and acting to control or eliminate them.

The most successful companies are able to quickly respond to new opportunities in products and services delivered to customers. Demands from customers require that your business processes be changed rapidly. These changes can often result in adverse effects by increasing waste and defects in your product or service. The finished delivered products or services influence customer confidence and satisfaction. Defects result from not truly understanding customer expectations and how to measure the results of these changes that adversely affect your customers. The reason to Do Six Sigma is to understand the source of variation in the quality of your processes and products and make them predictable. Finally, you will develop a sense of urgency for changes to improve the process, resulting in adding more money to your bottom line.

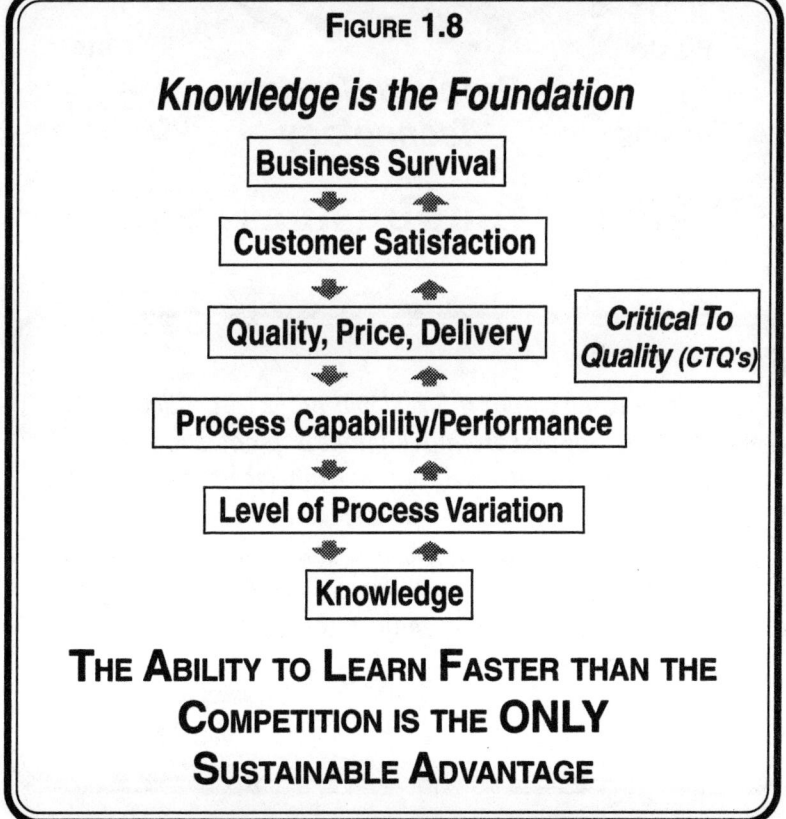

FIGURE 1.8

Knowledge is the Foundation

Business Survival

Customer Satisfaction

Quality, Price, Delivery

Critical To Quality (CTQ's)

Process Capability/Performance

Level of Process Variation

Knowledge

THE ABILITY TO LEARN FASTER THAN THE COMPETITION IS THE **ONLY** SUSTAINABLE ADVANTAGE

FIGURE 1.9

Directions of Knowledge

"I Think, I Feel"

Chaos

Waste

Fire Fighting

Problem-Solving Technology

Knowledge

Data

Good Decisions

Where is your business today?

> "Early results from a Six Sigma project at AlliedSignal's Pendlelton, South Carolina laminates plant showed a 50 percent reduction in inventory, and an increase in on-time delivery from 90 percent to almost 100 percent. GE Plastics has generated the equivalent of a plant's worth of capacity through its use of Six Sigma. One project in its polybutylene terephthalate business solved an extrusion surging problem, giving runs that are defect-free."
>
> *Chemical Week*
> *October 8, 1997*

Do It Faster, Better, Cheaper Than The Competition

Six Sigma companies produce exceptional, reliable, and customer-satisfying products and services *faster* (shorter cycle time), *better* (highest-quality), *cheaper* (lowest-cost), and *more efficiently* than their competitors. They are able to translate higher product quality for their customers into lower costs for themselves. Average companies are at Three or Four Sigma at best, and they are not aware of the opportunity which is right in front of them. These companies are often stalled and complacent, wrestling to stay inches in front of their competitors, and have no desire to know how poorly they are performing.

Basically, *they do not know their industry benchmarks.* They also typically do not believe Six Sigma performance is achievable or cost effective, and therefore are stuck in being just an average company.

Do It To Attain "World Class" Status

Using a set of rigorous statistical tools, with a project-by-project focus, and a disciplined approach to problem-solving, Six Sigma organizations perfect their processes to the point where they consistently produce no more than 3.4 defects or errors per million opportunities! That means:

3.4 defects out of 1,000,000 orders received;

3.4 defects out of 1,000,000 items shipped;

3.4 defects out of 1,000,000 parts produced;

3.4 defects out of 1,000,000 invoices processed.

The Six Sigma management process represents the peak of quality — the virtual elimination of waste and costly defects from every product, process, and transaction in a company. That's right! There are waste and costly defects in **all** of your business processes.

Waste, once identified and eliminated, is the investment currency for growth.

Those defects are not insignificant. They cost your company everyday they are in existence when rework is performed. You must think of the defects as the enemy that must be stopped or you will experience a flat growth plateau and the competition will eventually get the best of you.

The implementation of Six Sigma in your company will result in major shifts in how your management team thinks and how your company does business. Six Sigma will ultimately lead to quantum gains in process and product quality, enabling you to provide preferred products and services, delivered in a timely manner and at the best possible price. This commitment to excellence will translate into highly satisfied customers, increased profit margins, and steady growth in market share.

DO IT TO DEFEAT THE ENEMY: VARIATION

The **Seven Principles of Problem-Solving Technology** focuses on the radical reduction of process variation (both transactional and manufacturing type of processes) and product defects. Variation is your enemy! Principle #4 in our **Problem-Solving Technology** is "Exposing the Vital Few." You must identify those **Vital Few** factors that result in excess variation, then measure, analyze, improve, and control them.

The resulting process is very **robust**; one which makes very efficient use of resources and assets, and which results in a highly efficient organization. Robust processes simply mean that if you <u>do</u> have a glitch or a defect in your process, the customer is not adversely affected — the defect is not seen — it is not translated into a "cost of poor quality" or a lost customer.

Six Sigma takes away the guesswork and eliminates questions about which actions are the best way to improve quality. Six Sigma is based on data, not the "I think," "I feel," or "I believe" statements that decisions used to be based upon.

> *"This is not about sloganeering or bureaucracy or filling out forms. It finally gives us a route to get to the control function, the hardest thing to do in a corporation."*
> *Jack Welch, CEO, General Electric*
> *Forbes Magazine*

Do It To Get Maximum Results In The Shortest Period Of Time

Six Sigma teaches you how to leverage the **Vital Few** factors that impact your customers' satisfaction, allowing companies maximum results in the shortest period of time. Total Quality Management (TQM) does not distinguish between a process that is vital to the bottom line financial performance of your company and one that is not. Six Sigma tools enable you to ferret out the processes that give the most "bang for the buck." You can show excellent returns on investment in a very short time.

The average Six Sigma Black Belt project saves a company $175,000, and is completed in about five and a half months. A Black Belt can complete 4 to 6 projects per year: This is a full-time job. ***Each Black Belt delivers $1 million per year to your bottom line!***

DOING SIX SIGMA - Black Belt Results

The following Black Belt project is an excellent example of uncovering the real problem. The production line for a surgical instrument was running at 18 percent scrap and the time to build each unit was six hours instead of the projected two — which are both costly defects. Initial review of data showed that the main problem was failing the capacitance test. An ultrasonic electrical component (disk) appeared to be the largest contributor to the failed test. However, changing the disk would have delayed production of the instrument by eight months. The Black Belt candidate found that the disks were coming in cracked and dirty. Improved cleaning and packaging seemed to be the answer.

Six Sigma statistical analysis unexpectedly found that the FIC (Frequency, Impedance, Capacitance) meter itself was the source of variation and was affected by which operator set it up! After repeated experiments and testing, a different meter was found which produced far less variation and was unaffected by who was using it.

*Implementing the use of new FIC meters and the improved condition of the disks improved Ppk (long-term process capability) from 0.4 to 2.2, which took the process from 1.2 sigma to 6.6 sigma — reducing the defect rate from 95,000 to effectively zero. Reducing the time to build the unit was also accomplished by stabilizing the process to run in continuous flow mode, reducing time to 3.8 hours per unit and saving $16 per unit in labor. **Sometimes fixing the measurement system fixes the entire problem!***

TOTAL SAVINGS: $364,000
TIME: 11 months

"Quality is the next opportunity
for our (your) company
to set itself apart from its competitors.
Dramatically improved quality will
increase employee and customer
satisfaction, will improve share and
profitability, and will enhance
our (your) reputation.
This quality drive will require
the passionate commitment
of all of you to make it happen.
A Six Sigma 2000 target will require
a significant commitment of resources
and your strong, highly personal
commitment to the objective."

Jack Welch, CEO
General Electric

He's talking to you.
Are you listening?

APPLYING
PROBLEM-SOLVING TECHNOLOGY
TO YOUR COMPANY

Questions to Ask Yourself

How does *Problem-Solving Technology* differ
from the way we "do quality" in our company?

Are we committed to doing what is
necessary to get the financial results?

Where will we find the greatest opportunity for cost
savings in our company?

How reliable are the products our company produces?

How long is the useful life of our product?

Are warranty costs an issue with our company?

Do we know where we are compared to the competition?

Do we want to be "World Class" at what we do?

APPLYING
PROBLEM-SOLVING TECHNOLOGY
TO YOUR COMPANY

Action Items

Do a first-pass analysis on the cost of poor quality.

Audit the defect for a critical product or service that is a large percentage of your business.

Get a warranty report on your critical products.

Ask tech support or customer service what the biggest customer complaint is.

The advertising agency and
the lawyer call them clients;
the doctor calls them patients;
the hotel calls them guests;
the retailer calls them shoppers;
the manufacturer calls them dealers;
the politician calls them constituents;
the bankers call them depositors;
the sports promoter calls them fans;
the railroad and airline
call them passengers;
no matter what you call them,
they are always your customers
and they are the most important
people in your life.

-Unknown-

CHAPTER 2

The Seven Principles of Problem-Solving Technology

Six Sigma uncovers the true value to the customer by implementing a data-driven process that relentlessly focuses on bottom line results.

The tools and concepts of Six Sigma are not new. In fact, this stuff is older than dirt. For example, in 1890 Pearson described the standard deviation as standard divergence. The application of statistical methods to quality improvement is more recent. W. Edwards Deming pioneered the quality management paradigm shift from quantity management during World War II, and his philosophy is a part of the culture of many companies today. Then why have so few companies attempted to achieve exceptional quality levels approaching Six Sigma?

The majority of businesses are still stuck in the Four Sigma quagmire. Case study data show it is because quality improvement efforts of many companies exist without the support of senior management. Until senior management believes that quality and customer satisfaction are as critical to the success of the business as business goals are, efforts to improve quality will be met with limited success. It is the "charge" of senior management to link Six Sigma to the strategy of the business and build an overwhelming case for change that drives urgent action to improve quality and make it a ***PROFIT CENTER.***

PRINCIPLE #1: COMPELLING LEADERS
The Vision to Do Six Sigma

"One of the things about leadership is that you cannot be a moderate, balanced, thoughtful, careful articulator of policy. You've got to be on the lunatic fringe."
Jack Welch, CEO General Electric
Washington Post, 3/23/97

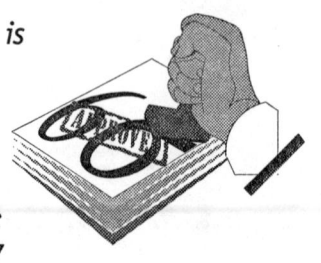

Achieving Six Sigma quality requires a commitment in the form of **time, energy, and resources.** Commitment must come first from the top of the organization and then everyone should be encouraged and supported to participate.

Leadership's commitment is to create a **compelling personal vision** for their company, then align the organization to achieve it. Six Sigma is a vehicle to achieve the vision of excellence. This vision of excellence sustains you through the hard times and provides a long-term focus, not a 24-hour or quarterly focus. Only when you create a compelling personal vision do you achieve excellence — the vision becomes the magnet which pulls you through.

> **"Without a vision, the people perish."**
> Proverbs 29:18 KJV

The cause of quality improvement must be "championed" at all levels of the company. The message must be clear and the commitment of senior level management visibly strong. Once such an urgency is established, company leadership needs to invest the appropriate dedicated resources to improve quality. This also includes time commitment from the CEO and those who report directly to him or her.

Improving quality to Six Sigma levels requires a totally new way of thinking about quality which takes you well beyond Total Quality Management. Your Six Sigma journey asks you as the leader of your company to recognize and mobilize your **people resources.** You must identify the best leaders, organizers, problem-solvers, communicators, coaches, and teachers. You must infuse them with your vision of quality improvement and customer satisfaction. "Stretch goals" are required to force people to rethink how work is done, not just "tweak" the existing process. You and your entire team are forced to think outside of your existing company box!

In order for Six Sigma to be successful, total management support must be in place, starting at the top with the CEO, executive directors, and Senior Management acting as **Champions** of the process. When you appoint a Six Sigma "Champion" from Senior Management you send a message throughout the company that you are serious about quality improvement.

This senior manager "Champion" provides day-to-day leadership and support for the implementation of Six Sigma. The Champion asks the difficult questions that generate innovative thinking about quality and customer satisfaction. You must link pay performance and bonuses to the outcomes of the Six Sigma implementation. For example, 40 percent of an executive's bonus at GE was based on the results achieved with Six Sigma.

> *"What we call 'stretch' simply means figuring out performance targets, from profitability to new product introductions, that are doable, reasonable, and within our capabilities, then raising our sights higher, much higher, toward goals that at the outset seem to require superhuman effort to achieve. We have found that by reaching for what appears to be the impossible, we often actually do the impossible; and even when we don't quite make it, we inevitably wind up doing much better than we would have done."*
>
> Jack Welch, CEO, General Electric
> 1996 Annual Meeting

FIGURE 2.1

Example of a Company-Wide Introductory Letter

From: (President & CEO) or Executive Staff
To: All Employees
Subject: Six Sigma

The world that we compete in today is much different from the one we once competed in. The opportunity to widen the gap between us and our competitor is at an all time high. Our customers are more demanding and have more options on where to spend their money. In order to thrive in this kind of environment and deliver on the financial commitments we've made to ourselves and to our public shareholders, we have to constantly and relentlessly look for new ways to improve our performance. Our goal is to be a growth company with our first target to be a $__ billion company.

For this reason we have started Six Sigma. Six Sigma is a way to break through to the next level of cost savings and to delight our customers by rapidly accelerating improvements in our processes, products, and services. It's the next step in our continuous process business model.

The term Six Sigma is actually a measurement that will tell us how rapidly we are eliminating waste and reducing defects and variations in our processes. But Six Sigma is more than a measurement. Building on our existing quality systems, Six Sigma is the way we are going to take productivity to the next level. Everyone will receive some basic training in this methodology, and some people will receive advanced training. The focus at all levels will be to generate productivity which is directly tied to our bottom line performance. We will develop appropriate ways to reward and recognize individuals and teams as part of our Six Sigma efforts.

The executives of (company) are committed to this program and have already received an executive briefing in the methodology of Six Sigma. We will now go to the next senior level to train managers in the methodology, and finally we will start our Black Belt training on (date). Your commitment and support is required to ensure the success of this key business initiative for (company). Each key business unit needs to identify potential resources and projects in his or her respective areas. (Name) Consultants have been selected as our business partner to help us implement Six Sigma.

Please join me in supporting this exciting effort.

It's critical to understand that executive level "buy-in" is crucial to the success of Six Sigma. Upper level management needs to institute rigorous program controls, assure proper training and coaching, and ensure that projects are properly designed to achieve the most effective use of resources. *If you can't see yourself as a Champion of Six Sigma, you can stop reading now.* You're wasting your precious time. If you do see yourself as a Champion, read on and see how your company can reap the benefits of being the *highest-quality and lowest-cost provider of goods and services; a "best-in-class" competitor in your market sector!*

"Champions within an organization must be ducks who don't want to fly with the flock. Being politically correct is not going to make these people a success. We need leaders who can look beyond the norm, beyond the way things have always been done and who are willing to test new waters."

Mikel Harry, Ph.D.

PRINCIPLE #2: EMBRACING CUSTOMERS
Delivering and Anticipating What the Customer Wants

Customer satisfaction is a function of consistently meeting customers' standards for quality, doing it better than the competition.

Customers have critical-to-business expectations. Are *you* in business to achieve a phenomenal customer satisfaction rate that *exceeds* critical-to-business expectations?

Business growth depends on how well a company meets the expectations of its customers in terms of quality, price, and delivery. In turn, the ability of a company to satisfy these needs with **predictability** is controlled by process **capability** and the amount of **variation** in the business processes, from administrative to manufacturing. Stock analysts base their recommendations about a company's stock on how reliably a company predicts its performance. Six Sigma provides a way to understand your system so you can reliably predict performance.

The key paradigm shift Six Sigma brings to the business world is to change from activities such as inspection, testing, reworking, etc. that keep defects from reaching the customer and focus instead on preventing defects from occurring in the first place.

CUSTOMER SATISFACTION

Today, focusing on the customer is absolutely essential. Of course, we all recognize this. But do we really internalize the idea? Do we really believe that such a focus has the potential to drive business growth and impact the level of prosperity which we should come to expect? Closely linked to the idea of customer satisfaction is the concept of operational excellence — the kingpin of success. Without a focus on excellence, it becomes easy to accept the position of second or third best. Being the best means embracing change and reaching out for newer and higher standards of performance. Only then can one break the chains of complacency and pave the way for breakthrough. The attainment of excellence is no longer a lofty goal or ideal, it is now a fundamental requirement — the ante for entering the game of business.

Mikel Harry, Ph.D.

Six Sigma builds on W. Edwards Deming's Total Quality Management (TQM) philosophy — the first management technique to gain acceptance for the principle that the customer's needs and wants mattered to the bottom line. Deming's philosophy changed the way many companies go about doing business. Six Sigma *turbo charges* the focus on quality, providing a well-defined process to determine which factors are critical to the customer's satisfaction.

FIGURE 2.2

Definition of Customer Satisfaction

Customer, n [O Fr. Coustumier, L.L. custumarius, custom.]

1. A **person** who buys, especially one who buys regularly.

2. A **person** with whom one has to deal.

Satisfaction, n [O Fr., from L. satisfaction (-onis), from satisfactus, pp. of satisfacere, to satisfy.]

1. To gratify fully the wants or desires of; to supply to the full extent

2. To free from doubt, suspense, or *uncertainty*; to give full assurance to.

3. To comply with rules or standards.

Adapted from "The Vision of Six Sigma" by Mikel Harry, Ph.D.
©1994 Sigma Publishing Co.

What is customer satisfaction? Embedded within the definitions listed above are two key ideas. First, the notion that the customer is a *person*, not an organization, corporation, etc. Secondly, the idea that satisfaction reflects how certain that customer is that his or her standards for quality, cost, and delivery will be met. Standards that are critical to *your customer,* not standards that you *think* are what the customer wants. If we cannot express this knowledge in numbers (statistics), then we don't know our customer.

Customer satisfaction is a prerequisite to business survival and growth. When customers are uncertain about the quality of your product and experience variation from what they expect, you have a costly quality problem. *To ensure customer satisfaction, we must focus on the root cause issues* that make your company's internal processes inconsistent and variable. The only way to ensure that this happens is to place a value and emphasis on what the customer cares about. This requires *measurements*, since, as the old cliché goes, "what gets measured, gets done." If you don't measure, or don't know how to measure variation and defects consistently, then how will customer satisfaction be achieved? If you don't measure variation and defects, customers will measure them through their experience with your product and service and choose the other guy next time.

Six Sigma requires company leadership to understand in quantifiable terms, the needs and expectations of their customers, and to translate these needs into the measurable outcomes of processes. Then, leaders must focus on understanding and measuring the inputs to the process and looking for the root causes of variation in that process.

If you don't measure, or don't know how to measure variation and defects consistently, then how will customer satisfaction be achieved?

What Is Critical to Your Customer's Satisfaction?

It is important that we understand and can measure those factors about our product or service that are critical to the customer's satisfaction. We can't make educated guesses about what those factors are, we have to *ask our customers what is important to them.* We want to avoid working on things that our customer doesn't think are critical. A good example occurred when I worked at Compaq Computers. They had an inlaid gold logo on the keyboard of their desktop computer; a feature they were very proud of which they thought was important to the customer. This feature was a costly but non-functional component of their computer. Did the customer care about the logo? Not really! When Compaq surveyed their customers, they found out that the customer *only* cared if the keyboard worked!

How easy is it for your customers to do business with you? Are you making assumptions about what your customers need, rather than basing your decisions on *facts*? How often do you *ask* these questions of your internal and external customers? When was the last time you, as a leader, initiated conversations with your customer vs. handling a complaint from a "good" customer? Is this knowledge communicated throughout your organization? How is it translated in direct correlation to your internal actions?

Linking Customer Expectations With What You Provide

The idea of expectations and fulfillment runs throughout Six Sigma. We must understand the customer's expectations and translate this into fulfilling those expectations with what we produce in products and services. Maximum value, both to the customer and to the supplier, is achieved when expectations and fulfillment have a maximum overlap. When we do things that customers don't expect or want, then we are not adding value to our product. We exist as businesses only to supply value for what the customer expects, wants, and needs.

Unless we satisfy customer needs through processes that are consistent, we may satisfy the customer on product quality, but disappoint the customer in another vital area, namely price. As we will see, achieving quality with inconsistent processes is very costly.

An important concept that drives Six Sigma quality is that defective products which get into the field — those which the customer sees and experiences — are often products that have been inspected, discovered to be defective, and reworked.

FIGURE 2.3

A customer complaint is just the tip of the iceberg

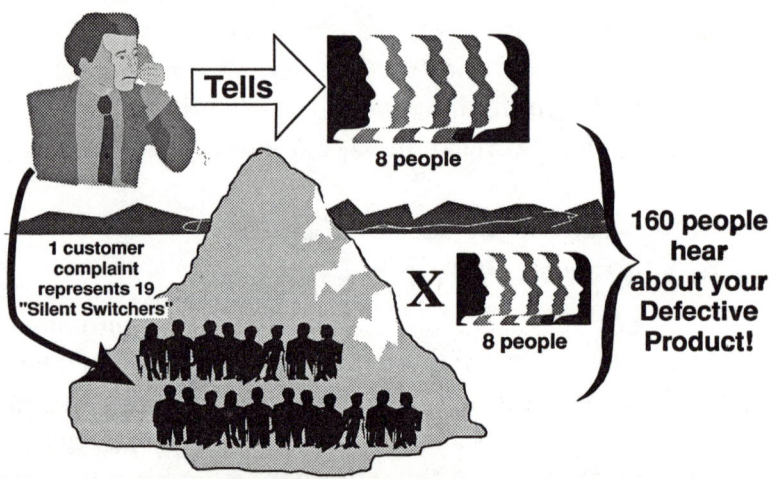

Tells

8 people

1 customer complaint represents 19 "Silent Switchers"

X

8 people

160 people hear about your Defective Product!

Historically 1 in 20 dissatisfied customers actually tells you about it — the others prefer to switch! That one dissatisfied customer starts a domino effect, and typically tells at least eight other people about their experience. If you hear one complaint, you can bet on the odds that at least another 19 people have experienced the same defect and that 160 people have heard about it!

Source: *The Service Edge*, by Ron Zemke and Dick Schaaf

FIGURE 2.4
Supplier Fulfillment of Customer Expectations

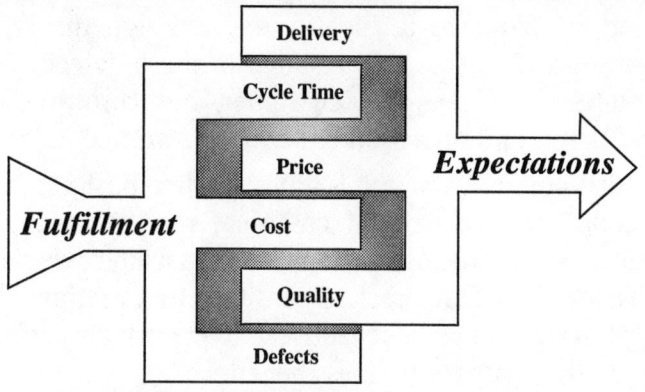

Delivery
Cycle Time
Price
Expectations
Cost
Fulfillment
Quality
Defects

Your goal is to minimize the gap between what your customer expects and what you provide.

Adapted from "The Vision of Six Sigma" by Mikel Harry, Ph.D.
©1994 Sigma Publishing Co

Maximizing the Interaction

Customers want quality, price, and delivery in order to receive value from us as a supplier. If we meet the customer's requirements on these three factors, we also benefit in terms of fewer defects, lower costs, and reduced cycle time. Reduction of defects leads directly to reduced cycle time since we eliminate the time to look for and fix problems. It also leads directly to cost reductions by eliminating all the resources tied up in inspecting and reworking defects.

Fixing the same recurring defects is like looking over your shoulder and trying to permanently change the past. It reminds me of the definition of a fanatic as one who, once losing sight of the goal, redoubles their efforts. Let's not get caught in the downward spiral of getting better at fixing things by working harder and believing that this is real work. Eliminating defects is thoughtful, purposeful work. This is the focus of Six Sigma.

The "stealth factory" of reworking defective products costs time, energy, and resources. Since a reworked product is more likely to fail, the customer will be dissatisfied. In addition, dissatisfied customers tell other potential or current customers about their dissatisfaction with your product. The driving idea behind Six Sigma is to identify and redesign the **Vital Few** processes and factors that resulted in these defects. Not just products that reach the customer, but throughout the manufacturing, transaction or service environment.

Customer satisfaction is a bottom line business issue! By focusing on well-defined customer requirements and by utilizing known processes and material capabilities, we can create robust designs that are less sensitive to variations. Robust designs remove uncertainty and lead to predictable performance with all the resultant business benefits.

The end result and driving force of all our efforts in Six Sigma will be to improve customer satisfaction and therefore the business results of improved financial performance.

DOING SIX SIGMA: Customer Satisfaction

On an airplane, the person sitting next to me had the same exact model of portable computer that I use. He degraded the computer because of all the hardware problems he had from the beginning even with the assistance from technical support. Maybe he had a reworked item. My computer has had no problems for five years. Yet, he was degrading the model and vowed never to buy from that company again. His dissatisfaction had cost the company a customer today, tomorrow, and probably many more potential buyers because of this experience. If the computer had worked properly from the beginning, the company would have saved the cost incurred in technical support as well as reaped the benefits of a satisfied customer.

FIGURE 2.5
CUSTOMER-BASED MANAGEMENT

Everything you do or produce effects more than one customer. As a CEO, who are your customers and what are their top three requirements?

Customers	_Requirements_
Shareholders (analysts)	1. _____
	2. _____
	3. _____
Customer base	1. _____
	2. _____
	3. _____
Employees	1. _____
	2. _____
	3. _____
Union	1. _____
	2. _____
	3. _____
Suppliers	1. _____
	2. _____
	3. _____
Federal government	1. _____
	2. _____
	3. _____
State/local government	1. _____
	2. _____
	3. _____
Other_____	
	1. _____
	2. _____
	3. _____

PRINCIPLE #3:

DISCOVERING THE $TEALTH FACTORY

The REAL Cost of Doing It Wrong

The **Seven Principles of Problem-Solving Technology** presents a way to look at company performance and profitability, uncovering and measuring the true hidden "Costs of Poor Quality" (COPQ). A more descriptive term for this is the "Cost of Doing It Wrong" (CODW).

The Stealth Factory represents the visible and less visible costs of all the defects that exist in your processes. It's like an iceberg — you only see the visible, tangible, obvious tip of your controllable costs. Whenever the true total cost of poor quality is accounted for and corrective measures taken, **the highest-quality provider of goods and services is shown to be the lowest-cost provider of goods and services.** Every time there is a defect (which is any result that is not what the customer of the product or service wants), companies expend time and resources to find, fix, and try to prevent these defects. To reduce these costs (such as rework, inspection, scrap, warranty claims, lost customer loyalty), the root issue — defects and process capability — needs to be addressed.

This Stealth Factory is the **black hole** sucking your best resources away from new product development just to keep surviving. **When you're in trouble, your brightest people end up working on the problem** — and you've drained away your best resources to work on the past, not the future. This is also known as fire-fighting!

Is it your common practice to include your an estimate of the 'stealth costs' in the price you charge for your product and just consider it a normal cost of doing business? Maybe you have no idea what the stealth factory is costing you — just know you are losing profit. You are not alone — many successful companies do. After all, it's not a lot of money per unit produced, and your competitors do the same thing. Right? **Wrong!** When you understand that there is a higher failure rate in the field for reworked products, and the cost of a lost or dissatisfied customer is substantial, ***redesigning the process to eliminate defects will obviously improve your bottom line.*** Product quality, customer satisfaction, and your profit margin all benefit from the application of ***The Seven Principles of Problem-Solving Technology.*** Customers will not continue to finance a company's COPQ indefinitely. Unlike your competition who still factors in the cost of poor quality in their price, you will become the ***highest-quality and lowest-cost provider of goods and services!***

FIGURE 2.6

COST of DEFECTS

The Stealth Factory — the Real Cost of Defects. Those things below the surface represent the bulk of the cost of poor quality. The tangible defects are just the "tip of the iceberg."

Rolled Throughput Yield (RTY) tells you the real productivity and quality of a company. It represents the yield through the entire process, and is the product of the individual yields at each step of the process. It tells you the probability of getting through the process defect-free. Standard practice and knowledge today is like going to a doctor who says "you look fine" without doing any tests or digging deeper into your actual condition. Improvement must begin with what is your baseline condition. RTY is a metric that enables you to learn what's really going on and fix it, saving millions of dollars in waste and poor quality. ***RTY is a metric used in Six Sigma that distinguishes this methodology from the rest.*** RTY is discussed in more depth in Chapter 3.

FIGURE 2.7

Methods vs. the $avings

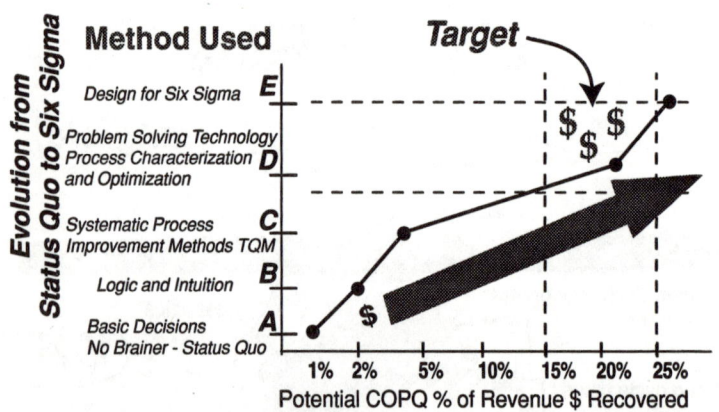

What methods do you deploy now? Where do you want to be?

Six Sigma results are found in the target zone of 15 to 25 percent COPQ.

If you are a billion dollar company using just basic management decision-making processes, no statistical measurement tools whatsoever, you'll probably realize one percent of that one billion dollars as profit. That's your bottom line.

With the **Seven Principles of Problem-Solving Technology,** using process characterization and optimization, you will begin to understand your processes and the real cost of poor quality. By identifying and eliminating the defects, you can realize between 15 and 25 percent of that revenue stream. That is between $150 million and $250 million added to your bottom line. **The question is, do you want the money?**

PRINCIPLE #4: EXPOSING THE "VITAL FEW"

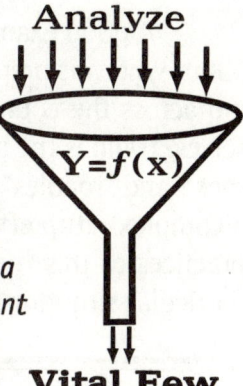

The Six Sigma Problem-Solving Technology's focus is to extract the knowledge of the VITAL FEW factors (the Xs) that predict the outcomes for a process with a greater than 95 percent confidence that you will get that outcome.

Once you have predictable outcomes, then you can reduce your cost. Why? Because you identified what you didn't know.

Is your company the best in what you are doing? **Really?** How do you know? What are your competitors doing? How do you compare with them? Benchmarking allows you to find out if you are **WORLD CLASS** at what you do. Benchmarking is the process of continually searching for and learning from the best methods and practices anywhere in the world, then adapting the good features to your own situation.

If your company is like most others, this process will clearly show that you are stuck in the Four Sigma (or less) trap along with most of your competitors. You are just **AVERAGE,** and that is nothing to celebrate. Especially when you realize that one of your new competitors is in the Six Sigma group of **WORLD CLASS** companies! You may suddenly understand why this competitor is giving your sales manager such difficulties in the marketplace. They aren't "dumping" their product at an artificially low price. Instead they are able to underprice you because

**the Highest-Quality Provider of
Goods and Services
IS the Lowest-Cost Provider!**

How to Benchmark

A good example for benchmarking is a company I heard about who was preparing to move their corporate manufacturing across the country to another location. They asked themselves, "Who is the best in the world at moving?" They selected rock band "roadies" as the benchmark for excellence in moving a complex setup efficiently from city to city! They studied the practices of this "best of the best" and adapted them to their particular situation.

FIGURE 2.8

Benchmarking Guidelines

- Select a topic you want to establish a benchmark for.
- Estimate the costs of doing a benchmarking study.
- Select and train a team to complete the study.
- Choose the key metrics you want to study.
- Select or design a survey and develop questions.
- Develop tools to collect the data.
- Test the methods you plan to use to analyze the data.
- Analyze yourself for the key metrics.
- Identify companies and contact them.
- Collect and analyze data from public domain sources.
- Formulate a benchmark plan and analyze information.
- Conduct gap analysis.
- Develop recommendations and plan to implement.
- Identify departments that are needed for support.
- Present the plans to management.
- Implement the plan and monitor the progress.

> ### "You can see a lot by looking."
> Yogi Berra

There is a lot of information available about what you are trying to benchmark from public domain sources. These sources include:

Library database	Internal reviews
Internal publications	Professional associations
Industry publications	Special industry reports
Functional trade publications	Seminars
Industry data firms	Industry experts
University sources	Company "watches"
Newspapers	Advertisements
Newsletters	Original research
Customer feedback	Telephone surveys
Inquiry service	Networks
Literature searches	Website searches

An excellent organization that can help with your benchmarking exercise is the American Productivity and Quality Center (APQ). You can reach them at www.apqc.org or by phone at (713) 685-4670.

Identifying the Vital Few — Y =f (x)

After the ego-shattering experience of benchmarking, when you realize where you **really** are in relation to your competition, it's time to identify those **Vital Few** factors (Xs) that can be leveraged to provide maximum results in the shortest period of time. Six Sigma helps you uncover those factors which are critical to the satisfaction of your customers. You can then identify the **Vital Few** processes upon which to focus your Six Sigma improvement efforts to get the most bang for the buck.

The question that needs to be constantly asked is "What is this a function of?" For order entry defects, manufacturing defects, processing defects, "What is this a function of?" That is the **Vital Few** we are looking for.

We want to work on the vital few, not the trivial many.

It may seem overwhelming to consider where to start when a process has a hundred or more steps where defects can occur. However, data shows that there are always **six or fewer key Xs for any product or process,** even if there are hundreds of steps that could play a role. Six Sigma Black Belts apply the statistical tools and analyses to determine the **Vital Few** that will truly make a difference to your customers' satisfaction and the company's bottom line.

> **Definition:** Y=$f(x_1$-$x_n)$ The characteristic of quality in a product or service you are trying to achieve (Y) is a function of or is controlled by several key process variables, or Xs. Six Sigma **Problem-Solving Technology** allows you to identify these "key knobs" and control them. The Xs are the **"Vital Few"**

DOING SIX SIGMA:
"Price Check on One, Please"

A major discount retailer's goal is to maximize the average "items per hour" through their stores. What I try to do as a Six Sigma consultant is to understand the equation for that process. If their key metric is items per hour (Y), what is that a function of (Xs)? How many factors play a role?

I can mathematically find the answer by using Six Sigma statistical tools, which I did for the client. The company executive said, "That's interesting! How did you do that? You only spent a couple of days in our store." My answer was: Through data.

I didn't have any previous experience with retail operations. I just know how to solve problems using statistical measurements. In the example above, their critical problem was price checks. When you had to check an item's price, it blew the measurement of items per hour out of the water.

The killer factor was properly pricing items on the shelf. Why is the pricing wrong? Why hasn't it been changed? Is it a procedural issue? Is it that the corporate office is holding back the pricing? No one knew. And those are the issues for which we had to get answers.

PRINCIPLE #5:
EMPOWERING PEOPLE
The "Best of the Best"

Six Sigma empowers your key human capital assets with powerful statistical tools to deliver impressive financial results.

Would you hesitate to invest in an expensive piece of equipment you knew would save your company millions of dollars? In Six Sigma, you invest in your employees as assets who can provide substantial returns on your investment.

Six Sigma offers a data-driven thought process that applies measurements to problem-solving. The implementation is assured when management embraces the **Seven Principles of Problem-Solving Technology,** allocating resources and empowering individuals to take ownership of projects. The selected individuals become Six Sigma Black Belts after thorough training by an experienced Six Sigma training partner and after demonstrating sucessful results with a Black Belt project. Black Belts are given the freedom to make change happen by using the Six Sigma process performance metrics and the four-phase system of <u>M</u>easure, <u>A</u>nalyze, <u>I</u>mprove, and <u>C</u>ontrol (MAIC).

Six Sigma training creates practitioners who exploit the full power of statistical quality control tools. **Problem-Solving Technology** has been developed for rapid transfer of knowledge throughout your company. It puts quality tools in the hands of a large number of workers and managers within a company. Six Sigma training partners "clone" themselves, teaching your people to be full-time quality scouts who uncover that pot of gold beneath the waste throughout your business processes. They become your **internal consultants,** able to be relentless on the constant journey towards Six Sigma quality.

In order to empower your people to find and fix the business problems that mean the most in terms of money, you must make sure they have the resources to do whatever is necessary. Six Sigma Black Belts should have no barriers. That is what company leaders need to understand and it is critical. That means that once the Black Belts have the data they can get the resources they need to implement their project. In turn, they will show you the data for what they will need.

As a leader, the request for resources to solve a problem is the first real test of your commitment to achieve Six Sigma results. Move quickly to line up the resources for the initial Black Belt projects. It will speak volumes to the Black Belts, as well as send the message throughout the organization that things are really changing.

FIGURE 2.9

A Possible Scale of Empowerment

Increased Capability		
.0σ	A lowly slug. You have no grade point.
.1σ	I will tell you what to do next.
.2σ	You will ask what to do next.
.5σ	Bring me your problems.
1σ	Bring me your problems with your ideas.
2σ	Bring me your problems with your recommendations.
3σ	Bring me your problems with your recommendations. If you don't hear from me, just proceed.
4σ	Take action, but let me know what you did.
5σ	Take action, and let's talk if it doesn't work out.
6σ	Take action and report as you deem necessary.

How much do you empower your people?
How much are YOU empowered?

Six Sigma Black Belts need to operate at a Four to Six Sigma level of empowerment.

Training and Cultural Change

Improved performance does not and will not happen automatically. High-caliber training is required. You are only as good as the people you have in your company. Your company should invest in people as an asset. The cost to train a typical Black Belt ranges from $8,000 to $30,000 depending on the number trained and the size of implementation within a company. If that asset — your employee — makes a million dollars in hard bottom line savings, then the return on investment is about 1,000,000/100,000 for a fully burdened employee — or roughly 1,000 percent.

Most equipment assets don't come close to that! Disciplined implementation of Six Sigma must follow the training period. People at all levels have to change the way they go about doing their jobs. In short, new ways of thinking, new questions, new ways of communicating and operating must spread to the entire organization.

PRINCIPLE #6:

HARNESSING THE MAGIC OF DATA
The Method (MA¢IC) without the "G" for Guesswork

Six Sigma statistical tools work like magic to uncover what we don't know. But we don't have to be statisticians. Computers and software do the work while we focus on tool selection, use, and interpretation of data analysis.

At one time, performance and decision data were available only to managers. With the advancement of the information economy, today data can be available to virtually anyone in a company. Data alone tells you nothing — you must torture, slice and dice the data (analyze it) to obtain the answers. The Six Sigma method uses data to **_Measure, _Analyze, _Improve, and _Control** performance. ***To me, MAIC is MA¢IC — the method without the "G" for Guesswork!***

The impressive success of Six Sigma **_Seven Principles of Problem-Solving Technology_** comes from the use of statistical measurements as a basis for decision-making. These measurable statistics are called indicators or **_metrics_**. Because of the use of the Sigma terminology, Six Sigma is frequently perceived as a statistics program. This is not the case: Statistics are used solely as tools for interpretation and clarification of data and decision-making.

The focus of Six Sigma is on tool selection and interpretation of data, using inferential statistics to make decisions. **_Calculations are left to computers and software._** Black Belts do get a working knowledge of the tools, but we don't do triple integral and derivation of the formulas and equations. We are practitioners, not theorists.

It's easy for you to see the challenges your company faces. However, it is more difficult to discover the hard facts behind the challenges. Biased, unclear reports and irrelevant data create a layer of fog that obscures reality. The first priority is to get rid of the fog with **accurate data.** Six Sigma tools have been used by quality management practitioners for decades. These are conventional methods applied unconventionally. In short, we use these tools for one primary purpose:

to make quality problem-solving
a profit center in your company.

As a business leader, you need to have **at least** a working knowledge of the Six Sigma tools and resources. These tools assist in moving a company from a Four Sigma 'average' player to being a Six Sigma "World Class" quality and price leader in its market sector, based on key business metrics. In the end, what we are talking about is establishing the proper "cockpit of metrics," measures to help us understand our business situation and keep us "on course" to our Six Sigma goal. This information can provide a sense of urgency and point out the actions needed to correct the root issue: **the defects!**

When your company has a goal or target of near perfection, it forces you to stop working with minor adjustments as to how you run your business processes. It confronts you and opens your eyes to an entirely new set of ways of performing the same process.

But we would all agree that reading about statistics is boring to anyone but a statistician or an engineer! However, there is money in the proper application of these methods. **It's not necessarily exciting, but the results are dramatic,** so as business leaders we must be able to at least interpret the results.

Business leaders must also be willing to ask new questions – questions about process capability, product design, and overall quality. Only then will new measures, new behaviors, new knowledge, and new values for quality start to appear. We must create an environment where we and our employees can ask questions that challenge the "sacred cows" in our world. A secure leader understands the importance of humility, and should demand dissent and truth about the business with no adverse effect to employees.

Statistical tools are imperative in order to discover *why* variation occurs and to find ways to improve and control it. A Ph.D. in mathematics or statistics is not required to implement Six Sigma, nor is it necessary to have an engineering background to understand what the data means to the quality improvement process and your company's bottom line.

The methods and techniques taught to and applied by Six Sigma Black Belts are not industry-specific. These methods have been used successfully by companies representing a variety of industries ranging from satellites to tennis balls, all with positive bottom line financial results and improved performance. ***Remember, Six Sigma Black Belts are problem-solvers.***

The difference between failure and success
is doing a thing *nearly* right
and doing it *exactly* right.

Edward C. Simmons

$Y=f(x)$

MA**G**IC = Methods Without the "G" for Guesswork!

The "Magic" of MAIC

The four-phase process of _**M**easure, **A**nalyze, **I**mprove, and **C**ontrol_ (MAIC) is the heart of the **Seven Principles of Problem-Solving Technology.** MAIC allows you to attain excellence in quality and customer satisfaction and make quality improvement a profit center. MAIC is magic — methods without the "G" for guesswork!

We have developed a detailed map of the process that leads you to your goal. It is described in detail in Chapter 3. This structured process of applying conventional statistical tools to both improve quality and make money is what makes Six Sigma different from other quality improvement methods. Each phase of _**M**easure, **A**nalyze, **I**mprove, and **C**ontrol_ uses a collection of tools, and each phase serves as a logic filter that leads you to the **Vital Few** causal variables (the Xs).

Performance metrics and the skills, experience, and knowledge of how to apply them are the most important tools Six Sigma has to offer your business. The Six Sigma Champion and Black Belt training familiarizes you and your people with the different types of tools that are useful, teaches you how to decide which ones to use, and shows you how to interpret the results.

PRINCIPLE #7:
RELENTLESS, CONSTANT JOURNEY
"The Will"

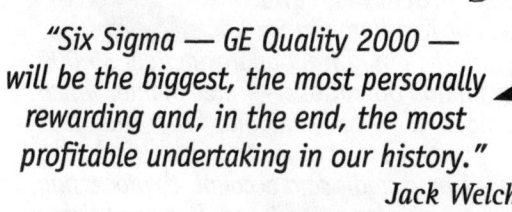

"Six Sigma — GE Quality 2000 — will be the biggest, the most personally rewarding and, in the end, the most profitable undertaking in our history."
Jack Welch
CEO, General Electric

Implementing Six Sigma will test your true strength as a leader. It will test your personal fortitude and strain your "friendships" to the breaking point. Many of your managers won't make the change. What will *you* do?

Just as Deming taught continuous improvement, Six Sigma is a relentless, constant journey towards the goal of 3.4 defects per million of the "Critical-to-Quality" factors that your customers have determined. As a compelling, visionary leader, you must be relentless on this constant journey.

In summary, Six Sigma is a process and structure that can provide a leadership and management foundation for the next millennium by changing a company's focus from the use of opinion in decision-making — those "I think," "I feel," and "I believe" statements — to quantifying issues and using statistics to provide a means of determining probabilities of success and failure. ***Don't you think your company should be there?***

The secret of success is constancy of purpose.
Benjamin Disraeli

GE's Relentless Journey

Three and one half years ago we made a decision to immerse this Company in the science and culture of Six Sigma quality, which is a disciplined method of eliminating virtually all defects from every one of the Company's products, processes, and transactions. For those not familiar with Six Sigma, it means, very briefly, going from approximately 35,000 defects or mistakes per million operations —Three Sigma, which is average for most companies — to Six Sigma, fewer than four defects per million, in operations that range from manufacturing a locomotive part to servicing a credit card account, to processing a mortgage application, to answering a phone. It means fixing processes so they are nearly perfect and then controlling them so they stay fixed. The common objective in virtually all Six Sigma projects is the elimination of variance.

During the first two years of Six Sigma we invested about half a billion dollars in the training of our entire professional work force. But the commitment, the big bet, was much more than financial. It involved the diversion of the very best talent in the Company — thousands of our best people, high-potential men and women — to multi-year tours of full-time Six Sigma work.

The short version of our progress from a standing start three and a half years ago is this: Virtually every professional in the Company is now what we call a "Green Belt," with three full weeks of training and a completed Six Sigma project under his or her belt. Five thousand full-time Black Belts and Master Black Belts are now initiating and coaching projects across the globe. Most importantly, the Master Black Belts and Black Belts are now being promoted to key leadership positions in the Company — big jobs — and they have begun to irrevocably change the DNA of GE to one whose central strand is quality.

The financial returns from Six Sigma have exceeded expectations. In 1998, we achieved three quarters of a billion dollars in Six Sigma-related savings over and above our investment, and this year that number will go to a billion and a half, with billions more to be captured from increased volume and market share as customers increasingly "feel" the benefits of GE Six Sigma in their own business.

Jack Welch, CEO, General Electric
1999 Speech to Shareholders

Applying
Problem-Solving Technology
To Your Company

Questions to Ask Yourself

Can I see myself as a Six Sigma Champion?

Do I believe that quality and customer satisfaction are as critical to our success as our strategic goals are?

Do we embrace customer needs as our business focus?

Do we know what those needs are?

Is that knowledge based on facts?

Are we doing things the customer doesn't need or want in producing our product?

Do we lose customers from bad experiences with defective products that we "fixed?"

How big is our stealth factory? Do we know what it costs us?

Do I empower my employees?

"When you can measure
what you are speaking about
and express it in numbers,
you know something about it,
but when you cannot
express it in numbers,
your knowledge is of a meagre
and unsatisfactory kind:
it may be the
beginning of knowledge,
but you have scarcely,
in your thoughts, advanced to the
stage of science."

British Physicist
Lord Kelvin
1891

CHAPTER 3

Harnessing the Magic of Metrics for Improved Performance

The utopian goal is NOT to produce statistics,
but to produce Six Sigma outcomes and results
for companies: to show the company the money.

This is the chapter no one wants to read. After all, who do you know that really liked their statistics class in college? But it is a misconception that Six Sigma is about a statistics program. Yes, you need to understand the *value* of statistical measurement, but the computers and software actually do all the work. You don't even have to remember or look up the formulas.

In fact, MINITAB™, a popular business statistics software program, has been the tool of choice for Six Sigma implementation. (See included 60-day trial CD.) As a business leader, you need to understand and interpret the kinds of information that business metrics can provide you: Factual data that provides a strong foundation for decision-making.

This chapter will provide you with the contextual overview of *process performance metrics* and tools so you'll understand the magic of their power and application. Detailed examples of the metrics I discuss are presented in the CD included with the book, and of course they are extensively covered in Six Sigma training when you choose to lead your company to **world class performance levels.**

Six Sigma Measures Quality Variation

Unless we can measure something, we cannot improve our performance. "Sigma" as a unit of measure gives us a way to determine the extent of variation and the capability of our processes to meet customer expectations consistently.

For a business, engineering or manufacturing process, the Sigma value is a measurement that indicates how well that process is performing. The higher the Sigma value, the better. Sigma measures the capability of the process to perform defect-free work.

To calculate Sigma, we use a common measurement — Defects per Million Opportunities (DPMO). An opportunity can be virtually anything: component specifications, a line of computer code, a customer service telephone call, an invoice or billing statement. The Sigma value indicates how often defects are likely to occur. A defect is anything that results in customer dissatisfaction and in turn costs you money. The higher the Sigma value, the less likely it is that a process will result in a defect. **As Sigma value increases, costs go down, cycle time goes down, and customer satisfaction goes up.**

Figure 3.1

What is a Sigma? *Sigma is a Greek letter that represents a measure of variation and which describes the distribution or spread around the mean. Sigma could be any measurement: inches, volts, pounds, meters. It is used to assess the variability of any process or procedure in manufacturing, engineering, services or transactions. When we say that something is Six Sigma, we are saying that there is an extremely small amount of variation, relative to the specification width for the process. Six Sigma is 3.4 defects per million opportunities (DPMO).*

OPPORTUNITY COUNTS

The purpose of opportunity counts is to establish a common denominator in the equation for calculating defects per million opportunities (DPMO). This metric reflects the complexity of the process. A locomotive, a jet engine, and a light bulb all manufactured at one defect per unit (DPU) would have an equivalent rolled throughput yield (RTY). These two metrics do not reflect the complexity of the process. There are more opportunities for defects when manufacturing a locomotive than in a light bulb.

Using the opportunity count allows for the complexity to be reflected in the DPMO or subsequent sigma calculation. *This denominator allows for comparison of vastly different process technologies an industry is using.* Sigma is derived by first determining DPMO. Defects per Million Opportunities can be converted to the area under the right hand tail of a normal distribution curve, or the additive of both tails depending on where the defects end up relative to the specifications.

Sigma is then equal to the Z value for the corresponding tail area, or the sum of two tail areas. (The Z value is equivalent to the Sigma value.) Therefore, the objectivity and fairness of the Sigma metric is tied to how well the rules for opportunity-counting are developed and applied. *A highly structured approach is essential.* Once you set the rules, don't change the approach.

Figure 3.2 SIGMA DEFECT CURVE

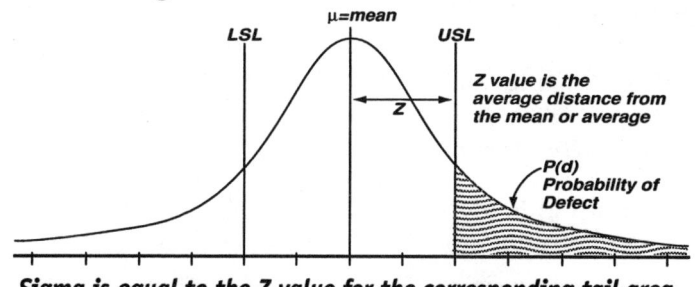

Sigma is equal to the Z value for the corresponding tail area.
Adapted from <u>The Vision of Six Sigma</u> by Mikel Harry, Ph.D., 1994

What constitutes an opportunity? An opportunity count should never be applied to any operation which does not add value to the product. Testing, inspection, gauging, etc. should rarely be included in an opportunity count. In most cases the product is unchanged after any of these processes. An exception would be an electrical test where the test is also used to program electronic testing equipment since the product was altered and value was added.

Another acid test for opportunity counts is the question, "Will applying counts in these operations take my business in the direction it is intended to go?" If counting each dimension checked on a coordinated measuring machine (CMM) inflates

---

FIGURE 3.3
Guidelines for Opportunity-Counting

COUNTS

- Each supplied and made part counts as one opportunity (the bill of materials).
- Each machined feature counts as one opportunity, but only if it is inspected frequently.
- Each fastener creates one opportunity in assembly. This includes bolts, nuts, snap rings, clips, rivets, spot welds, forming, swaging, etc.
- Paint counts as one opportunity per color.
- Each field on a data entry form counts as one opportunity.

DOES NOT COUNT

- Consumables such as supplies, oil, temporary plugs or covers, packaging, etc.
- Non valued-added processes or steps such as inspection, testing (except for trim or adjustments), deburring, material handling, packaging, shipping, warehousing, etc.

Adapted from a White Paper on Opportunity Counting by Mike Carnell

---

the denominator of the equation, adds no value, and increases cycle time when the company objective is to take cost out of the product, this type of count would be counter to the company objective.

Each supplied part should provide one opportunity since you can receive a correct or incorrect part each time. Supplied materials such as solder, machine oil, coolants, plater's tape, etc., do not count as supplied parts.

Each attachment should count as one opportunity. If a device requires four bolts, that counts as four opportunities. A sixty-pin integrated circuit, surface mount device, soldered to a printed circuit board would count as sixty. A sixteen-pin dual in line package (DIP) with through hole mounting would count as sixteen. A solder joint on the top and bottom side would count as one opportunity, not two.

In a machining operation there should be a count for each machined surface. If one tool makes five separate cuts the opportunity count is five. When a hole is drilled and counter-bored, the count would be two because there are two separate operations.

A drilled hole that is drilled and honed because the drilling operation is not trusted to hit the dimension is only one opportunity. The honing operation is the rework of the drilling operation. Filling out a form would count one opportunity per entry, not each alphanumeric entry (see Figure 3.3 for guidelines).

Once the opportunities have been established they should not be changed without a significant process change. The purpose of the metric is to **_allow for assessment of process improvement efforts._**

Small changes to the count will divert the energies of the organization from process improvement to mathematical exercises, or accounting gymnastics. The true benefit is in the continuity of the metric for evaluation of the defect reduction efforts when implementing Six Sigma.

PROCESS PERFORMANCE METRICS

Many performance metrics are available to define and communicate the *capability* of any manufacturing, service or transaction process. Each measurement has a unique function, and each individual, department, or organization will have its favorite ones that are used in particular situations.

Combinations of metrics are often useful, and many times we have to use several metrics together or use a specific order of metrics to gain in-depth knowledge of a process.

The appropriate metric to use in a particular situation is a function of the type of data involved — discrete (attribute) or continuous (variable) — and whether the capability being evaluated is short-term or long-term. Each metric has its own merits, but often several are needed to fully understand a process. It is difficult or impossible to compare processes with each other if they use different metrics. Without using similar metrics, it is impossible to say which process under investigation is better than the others.

Key metrics for process capability are:

Continuous (Variable) Data The measures Cp, Cpk, Pp, Ppk are most commonly used for describing continuous data. Cp is used to signify short-term potential capability, while Pp is used to signify long-term capability. Cpk and Ppk indicate if the process is centered and capable of producing to specified limits. Cp and Pp describe the *potential* of a process but do not necessarily reveal whether or not the process is under control and is generating a high product yield. Cpk and Ppk address the issue of whether a process is under control and generating good product yield *in relation to the specification limits.* They do not tell us the theoretical potential of the process if it could be precisely controlled. For this reason, these metrics are often used together as a complementary set.

Process Entitlement Cp represents process entitlement, or the best the process or product can be in the short-term. Cp assumes the process is centered or that the mean/average of the process is right on the design target. Cp only takes into consideration the tolerance or the width between the specification limits, not the location or the mean of where the process is performing. As a result, Cp can be very misleading since the process seldom operates right at the design center or target of the process. Sigma short-term is Zst which equals Cp x 3. For example, if Cp = 2, your Sigma short-term is Zst = 2 x 3 = 6; the process is operating at Six Sigma. (Cp uses a sample size of 50 over a short time.)

Process Capability Cpk represents the true short-term capability of your process, and takes into account the shifted condition. If the data is long-term, Ppk is an estimate of the quality that the customer receives from your company, or that your company receives from its suppliers. (Ppk uses a sample size of 500 over a longer period of time, rationalizing subgroups about the process.)

Discrete (Attribute) Data The measures DPO, PPM, DPMO, and DPU are the principal metrics unique to discrete data. They describe the number of defects produced by a process. Discrete data is long-term by nature.

Sigma Value The Sigma value (Z) is considered to be one of the best metrics, since it can be used to compare the capability of processes that are very diverse in nature. It is also used to "roll up" or "pool" many processes across a business unit into one top-level metric. The Sigma value (Z) can be calculated for any process, no matter what type of data is used.

The Sigma value (Z) is the only metric that applies in ALL cases (which includes opportunity), allowing direct comparison of one process to another, or one product to another, or one industry to another, regardless of their characteristics or complexities. It is the ***universal metric,*** ideal for comparing the capability of one process to another, no matter how dissimilar they may be. In this way, the capability of many processes can be 'pooled' into one top-level metric for a business unit. Using the pooled Sigma value, we are able to track overall improvement as it relates to the detailed processes.

The Sigma value (Z) is the only metric that applies in all cases, allowing direct comparison of one process to another, one product to another, or one industry to another, regardless of their characteristics or complexities.

Rolled Throughput Yield The concept of yield (Y) is the percentage of good products produced by a process. It applies equally to continuous or discrete data. Throughput Yield (TY) or Rolled Throughput Yield (RTY or Yrt) are the most meaningful metrics for yield since they take into account the "Stealth Factory," i.e. rework, scrap, failure analysis, etc. It is the yield throughout the entire process, not just the end or first pass yield.

First-Pass Yield The percent of good pieces resulting from a process step. This is equivalent to the number of good pieces divided by the total pieces started into the process. Rolled Throughput Yield is a multiplication of the first pass yield of each process step. A comparison of the two yield measurements follows.

The use of RTY distinguishes Six Sigma from other quality management processes. As Figure 3.5 demonstrates, average yield may look good, but RTY is poor.

FIGURE 3.4
ROLLED THROUGHPUT YIELD (RTY)

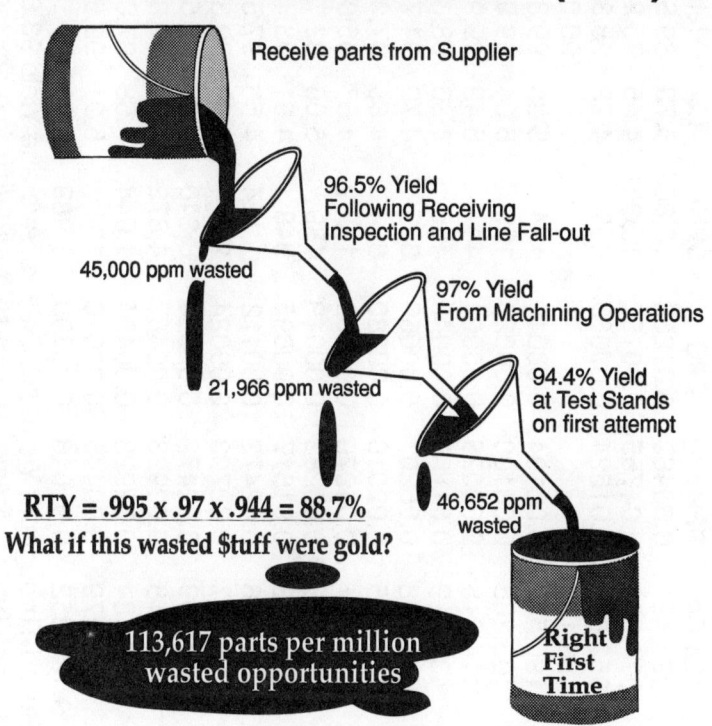

Receive parts from Supplier

96.5% Yield
Following Receiving
Inspection and Line Fall-out

45,000 ppm wasted

97% Yield
From Machining Operations

21,966 ppm wasted

94.4% Yield
at Test Stands
on first attempt

$RTY = .995 \times .97 \times .944 = \underline{88.7\%}$
What if this wasted $tuff were gold?

46,652 ppm
wasted

113,617 parts per million
wasted opportunities

Right
First
Time

How much "stuff" (Y) do you need at the beginning? To calculate,
$Y = 1 + (1 - Y_{RT}) = 1 + (1 - .887) = 1.113$ *or 111%.*
Approximately 11 MORE units need to be put into the process
at the beginning to get 100% yield at the end.
The 111% more "stuff" = effort, inventory and time.

Rolled Throughput Yield (RTY)

Yield taken at each step of the process.

Includes rework and scrap.

Will always be less than first-pass yield.

Gives you the probability of zero defects.

Looks at the quality of all the parts that make up the end product.

Gives the probability of a unit going through steps of the process with zero defects.

Takes into account the process complexity.

First–Pass Yield

Yield at the end of the process.

Doesn't include rework and scrap.

Will always be more than RTY.

Gives probability of zero defects.

Only looks at end product quality.

Gives the probability of a unit going through final assembly with zero defects.

Does not take into account the complexity of the process.

Figure 3.5: Metrics Performance of a Small Product Line

Line	Type	Def	Units	Op	Total Op	DPU	DPO	DPMO	σ+1.5σ*	Yield%
1	Tank Line	11,520	19,053	47	895,491	0.60463	0.01286	12,864	3.73	39.54
2	Paint Line	906	19,053	30	571,590	0.04755	0.00159	1,585	4.45	95.24
3	Core	619	38,106	25	952,650	0.01624	0.00065	650	4.72	98.38
4	Insulation	0	19,053	2	38,106					100.00
5	Small Coils	37	19,053	10	190,530	0.00194	0.00019	194	5.05	99.81
6	Small Coils	19	19,053	5	95,265	0.00100	0.00020	199	5.04	99.90
7	Core/Coil	5	19,053	6	114,318	0.00026	0.00004	44	5.42	99.97
8	Mount	213	19,053	23	438,219	0.01118	0.00049	486	4.80	98.88
9	Tanking	992	19,053	76	1,448,028	0.05207	0.00069	685	4.70	94.79
10	Test	383	19,053	25	476,325	0.02010	0.00080	804	4.65	97.99
11	Fit for Shipment	948	19,053	47	895,491	0.04976	0.00106	1,059	4.57	95.02
12	Repair	54	19,053	15	285,795	0.00283	0.00019	189	5.06	99.72
13	BlockBraze	289	19,053	16	304,848	0.01517	0.00095	948	4.61	98.48
14	Tank Storage	471	19,053	22	419,166	0.02472	0.00112	1,124	4.56	97.53
15	Cust Sat Co	134	19,053	29	552,537	0.00703	0.00024	243	4.99	99.30
16	Fact Sm Prod	471	19,053	3	57,159	0.02472	0.00824	8,240	3.90	97.53
17	Unknown	557	19,053	6	114,318	0.02923	0.00487	4,872	4.08	97.08
18	Engineering	557	19,053	28	533,484	0.02923	0.00104	1,044	4.58	97.08
19	Purchasing	85	19,053	43	819,279	0.00446	0.00010	104	5.21	99.55
	TOTAL	18,260	20,056	458	9,185,552	0.91046	0.00199	1,988	4.38	

Rolled Throughput Yield 28.62%   vs. Average Yield 93.63%

*1.5 σ is used to estimate long-term process capability. Six Sigma assumes shift and drift in a process or product and 1.5σ has been proven to be the approximate amount of shift over time.

Precision is Not the Same as Accuracy

Let's follow the performance of a field-goal kicker to explain the difference between the precision of a process and its accuracy. The goal posts represent "the money," or the limits within which your process or product needs to perform. Each post represents an upper and lower specification limit for a process, in this case, the process is kicking a field goal.

Our team is really lucky! Our kicker can kick the ball 75 yards within a 20-foot width. His contract pays him $50,000 for every kick that goes between the goal posts, not to the right or the left. This 75-yard field-goal kicker is very **precise**, but he's not always **accurate** in his orientation! His kicks often go off to the right.

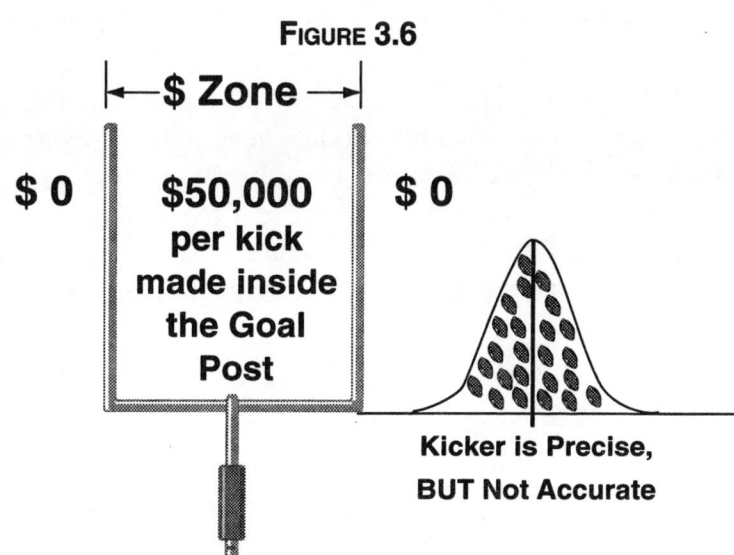

FIGURE 3.6

|←— **$ Zone** —→|

$ 0 **$50,000** per kick made inside the Goal Post **$ 0**

**Kicker is Precise,
BUT Not Accurate**

*Precision is Not the Same as Accuracy.
The plot on the right shows where the ball went.*

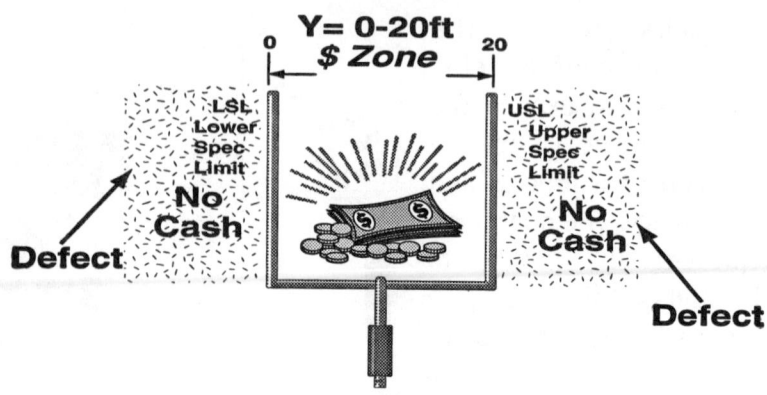

The Money Zone.
The kicker must kick into the zone to make money.

So this kicker needs to know what Y (kicking accurately) is a function of $[Y = f(x)]$. Y can be defined as kicking the football into a specification between 0 and 20 feet, the upper and lower specification limits represented by the goal posts.

Cp is a capability index which describes how capable a process is to give a specification width that is ***not anchored down.*** It takes into account only the ***width*** of the process or design tolerance (20 feet between the goal posts), not the upper and lower limits (the location of the goal posts). If we could pick up the goal post and move it around to where this kicker sends the ball, he's very capable of kicking 75 yards in a 20-foot width. He's just not ***accurate.*** Cp only states what the actual capability could be if you could move the specification around, and it only describes the ***precision*** of the process, not the ***accuracy.***

Another capability index is Cpk, which is an index which describes ***accuracy*** and is anchored to a specification. You can't pick up the goal posts and move it around. If Cp = Cpk then the kicker is both ***precise*** and ***accurate.*** If you look at this on an annual basis, kicking around three kicks per game for 20 games, the precise and accurate field-goal kicker would make a lot of money.

92   *Six Sigma for Leadership*

FIGURE 3.8

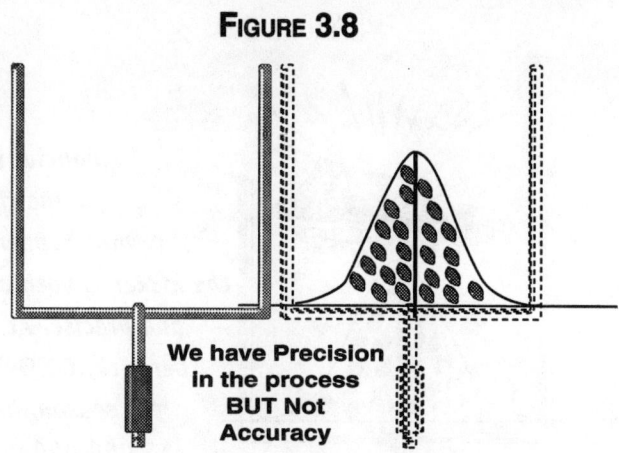

Process Precision. Kicking to the right is not accurate, but the kicks meet the precision requirement.

When he kicks off to the right, the Cp of the process is the same as when he kicks it through the goal posts, since Cp does not take into account where the process is performing, only the design tolerance and the standard deviation. It measures whether the kicks are within 20 feet of each other. His Cpk is terrible, since the process is running outside the upper specification limit (the right goal post): the team doesn't score and the kicker makes no money. This situation gives you a product that has little variance but is out of specification.

The kicker needs to determine what factors – the Vital Few – determine his **accuracy**. What are the Xs in the equation $Y = f(x)$?

X_1 = Force of the kick

X_2 = Height of the launch

X_3 = Angle of the ball on the ground

X_4 = Shoe type

X_5 = Foot to ball hit location

X_6 = Ball lace position at time of kick

X_7 = Follow-through eye position of the kicker

X_8 = Follow-through position of the leg

FIGURE 3.9

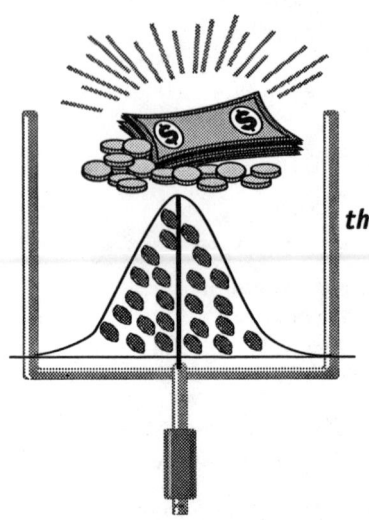

Financial Reward.
The financial
reward happens when
the kicker is both accurate
and precise. At $50,00
per kick, 60 field goals
per season, he makes
$3,000,000 annually!

When the kicker is able to determine the **Vital Few** that affect his **accuracy,** both the kicker and the team will be happy — Cp and Cpk will be identical when his process (kicking a field goal) is operating with precision and right at the design target (the center of the goal posts). And finally the financial reward happens! For the kicker it is 60 field goals at $50,000 or $3,000,000 annually.

USING PERFORMANCE METRICS

How often does management typically look at the business consequences of quality performance? That is, gains in market share or profit resulting from quality improvements? Japanese companies do so 70 percent of the time vs. 50 percent in Canada and 55 percent in Germany and the U.S. And it is well known that Japan has been ahead of the quality and cost game for years. So how do we go about looking at these consequences in a factual way?

A fundamental concept of the Six Sigma quality improvement process is that performance metrics, or the measurement of what is happening in every sector of a business, are critically important to the bottom line. Performance metrics allow you to select something about your business that you value (Y), measure it, and translate it into statistical "pictures," put a goal line in place, then measure it and assess it over time. Eventually, through Six Sigma you will predict what Y will be and reduce the costs that adversely affect defects in the customer's Y.

The benefit of performance metrics cannot be overstated! Using metrics is a proven means to guide the basic operation of a business. It provides feedback and a focus on business performance fundamentals. Six Sigma metrics make sure that management is focused on improving:

1) *Critical-to-Quality*
factors that matter to the customer, and
2) *The VITAL FEW*
factors that give the most "bang for the buck."

FIGURE 3.10

The Data Use Questionnaire

We use data to Measure, Analyze, Improve, and Control processes. ***What level of data do you use currently?***

1σ No data collection, we just use our experience.
2σ We collect data, but don't use it.
3σ We form charts and graphs with some collected data.
4σ We present charts and graphs,
        but make no decisions on the data.
5σ We collect data and use descriptive statistics. (μ, σ)
6σ We collect data and use inferential statistics,
        making decisions with data.

Six Sigma companies are at level six.

Adapted from "The Vision of Six Sigma" by Mikel Harry, Ph.D.

©1994 Sigma Publishing Co

Metrics show you where you've been, where you're going, if you're on course, and whether changes have achieved desired outcomes. Like the instrument panel of an airplane, performance metrics are essential: **Without them you are BLIND in the storm!**

MAIC = MAGIC WITHOUT THE "G" FOR GUESSWORK

The **Seven Principles of Problem-Solving Technology** are built upon the core Six Sigma principle of MEASURE, ANALYZE, IMPROVE and CONTROL (MAIC). This concept was first developed at Motorola, where it was called Define, Analyze, Optimize, and Control. It was then refined and perfected by Dr. Mikel Harry of Six Sigma Academy.

The first two phases **characterize** any process targeted for improvement, and the last two **optimize** and **maintain** it. This four-step process is taught to Champions and Black Belts in Fortune 500 corporations by certified Senior Master Black Belts. This process provides the framework for the application of performance metrics tools and enables you to **manage with data** and to identify and define the equation $Y = f\ (X_1 - X_n)$.

On the front-end of this process, you must identify customer-driven, critical-to-quality (CTQ) characteristics, then identify the processes that contribute to defects and waste in these characteristics.

**Deviate an inch,
lose a thousand miles.**

Chinese Proverb

Prior to going into the MAIC process, senior level managers must perform a macro-level project selection which identifies a list of chronic and high-impact issues affecting the business. This work is then handed over to the potential Black Belt candidate prior to the beginning of training. The Black Belt candidate further refines the scope of the project with his assigned Champion. Now the Black Belt candidate is ready to go to class. General Electric calls this the **DEFINE** phase. There is another phase prior to define which is the **RECOGNIZE** phase; this phase simply states that you recognize the **NEED** to do Six Sigma.

Phase 1: Measure

This phase is concerned with identifying one or more product or service characteristics. These dependent variables (Ys) describe the process by mapping the respective process, evaluating the measurement system, and estimating the baseline capability of the process. As a general output of the measure phase, a list of potential Xs should be identified, a current process capability determined, and a valid measurement system established.

The following are questions that Champions should ask their Black Belts during the MEASURE phase:

- What business problem led to this project? Where are the opportunities? How will this project improve the situation?

- What is the impact to the customer when this project is completed?

- Who are the process owner(s)? Who are your process improvement team members? Does anyone require additional training?

- What are the critical quality characteristics leading to the selection of this project?

FIGURE 3.11

Problem-Solving Technology (PST) Model

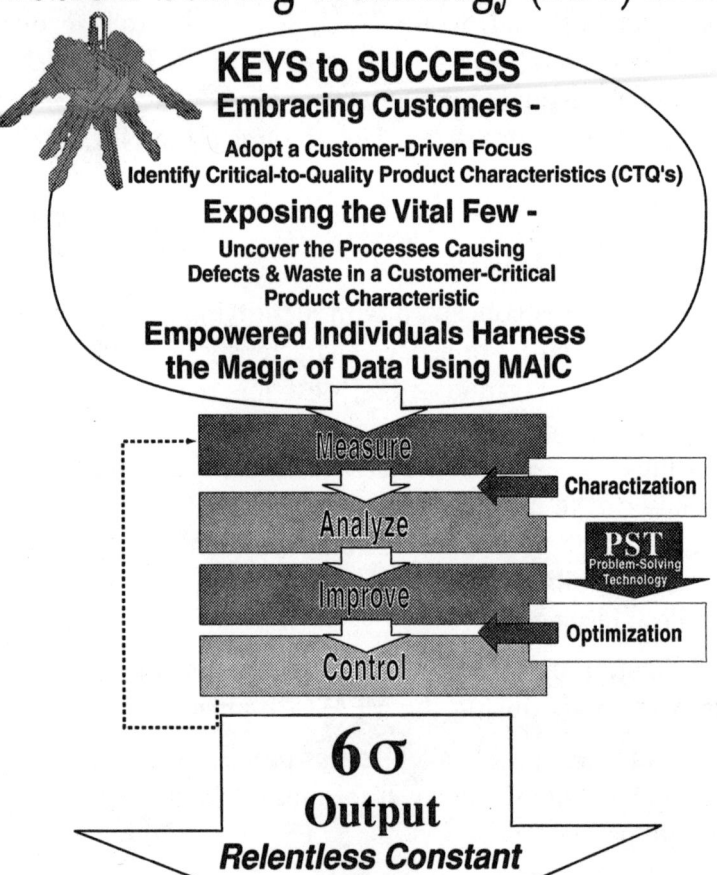

KEYS to SUCCESS
Embracing Customers -

Adopt a Customer-Driven Focus
Identify Critical-to-Quality Product Characteristics (CTQ's)

Exposing the Vital Few -

Uncover the Processes Causing
Defects & Waste in a Customer-Critical
Product Characteristic

Empowered Individuals Harness
the Magic of Data Using MAIC

Measure

Analyze

Improve

Control

Charactization

PST
Problem-Solving
Technology

Optimization

6σ
Output
Relentless Constant
Journey

- What do you hope to accomplish? What are your objectives as they relate to the baseline performance established?

- Have you completed your Project Status Form?

- Have the benefits of this project been quantified? If not, when can we expect to see this?

- How did you collect the data to support the project?

- How many parts, and why this number?

- How do you know that you took enough samples?

- How did you ensure that you have eliminated the influences of assignable causes (noise) within your subgroups?

- How did you ensure that you included noise between rational subgroups?

- What is the Gauge R&R (Repeatability & Reproducibility)? Who took the measurements? For supplier projects, who owns the gauging? If a better gauge is needed, what would be the cost?

- Do you have a process map (flowchart)? Who was involved in its development? Where are the tally points?

- What are the categories of defects as shown in your Pareto analyses?

- If a technology problem is indicated, what do you think it will take to improve it? Are there any other alternatives?

- What is the beginning level of defects (parts per million)? Do you have a chart showing where you plan to go and the necessary timing?

- What is the short-term capability (Zst) and long-term capability (Zlt) of the process?

- What are your next steps?

- Are you satisfied with the level of cooperation and support you are getting?

MEASURE - DELIVERABLES

(1) **Project Status Form**

(2) **Metric Graph**

(3) **Process Map w/Tally Points**

(4) **2- level Pareto Charts** (by line/cell & defect type)

(5) **Measurement [Zst & Zlt (capability short-term and long-term)], RTY, PPM, Gauge R&R for the Vital Few defect types and start of Failure Mode Effect Analysis (FMEA)**

(6) **Improvement Plans / Next Steps**

(7) **Completed Local Project Review prior to Six Sigma review.**

Phase 2: Analyze

The purpose of the analyze phase is to begin to passively evaluate the Xs identified in the measure phase using graphical analysis and hypothesis testing. The general deliverables of the Analyze phase are a reduced number of Xs from the list identified in the Measure phase. In some cases, there will be a more focused or re-scoped problem statement. In a few cases the problem can be contained but not solved.

The following are questions that Champions should ask their Black Belts during the ANALYZE phase:

- Have you updated your Project Status Form?
  Let's review it.

- How many significant ("Vital Few") variables influence the process, and what are they? What's on the list of ALL the variables initially analyzed?

- Who participated in the initial brainstorming about what the vital few COULD be?
- What is the potential contribution of each of the Vital Few? (Sum of Squares ratios.)
- What progress has been made on the PPM (parts per million) chart (projections and timing)?
- What new tools have you used in this phase? How were they helpful?
- What are your containment actions to reduce defects from the project process(es) until the final solution can be developed and implemented?
- Explain your improvement plans and next steps to get there (include timing, responsibility, and expected results).
- What was the basis for the improvement quantification calculations?
- Are you satisfied with the support you and your team are receiving from the process owner(s)?
- What other support actions or activities do you need to accelerate your progress?

FIGURE 3.13

ANALYZE - DELIVERABLES

(1) Project Status Form — updated

(2) Metric Graph — updated

(3) Tool Use as Applicable

    — DOE Plan, Gauge R&R, 3-level Pareto

    — Contingency Table, FMEA, etc.

(4) Solution (Root Cause)

(5) Improvement Plans / Next Steps

(6) Quantification of Improvement Plans

(7) Completed Local Project Review

FIGURE 3.14

The Six Sigma Problem-Solving Technology: Measure, Analyze, Improve, Control

	Focus
Measure Phase 	
1 Select Product or Process Critical To Quality (CTQ) CTQ Characteristics(s); e.g., CTQ Y	Y
2 Define Performance Standards for Y	Y
3 Validate Measurement System for Y	Y
4 Establish Process Capability of Creating Y	Y
Analyze Phase 	
5 Define Improvement Objectives for Y	Y
6 Identify Variation Sources in Y	$x_1 x_2 \dots x_n$
7 Screen Potential Causes for Change in Y and Identify Vital Few x_i	$x_1 x_2 \dots x_n$
Improve Phase 	
8 Discover Variable Relationships Between the Vital Few x_i	
9 Establish Operating Tolerances on Vital Few x_i	Vital Few X
10 Validate Measurement System for x_i	
Control Phase 	
11 Determine Ability to Control Vital Few x_i	Vital Few X
12 Implement Process Control System on Vital Few x_i	

The Six Sigma Problem-Solving Technology of Measure, Analyze, Improve, and Control (MAIC) is typically a 12-step process. Each step focuses on Y, the characteristic of quality that you are trying to achieve, or X, the key process variables that control Y.

Phase 3: Improve

In the improve phase, the reduced list of Xs are then actively evaluated through experimentation. The output of this phase should include identifying the Xs that explain (correlate) the variation of the process $[Y = f(x)]$.

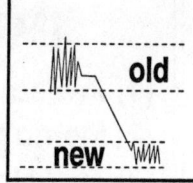

The following are questions that Champions should ask their Black Belts during the IMPROVE phase:

- Has your Project Status Form been updated? Let's review it.

- Will the production line be able to support your Design of Experiments (DOE)?

- What progress has been achieved to date in the PPM performance? Has your chart been updated?

- What impact will your DOE have on the line? What is the value of any scrap that will be generated?

- Has the Controller or his designate been involved in the process to fully understand any cost implications?

- What is the DOE method and why was this particular method chosen?

- What new tools have you learned that were used in this phase of the project?

- What does the DOE point to as possible root cause(s)?

- What are your next steps toward achieving your improvement targets?

- Have the improvement plans been quantified and has the Controller's office been involved in these discussions and calculations?

- Are you satisfied with the support you and your team are receiving from the process owner(s)?

- What other support actions or activities do you need to accelerate your progress?

Phase 4: Control

The control phase is the hardest and most important phase. This phase is related to ensuring that the new process conditions are documented and monitored with process-control methods. In addition, the process capability should be reassessed to ensure that gains have been realized and sustained over six months to a year. In some cases there are no controls because you eliminate the problem entirely.

The following are questions that Champions should ask their Black Belts during the CONTROL phase:

- Has your Project Status Form been updated? Let's review it.

- What process-control method is being implemented to assure that you are able to "sustain the gain"?

- What progress has been achieved to date in the PPM performance? Has your chart been updated?

- Who will take the responsibility for maintaining this process after your team has completed their Six Sigma effort? Are these people fully aware of this and have they agreed?
- Is there a plan to revisit this process in the future to ensure the new capability level is maintained? What new measurements are in place?
- What is the expected improvement in terms of cost reduction? Has the Controller or his designate been involved in the process to fully understand any cost implications? Are these costs being permanently driven out?
- What new tools have you learned that were used in this phase of the project?
- Are you satisfied with the support you and your team received from the process owner(s)? What recommendations can you offer to better support the next Six Sigma project? What are the "lessons learned" that will improve your next efforts?
- When do you plan to have your final report completed?
- What is your control and transition plan for this project?

FIGURE 3.16

CONTROL - Deliverables

(1) Project Status Form
(2) Metric Graph
(3) Specific Control Plan / Validation Plan
(4) Verification of Improvement / Results:
    metrics and $$ savings
(5) Transition Plan to "Sustain the Gain"
(6) Significant Lessons Learned
(7) Final Report
(8) Completed Local Project Review

Getting Away From I Think, I Believe, and I Feel

At the General Electric appliance plant in Louisville, Kentucky, I helped a Black Belt address a chronic problem: The washing machine agitator didn't fit. It took two factory assembly people to force the agitator into place, using a big cross-patterned auger. This was a source of carpal tunnel syndrome for the employees, a safety-related issue, and a Cost of Poor Quality. Also, there were two people doing what should have been a one-person job.

If the agitator did fit, it was often too tight. If the washing machine leaked in the field, the repair person couldn't get the agitator off. So the whole machine had to be taken in for the repair. The customer wasn't happy with the washing machine or with GE.

Some of the agitators didn't fit at all and became scrap, or the production line was stopped to make adjustments. The production, warranty and service costs were all increased because of this chronic problem of poor fit.

This whole problem added up to about $1 million annually. To solve it, we had to measure what was happening and understand the whole process. The Black Belt identified a strong correlation between the weight of the agitator and the fit. If it weighed just right, it would fit perfectly, with only one person doing the installation.

To really understand the problem, it is sometimes necessary to imagine that you are the defective part. In the case above the "agitator," is asking the question, *"Why don't I fit?"* The answer in this case was, *"If I am the right weight, I fit perfectly."*

The question then was, *"Why aren't all the agitators the right weight?"* We went to the supplier of the agitator for the answer. The agitators had never been weighed before, but since we now knew that there is a correlation between the weight of the agitator and the fit, they had to be weighed now. Remember $Y = f(x)$ or simply stated, **fit** is a function of **weight.**

In the past, the brainstorming sessions about this problem were done with "I think, I feel, I believe" statements. We were now going to get away from that and **actually weigh the agitators.** Then we did a comparison of the injection molding cavities. There were ten cavities making the agitators. The question we asked (the hypothesis) was, **"Are all ten plastic molding cavities producing the same weight agitator?"**

GE had never asked that question of the supplier before. We had to analyze it, to break the problem down into parts. First, we had to demonstrate that we could actually weigh things consistently and accurately, and we did. With this data, we identified the vital few issues.

FIGURE 3.17

WHICH AGITATORS FIT?

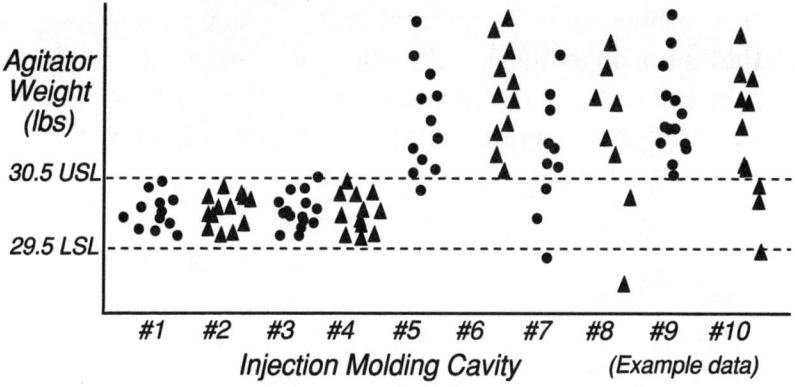

When the agitators were weighed, it was clear that cavities 1 through 4 produced agitators that were within specified limits. Fit is a function of weight. Only agitators from cavities 1 through 4 FIT.

The weight of each agitator is a function of each of the 10 different cavities. Now, leaving the world of "I think, I feel, I believe," we enter the world of facts and data or the "confidence interval question." We can say, "I am 95 percent confident of this," based on data that has been validated.

The specifications for a "good" weight were between 29.5 and 30.5 pounds. A correct agitator weight meant no warranty costs for repair, no carpal tunnel syndrome in the employees, and only one person per shift required to 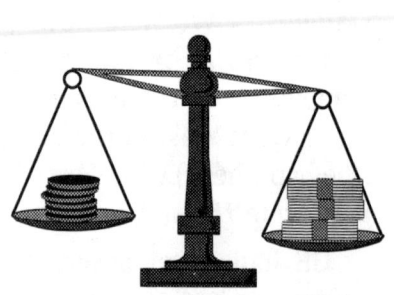 install the agitator. Controlling these costs would result in one million dollars in additional cash for GE. We were 95 percent confident that the first four molding cavities (represented on the graph) were going to produce properly weighted agitators. The other six were problem producers.

Now GE has identified one of the "vital few", the source of the problem, but hasn't yet fixed it. What can GE do to fix the problem which comes from the supplier base? They told the supplier they would only purchase agitators made from the first four cavities. The supplier then had to adjust the other six and prove that they were producing agitators that met GE's weight specifications.

The Measure and Analyze phases contained the problem at the supplier level. The supplier didn't like the solution, but he was not consistent with his production, so the problem had to be fixed. First we contained the problem by limiting the agitators to the first four cavities. Then in partnership with the supplier, we went on to fix the cavities of the other six machines.

FIGURE 3.18

The Quantum Gains of Problem-Solving Technology

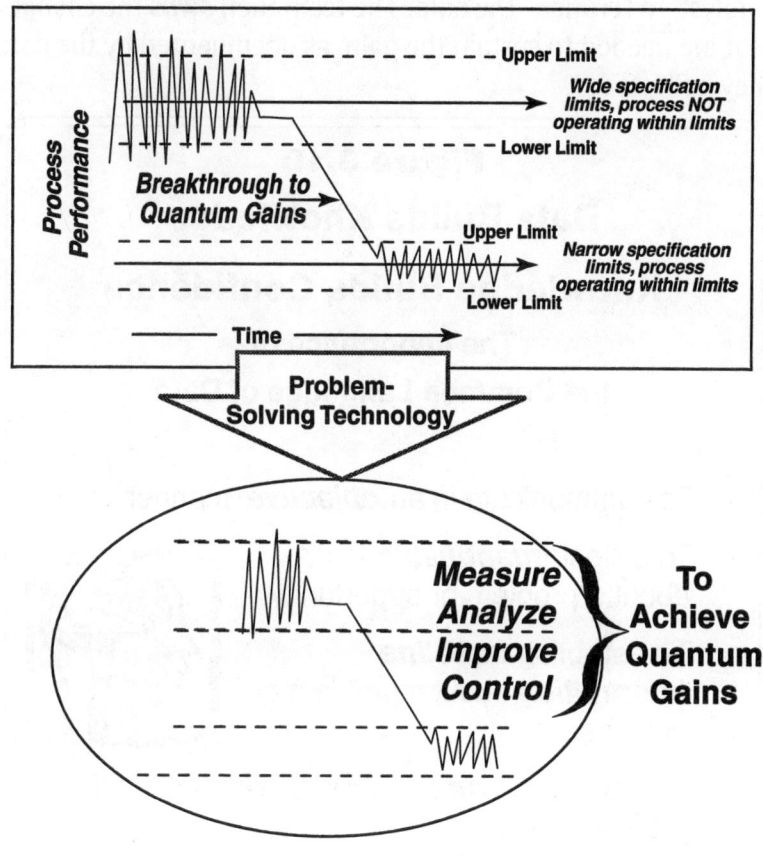

Adapted from Juran, 1964 *Breakthrough*

When you discover the "Vital Few" and control them, you can achieve Quantum Gains — breakthrough improvements in product quality — and set new standards.

When you discover the "Vital Few" and control them, you can achieve quantum gains in product quality and set new standards. During the *Measure* and *Analyze* phase, we characterize the problem and find the variables. Performance then *Improves* and you *Control* it over time. This ensures that the process remains at the new standard. The Black Belt and the project team gather the data, and the Black Belt acts as a catalyst to "crunch" the data. The team then *owns* the changes that are needed to sustain the gain, as documented by the data they collected.

Figure 3.19

Data Builds Knowledge

Knowledge Builds Confidence

The Importance of
the Common Language of Data

- To communicate in an *objective* manner.

- To collect *quantifiable facts* about a problem or opportunity.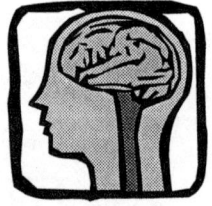

- To establish *baseline information* about a problem or process.

- To facilitate *cost-benefit analysis* of proposed solutions.

- To compare *before and after* - quantify the impact of a solution.

- To *justify extension* of the solution.

THE ROLE OF A SIX SIGMA PARTNER

Many times that I have been called in to consult with a company that has been trying to implement Six Sigma based on what they have read about it. A good example occurred when I presented our capabilities as a training partner to the quality department of a leading document company. They were impressed with the results experienced by other clients, but they decided to go it alone.

A year later, they paid me to come back just to tell them where I thought they should be after a year of doing Six Sigma. I showed them a spreadsheet that predicted where a company of their size would be after one year.

The projected savings from Six Sigma Black Belt projects were $150 million. Well, they weren't even close! Their best figure was less than $10 million — not even 10 percent of the projected figure. Yet they still couldn't justify spending less than a million to get it done right and save $150 million.

I tell this story because you need to understand that there is a proven process to implement Six Sigma in any company. The process that has a track record of success that delivers bottom line savings. You can try to go it alone, but your results are likely to look as sickly as that of the document company.

Experienced Six Sigma practitioners bring more than knowledge to the table. They bring **strategy** and **tactics** learned on the front lines during many cycles of implementation. They are able to build momentum, remove barriers, and light a fire for the vision of Six Sigma throughout your company. They should provide the **vision, velocity, and quantum gains** for your company. They have the knowledge,  the extreme sense of urgency, experience, and skills to transfer that knowledge to your people.

When your Six Sigma partners leave, they leave behind copies of themselves: Black Belt clones that work for you full-time. They are able to find out what you don't know about your stealth factory costs. You and your people are too close to the situation to see what is there. When you try to save money by not hiring a training partner, you never find out what you don't know.

> **Three fourths of the mistakes of man are made because he does not really know what he thinks he knows.**
>
> *James Bryce*

APPLYING PROBLEM-SOLVING TECHNOLOGY TO YOUR COMPANY

Questions to Ask Yourself

How much variation exists in our processes?

How many defects per million opportunities do we produce?

Do we generate good product yield?

Are our specification limits based on customer requirements?

Do our yield measurements take into account the "stealth factory?"

Do we know what we need to know to use performance metrics?

Can we calculate the RTY (Rolled Throughput Yield) of our processes?

"Good management consists in showing **average** people how to do the work of **superior** people."

John D. Rockefeller

CHAPTER 4

Creating the
"Best of the Best"
Six Sigma Champions and Black Belts

To become a Six Sigma company,
it takes more than technology, knowledge and
organization. This quantum leap in quality needs
REFOCUSING of people to make it happen.

As you have seen, the Six Sigma process is rigorous, requiring tremendous commitment from the highest levels of management. It requires a culture change in your company, using Champions and Black Belts as agents of change[1]. Through training and guidance, Six Sigma experts maximize potential, translate problems into solvable equations, and in the process transform your people assets into Champions and Black Belts of the Six Sigma vision. **We transfer "Do Six Sigma" know-how to your people permanently.**

We've referred to the terms Champion, Master Black Belt and Black Belt several times in this book. You are probably wondering where the term Black Belt comes from — visions of karate masters obliterating their opposition! That's not far from the truth. In fact, Dr. Mikel Harry appropriated the term "Black

[1] Champions, Master Black Belts, Black Belts, and Green Belts are service marks of Six Sigma Academy and are used with permission as a Licensee of the Academy.

Belt" while at Unisys. This company had a huge circuit board problem and Six Sigma tools were successfully used to fix the problem. Dr. Harry was discussing how to leverage Six Sigma throughout the company with plant manager Cliff Ames. Cliff was wondering what to call the Six Sigma tool masters. The term engineer or statistician didn't reflect how they were being asked to attack major challenges and develop creative solutions through the rigorous application of quality techniques.

Dr. Harry compared the Six Sigma masters to karate experts. They chop and kick with Six Sigma tools and beat the heck out of variation. The analogy made sense. Martial arts black belts are very skilled, are excellent tacticians, and have a precise command of simple but effective tools such as numchucks and throwing stars. Six Sigma Black Belts do the same with statistical tools, so the term stuck.

The classical model for quality improvement has been to find people with on-the-job experience and discipline-specific skills, and through trial and error, observation, knowledge, and reasoning they are expected to solve whatever problems arise. In addition, the complexity of quality improvement systems in the past has made the systems nearly irrelevant in practical terms. High-level executives have no time or motivation to study the systems since they don't seem to relate to bottom line, quantifiable financial gains.

To achieve Six Sigma performance, you need to add a couple of key factors to the classical quality improvement model. First of all, Black Belts need *statistical skills.* Not that your people have to be statisticians, but they have to understand how to select and use the tools available in order to uncover the processes that need attention. You can't battle process or product variation without these tools. Secondly, Black Belts need *leadership skills.* They need to know how to get things done, how to communicate the vision of Six Sigma quality throughout the company. They need to become *"Change Agents"* and be able to conquer the barriers they will find in their path.

FIGURE 4.1

Roles of a Six Sigma Black Belt

Classical Model for Quality Improvement

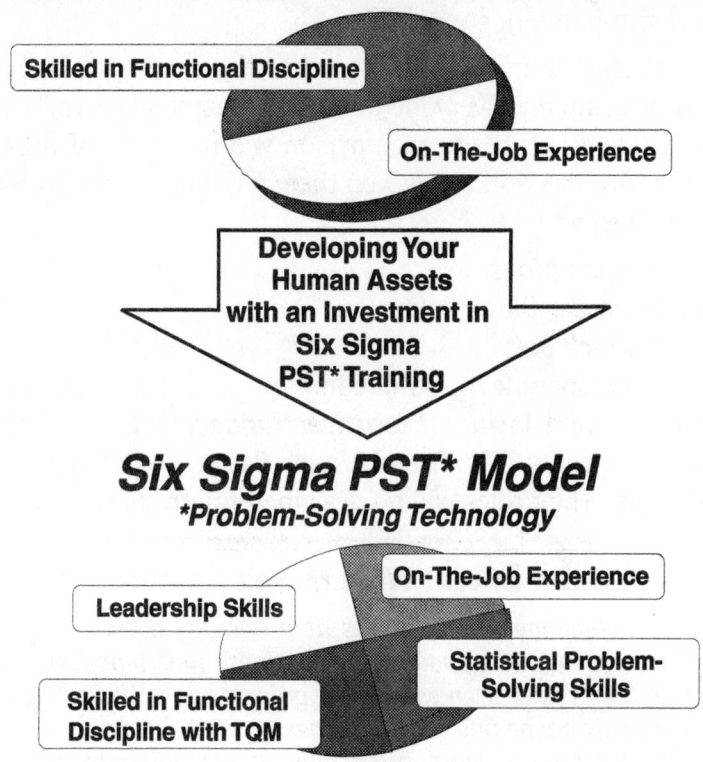

Skilled in Functional Discipline

On-The-Job Experience

Developing Your
Human Assets
with an Investment in
Six Sigma
PST* Training

Six Sigma PST Model*
**Problem-Solving Technology*

On-The-Job Experience

Leadership Skills

Statistical Problem-
Solving Skills

Skilled in Functional
Discipline with TQM

Being a Black Belt is a FULL TIME assignment!!

As discussed later in Chapter 6, Six Sigma training uses the PTAR process of Plan, Train, Apply, and Review. It is critical that your "human assets" be thoroughly familiar with the metric and statistical tools required by Six Sigma, with how to apply these tools to projects, and with how to accomplish their objective. ***The Seven Principles of Problem-Solving Technology*** follow a standard process to train your people and implement Six Sigma in your company.

Six Sigma is a sophisticated data-driven thought process that applies measurements to problem-solving. Implementation of Six Sigma is ensured by **empowering individuals to take ownership of projects.** That's what training is all about — **empowerment.** These individuals are then free to make positive change happen using the tools learned during their extensive training.

Clearly defined roles are vital to the success of Six Sigma in your company. Everyone in your company needs to "see the vision," and eventually each person will use some of the tools to improve the work. However, there are three major Six Sigma roles. They are:

- *Champions*
- *Master Black Belts*
- *Black Belts*

Other people in your company are also important as resources, and include **Executive Management, Supervisory-level Managers, Six Sigma Green Belts, and Project Team Members.** Their roles will be described briefly as well.

DOING SIX SIGMA: What Makes a Good Champion

A company president was at a one-day overview of Six Sigma for plant managers and business unit managers. He told us, "You've seen what we're going to do with Six Sigma. I see this happening within the next year. We're going to turn this company around financially. We're going to change everything. I'd like for you to all take part in it, but if you feel you're not going to take part in this effort, let me know right now so we can help you find other employment."

This is a Champion with commitment to the vision of DOING SIX SIGMA. There was no question about it. No one thought that Six Sigma was the latest management fad that they could ignore if they liked. He didn't give them a choice. It was DO SIX SIGMA or find another place to work.

Ray Everhart, Master Black Belt

Six Sigma Champions

Executive-level managers in your company (the Vice President and Director level) must own and drive the Six Sigma journey to quality improvement. At least one individual from this level must become a Six Sigma Champion to provide day-to-day leadership. Depending on the size of the company, several Executive-level managers may choose to become Champions.

The role of the Champion cannot be overemphasized.

Without Champions, the potential for success is far less. The Champion must thoroughly understand the strategy, discipline and tools of Six Sigma. Each Champion must promote Six Sigma strategy and methodology throughout the company, but especially in their area or function. It is the Champion's job to select Black Belt candidates, identify potential project areas for Black Belts, and establish clear and measurable objectives for those projects. It is up to the Champion to assign the necessary people resources to assist each Black Belt on these projects.

The Champion must encourage setting challenging goals, and targets high enough that people are forced to re-examine the way they do their job, not just tweak the existing process. *The Champion asks different questions and sees a better vision, forcing people to re-examine the status quo.*

Common sense is Four Sigma thinking.
To achieve Six Sigma we need <u>extraordinary</u> sense.
Six Sigma thinkers, not common thinkers.

Mikel Harry, Ph.D.

The Champion is extremely important to the Black Belts who are on the front line of implementation. The Champion acts as coach and mentor, provides reward incentives, removes any barriers, and makes sure that necessary resources are available. Champions truly "own" the process, monitoring and ensuring the implementation of Six Sigma in their area or function while leading and supporting project teams. They are responsible for monitoring the benefits of a project after completion and for tracking costs and savings realized.

Probably one of the most important roles a Champion plays is to run interference for their Black Belts. One thing management likes to do with Change Agents is take credit when things are going well and shoot them if they aren't! The Champion provides a shield for the Black Belt.

DOING SIX SIGMA: What Makes a Good Champion

At a Canadian glass manufacturing plant, we went in to do Six Sigma. This plant does not shut down for anything. Once the plant starts making glass, it runs continually for 12 years. The hot section is sacred — only people with a lot of experience work in that section because of the danger. Of course, we were told we had to do all our projects in the cold section, we were not allowed to go into the hot end to do anything. This Champion told us, "Let's demonstrate that Six Sigma works by starting in the cold end and then I'll get you into the hot end. I'll take you there." He essentially told the people in the hot section, "Here's what the Six Sigma Black Belts achieved over here in the cold end. Can you give me your numbers where you made this kind of improvement using your 'tribal knowledge' and experience? What have you done in the hot section to match what was done in the cold section?" This Champion took the data from the cold section projects and got us into the hot section of that plant, which was totally unheard of. That's a Champion who believed totally in Six Sigma and who made the time in his schedule to be a part of the effort.

Ray Everhart, Master Black Belt

An example of a bad Champion: I was working with a Black Belt on a project in a factory. The Black Belt had identified an area of tremendous savings — $22 million — and was not getting the cooperation of his Champion to remove the barriers. When the product this factory made was finished, it was going to an area of the plant where it was "messed with" unnecessarily, rather than going straight to the painting step. The Black Belt couldn't seem to get the line workers to change the way they did things and his Champion (the plant manager) wasn't helping. In cases like this, an outside influence is needed to move things along. I made a call to the CEO and soon the barrier (the plant manager) was removed.

Champions Accelerate the Change Process

Champions have to get involved — this is not a spectator sport! They have to work with their Black Belts to mobilize commitment and make change last. It's the job of the Champion to:

- Identify and remove the barriers and roadblocks to achieving high performance with Six Sigma.

- Ensure that the process owner's support is there during all phases.

- Focus Black Belts by asking many difficult questions (see Chapter 3 for examples).

- Encourage follow-up and monitoring activities.

- Carefully select high-impact projects.

- Help transfer project ownership from Black Belt to supervisory-level managers who "own" the process upon completion of the control phase.

DOING SIX SIGMA: What Makes a Good Champion

A VP of Manufacturing came to the Black Belt report-out meetings really trying to understand things. A Black Belt needed to buy a table so product defects could be sorted off-line. Currently, when the line got a certain level of defects they shut everything down and went in and sorted. In order to keep the line moving, the Black Belt wanted to divert the defects to a table off-line which would cost $17,000 to install. The controller told her to go through the normal process and she'd get the table in about four months. That kind of delay would have killed the program right there. At the report-out, the VP asked the Black Belt "Do you need that money? Where is your data?" She presented the data, and the VP said, "the $17,000 is not an issue, start digging the hole on Monday."

*When a Champion does this, his action sends a clear signal: We're serious about this. If she had had to wait four months to get a measly table it would have sent the wrong signal that you're just going to "hit the wall" when you do these projects. That's what **velocity** is about; moving quickly to get it done and removing the barriers to make it happen.*

Savings Statement:

Champions must take responsibility for removing the Cost-of-Poor-Quality. The Black Belts need your assistance. It's not a Black Belt's job to manage out the costs. That is your job. Be involved in the process. (This goes double for the Finance group!)

Figure 4.2

Champions need to make sure that transfer of knowledge happens

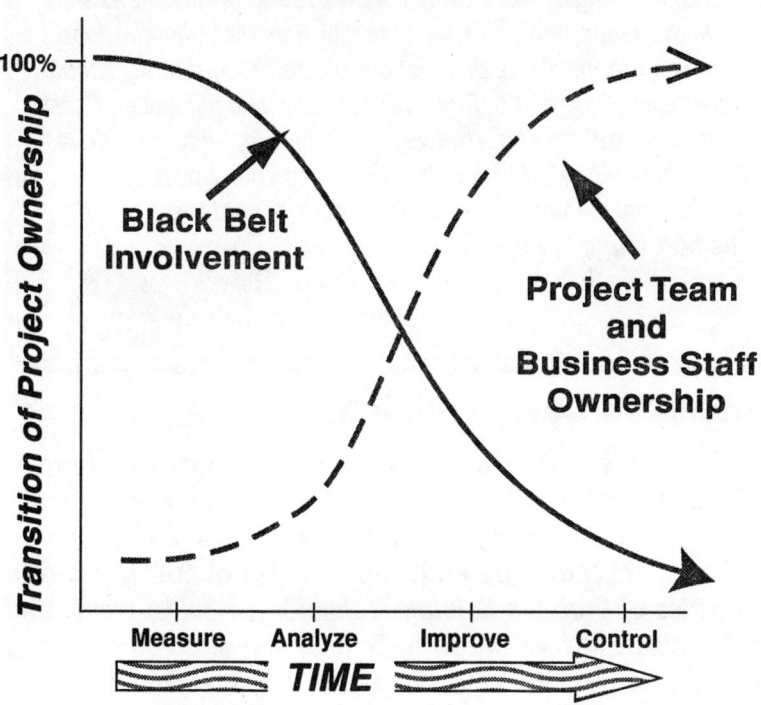

For a successful Black Belt project, knowledge must be transferred
from the Black Belt to project team members and business staff.
By the end of the control phase, the "Team" and business staff
have taken 100% ownership of the project
and the Black Belt has moved on to another project.

NOTE: During the control phase, the Black Belt MUST transfer
control to the Project Team. Only then will he or she become available
to initiate new projects.

Champion-Level Training

The Six Sigma Champion receives an abbreviated form of Black Belt training with an emphasis on managing the process. Training covers core Six Sigma concepts, basic and advanced statistics, the concept and implementation of **The Seven Principles of Problem-Solving Technology,** how to create and communicate the vision of Six Sigma, and strategic planning to maximize the benefit of Six Sigma projects. The Champion must be able to understand and interpret the things that the Black Belts do, especially the charts and statistics that will be generated during the process.

Champions need to make sure that Black Belts transfer knowledge to others in the company in order to get their ownership, involvement, and support (See Figure 4.2). The Black Belt becomes less involved in the project as it moves through the Measure, Analyze, Improve and Control phases, and the team support and business staff become more involved as time goes on.

FIGURE 4.3

THE CHAMPION'S COMMITMENT

- **To Support Your Black Belts**
  - Provide full-time training effort. Commit to maximize this new process improvement resource.
  - Make sure every operation participates and trains Black Belts. Fill up all available training slots.
  - Send the "Best of the Best."
  - Provide developmental plans and incentives. Make being a Black Belt a great career move, a key part of your organization.
  - Always keep renewing the technical infrastructure. Benchmark your processes.
- **To Establish a Business Unit Champion**
  - Choose a key business unit leader who:
    - Assigns Black Belts to maximize cross-product and service delivery systems.
    - Removes barriers.
    - Ensures local ownership of projects by using metrics.
- **To Demonstrate Commitment in Every Way**
  - Use the process as a strategic weapon to delight customers.
  - Keep enthusiasm at a high pitch.
  - Provide resources, motivate, reward and celebrate success.

If the Champion is not willing to dedicate the time to this, he or she should step down from this function!

When a Black Belt is finally on his/her own, it's like a mother bird who raises the chicks to a certain level and when it's time for them to fly, she kicks them out of the nest and they either fly or the cat gets them. This is where the infrastructure to support the Black Belt is of the most importance.

The Champion has to have a backlog list of projects that need to be done and can be assigned to the Black Belt. Reviews must continue; accountability must be built in. The attention that is there during training needs to continue, but often there is no defined structure after the training process. Phase 1 is the training process; Phase 2 needs to be co-created with your training partner.

Six Sigma leads to the democratization of management. Once people in the business have the data, they make good decisions.

MASTER BLACK BELTS

The Master Black Belt is to a Champion, as a Chief Engineer is to the Director of Engineering. Master Black Belts are a critical infrastructure element of Six Sigma implementation. The Champion is the management element, providing fundamental leadership for change. The Master Black Belt is the technical  counterpart who insures the formation of the Black Belt infrastructure and provides the necessary training and education for Black Belts.

Master Black Belts are 100 percent dedicated to the process improvement effort. They are the primary Change Agents for Six Sigma quality, with the vision and passion for change and improvement to drive their company to new levels of performance. They have become experts in the use of Six Sigma tools and tactics, and they have the experience to exploit the full value of the tools offered by Six Sigma.

Because Master Black Belts are the primary trainers and coaches for the company, over time they must develop *absolute mastery* of the methodology and philosophy of Six Sigma. They become "application discoverers," constantly upgrading their understanding of Six Sigma and how its tools can be applied to solve a variety of quality issues.

Master Black Belts are the training leaders, team-teaching Black Belts by using outside experts at their discretion. Master Black Belts oversee all Black Belt projects and are involved from the planning and selection stage. One of the most powerful tools Master Black Belts employ is in-depth project review, using this as a learning experience for Black Belts during their three-week application period after each week of training.

Master Black Belts are mentors and coaches to Black Belts: They set the example, "walk the walk," and lead the way. The role of Master Black Belt is NOT a desk job. They are in the trenches daily on the factory floor, in the service area, wherever they need to be, learning along with everyone else. Master Black Belts are there to provide practical guidance in how to use Six Sigma tools, anticipate problems and barriers, and advise their team in all aspects of Six Sigma.

You may choose to use Master Black Belts as consultants or advisors when planning Six Sigma implementation. *Master Black Belts are able to skillfully facilitate problem-solving without actually taking over a project.* They are facilitators, helping their team improve the quality of work by offering a well-defined problem-solving structure, new perspectives and ideas that ignite others. This is one of the more challenging roles of the Master Black Belt, requiring excellent people skills and judgment.

The Master Black Belt must be able to encourage others to leave behind long-held beliefs about the way things should be and to consider unconventional solutions. Change often elicits fear — fear of losing one's job, fear of being criticized for past performance, fear of the unknown. The Master Black Belt needs to be aware of the natural fears that arise during a change process and make sure that factual data is available to all.

The Role of the Master Black Belt

- Primary "Change Agent" for Six Sigma quality
- Ultimate "barrier removal tool" when needed
- Expert in using statistical tools
- Tactical expert and application discoverer
- Skilled facilitator
- Involved in planning and selection of projects
- Mentor, coach, and trainer of Black Belts
- 100 percent of their time is dedicated to Six Sigma

SIX SIGMA BLACK BELTS

Six Sigma Black Belts become the basic infrastructure within your company that supports *The Seven Principles of Problem-Solving Technology* and the use of Six Sigma tools to improve quality, cost, and customer satisfaction. Black Belts transfer the knowledge of how to "Do Six Sigma" to others. The aim of Black Belt training is to create technical leaders who can use the tools and methods to create quality improvement. Black Belts are usually individuals who are technically oriented, but not necessarily engineers. Their main skill is their *problem-solving ability.*

Black Belts carry a heavy load and face many challenges. They have to understand and apply their training immediately on projects that improve quality and return bottom line savings. They must lead and convince their team that the change they are recommending is the right thing to do

based on data. Black Belts assure that the rigor and discipline of the Six Sigma methodology is employed in the plants and within the processes. They are responsible for making sure the improved process *stays* improved. And they are the ones providing face-to-face feedback to management on projects and results, changing corporate culture one project at a time. Black Belts need the total support of their Champion to succeed.

Black Belt candidates must have the desire to succeed, the desire and will to practice, the environment in which to practice, the leadership backing for adequate resources, and access to mentoring from experienced Six Sigma practitioners.

FIGURE 4.5

The Role of the Black Belt

* Black Belts are contributors from various disciplines within your company.

Certified
Six Sigma Black Belt

✔ Black Belt training
✔ Complete two projects
✔ Final reports
✔ Sustain the gain
✔ Master Black Belt approval

* They are change agents for the company, bringing the philosophy and vision of Six Sigma to as many people in the company as possible.

* They should be **encouraged** to stimulate management thinking by posing new ways of doing things.

* Black Belts challenge conventional wisdom by demonstrating successful application of new methodologies.

* Black Belts carry a very high level of peer respect and are clearly seen as leaders.

* They manage risks, help set direction, and lead the way to **quantum gains** in product quality by implementing carefully selected and designed projects.

* Black Belts are the problem-solving leaders of project teams, and must understand the practical application of the Six Sigma tools.

* They must be able to instill rigor and a fact-based focus to the team's work.

* Black Belts don't have all the answers. They help others organize and analyze the vast knowledge of a process that usually exists in the experiences of people who work with the process.

* Each Black Belt is like a modern day Sherlock Holmes, finding out what information is needed to solve a critical issue and knowing where to find that data.

Warning!

A Black Belt is a valuable resource and NOT a part-time assignment!

It is absolutely vital that a Black Belt be empowered and allowed to devote his or her *FULL TIME* to the effort. *Part-time assignments do not work!* Management must allow time for training – typically four months – and expect full-time focus on Six Sigma during the training period and beyond. A Black Belt is typically a two-year career assignment.

Substantial time commitments are one reason why Six Sigma requires senior management commitment, linkage to the overall business strategy and goals, and a recognition of the extreme urgency and need for change.

FIGURE 4.6

Quantum Gains Require Time Commitment

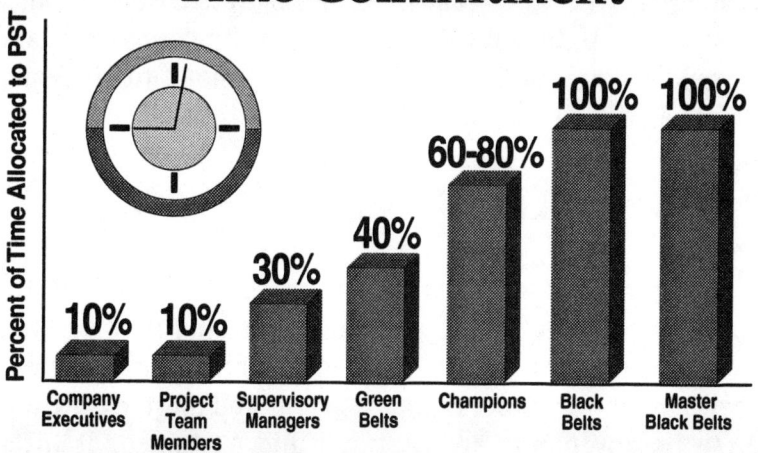

OTHER RESOURCES

Executive Management

It is absolutely vital that the top executives in a company become involved as supporters of Champions or by becoming Champions. These executives can be actively involved with this process through a *Management Committee* or a *Core Team.*

The *Management Committee* is composed of Champions and key Executives who are actively involved in leading and supporting Six Sigma implementation. The Committee sets the overall company goals and business objectives, and views Six Sigma as a major corporate initiative to reach these goals and objectives. Committee members are present at project and program review sessions. They provide vision and leadership for change, they understand and promote Six Sigma concepts and tools, and they act as role models to communicate the Six Sigma message throughout the company.

A Six Sigma *Core Team* is drawn from senior management in a business unit (Vice Presidents, Directors, etc.). The job of the core team is to establish goals for their business unit, set the key metrics to link to the business strategy, and represent their interests to the Management Committee. The core team is responsible for ensuring that a coordinated strategy is developed at their functional level and for guiding their business units as they respond to Six Sigma initiatives.

Supervisory-Level Managers

Supervisory-level managers are the "owners" of the business processes that may be targeted for Six Sigma improvement and must be willing to lead efforts in their areas. They benefit from process improvements and must ensure that these improvements are captured and sustained. It often

FIGURE 4.7

Executive Management Responsibilities

- Develop policy and procedures documents.
- Encourage the development of a quality environment.
- Lead Six Sigma implementation in their area.
- Ensure Six Sigma integration with other systems and initiatives.
- Coordinate the development of training materials by the Master Black Belts.
- Coordinate training sessions.
- Develop and approve project-tracking systems.
- Develop an implementation plan for their business unit, and coordinate its implementation.
- Set up and support certification of Master Black Belts and Black Belts.
- Coordinate the selection and approval of projects.
- Establish a governance process.
- Contribute to reviews to ensure the effective implementation of Six Sigma.

happens that a process will cut across organizational boundaries. In these cases, these managers must work together and coordinate efforts across functional or departmental lines. No "silo mentality" allowed!

The Six Sigma Project Team looks to the supervisory-level manager for project support. For example, in order to carry out Six Sigma experiments, they may need time on the production line or need to disrupt an information service. Or they may need the supervisory manager's help to obtain resources from some other area of the company.

Supervisory-level managers must communicate the vision of Six Sigma to all of their employees. Why is Six Sigma important to us? What projects are being worked on right now? How can we assist in the process? What are the implications for our jobs? How do we sustain the quality, cost and customer satisfaction gains we have made? The Black Belts are required to present a one-day overview to the supervisory-level managers along with their Champion to kick off their project.

Six Sigma Green Belts

Green Belts are people who assist Black Belts on specific projects. Many times the Green Belt projects deliver savings of a Black Belt proportion so they should not be treated as an addendum to the program. Green Belts are critical to the long-term success of your Six Sigma implementation and really integrate the methodology into daily work. Why? They apply the Six Sigma tools to a project on their regular job. When you train your people as Green Belts, you have spread Six Sigma to the masses.

Green Belts are also extraordinarily helpful to Black Belts in completion of their projects. They may help the Black Belt collect and analyze data, or help run experiments. Many projects must be completed before a company reaches consistent Six Sigma performance levels. Having the assistance of a Green Belt allows Black Belts to complete more projects, thus leveraging this important resource.

This is where your company
makes a culture shift,
bringing Six Sigma training
to the mass of employees to gain momentum.

Six Sigma Green Belts usually work part-time, but could be assigned full-time to a Black Belt project in order to learn how to apply the tools and methods. Six Sigma Green Belts could be used to collect and analyze data to help speed up the

Measure phase of a project. At General Electric, all salaried employees receive an equivalent of Six Sigma Green Belt training, even if they aren't officially designated as a Green Belt.

Role of Project Team members

Project Team Members work part-time on projects, providing necessary technical expertise. They represent the various areas that are directly or indirectly involved in the process, especially if they use the outputs from the process as inputs to their work or provide critical input variables to the process. Team members could work to gather and analyze data and help sustain long-term improvements.

FIGURE 4.8

FOOD FOR THOUGHT: The GE Experience

What happens when a corporation adopts a Six Sigma mindset? The following snapshot of General Electric shows how a committed organization infuses Six Sigma throughout the company, and receives bottom line results in return.

- *4,000 full-time Black Belts and Master Black Belts*
- *60,000 Green Belts*
- *1,000 people and $44 million in savings in GE Appliances*
- *16,000 people and 2,000 projects in GE Capital*
- *2,600 people and $47 million in savings in GE Lighting*
- *600 projects and $42 million in savings in GE Medical*
- *2,200 people, 3,000 projects, and $137 million in savings in GE Plastics*
- *2,500 projects and $94 million in savings in GE Power*
- *50 percent of the employees and $35 million in savings in GE Electrical Distribution*
- *1,000 people and $34 million in savings in GE Transportation Division*

Source: General Electric 1997 Annual Report

FIGURE 4.9
Problem-Solving Technology
Black Belt Training Overview
Generic Training Topics

Week 1

Cause & Effect Matrix
PST Strategy
MINITAB/Basic Stats
Process Capability
Measurement Systems
Multi-vari Analysis
Process Mapping

Week 3

2k Factorials
Fractional Factorial
*   Experiments*
Screening Experiments
Full Factorial

Week 4

Quality Systems
Control Systems
Evolutionary
*   Operation (EVOP)*
Response Surface
Mistake-Proofing
Measurement Systems
Lean Manufacturing
Control Charts

Week 2

Hypothesis Test
Design of Experiments
Advanced Statistics
Central Limit Theorem
Confidence Interval
Single Factor
*   Experiments*

Review the accompanying CD for full day-to-day content of the entire training sequence.

THE TRAINING ASPECTS OF SIX SIGMA

Human assets are the main factors; without them, business results are not achieved. The key to success is knowledge transfer through people. Breakthrough success and improvement cannot occur without new knowledge.

New knowledge will not be created without human resources applied to chronic, high-impact issues of your business. You need to keep asking new questions. Asking the same questions over and over yields the same old answers. Remember, don't be a fanatic. Different tools prompt new questions resulting in breakthrough outcomes. Motorola has found that training has a ten to one return on investment. In fact, they require every employee to receive 80 hours or more of training annually, and 40 percent must be in problem-solving skills.

The success of Six Sigma requires that ALL employees apply the concepts to their respective processes.

Your people are your primary resources for implementing Six Sigma. To reach Six Sigma performance we must harness the ideas of ALL employees. All employees should buy into the process, understand the Six Sigma philosophy and learn how to apply its tools to their work.

Providing training to all employees expands the resources available to your Black Belts and Project Teams. Basic Six Sigma training of all employees enables them to help when needed and to understand the reasons for data collection.

APPLYING
PROBLEM-SOLVING TECHNOLOGY
TO YOUR COMPANY

Questions to Ask Yourself

Do I have people who have the skills to become Six Sigma Black Belts?

Can I tolerate the questioning required? The challenge to the status quo?

Can I establish challenging stretch goals for my people?

Can I remove roadblocks and run interference for my Black Belts?

Am I willing to dedicate 100 percent of the time for Master Black Belts and Black Belts?

Am I ready to train ALL my work force in the basics of Six Sigma?

It is a paradoxical but profoundly true
and important principle of life
that the most likely way to reach a goal
is to be aiming
not at that goal itself but at some
more ambitious goal beyond it.

Arnold Toynbee

"The best Six Sigma projects
begin not inside the business
but outside it, focused on
answering the question:
How can we make the customer
more competitive?
What is critical to the
customer's success?
Learning the answer to that question
and then learning how
to provide the solution
is the only focus we need."

Jack Welch, CEO, General Electric
1997 Annual Meeting

CHAPTER 5

Selecting High-leverage Projects that Impact Your Bottom Line

*Just like building a house brick-by-brick,
Six Sigma is a project-by-project journey
with a set of resources focused
on the bottom line.*

Once you have made the initial financial investment to Do Six Sigma, the next critical decisions you must make are to select the first projects and the first Black Belts. Organizations expend extraordinary creative energy to maintain status quo. I am talking about the tiers of management three and four levels removed from top management. This is the level of management that will make decisions about projects and people.

If this level of management throws a poor combination of projects and Black Belts into the initial implementation, it can kill the program. Therefore, it is critical for the executive leaders to have a formal review of the initial projects and people selected. Your reputation is riding on the first six months of implementation.

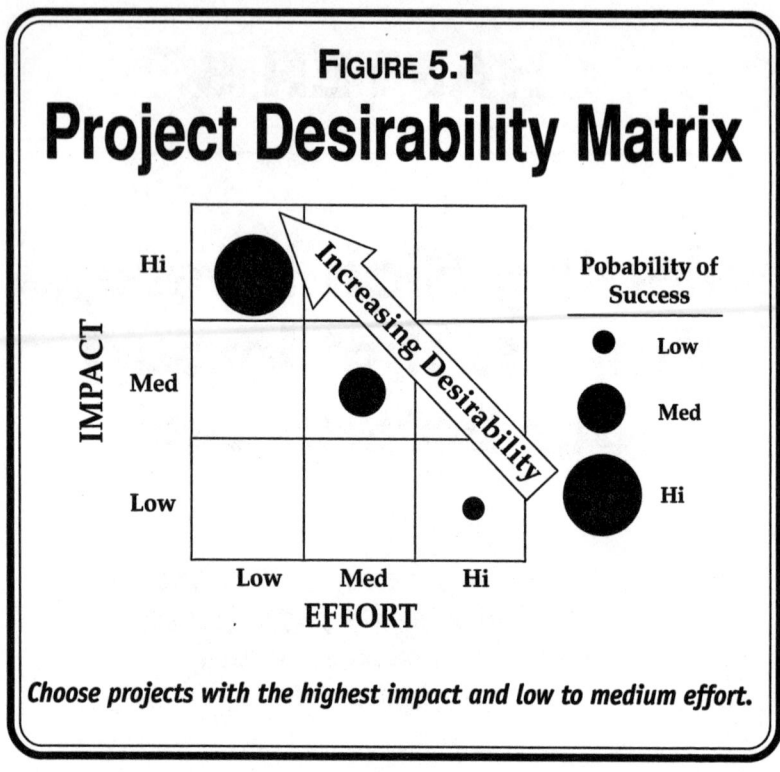

FIGURE 5.1

Project Desirability Matrix

Choose projects with the highest impact and low to medium effort.

There are two major attributes of projects that I consider when evaluating the desirability of a project. First is the *effort required.* This includes not only the effort of a Black Belt, but also the time required of team members and any expenditure of money. Second is the *probability of success.* You must look at an assessment of risk factors including:

TIME
Uncertainty of completion date

EFFORT
Uncertainty of the investment required

IMPLEMENTATION
Uncertainty of roadblocks

It is best not to try to "save the world" with a massive undertaking that is impractical and requires huge amounts of time and the involvement of multiple departments. Smaller, well-focused projects which target elements of a process are more likely to succeed and to provide a good return on your investment of time, money, and people resources.

High-leverage projects are those that improve more than one factor that is critical to your internal and external customers. Priority should be given to those projects that address more than one of the factors critical to the *quality, cost and delivery* expectations of your customer.

If a project can be designed to address all three factors, you can get maximum leverage to meet the Critical-To-Satisfaction expectations of the customer. However, strategic business objectives are often effectively addressed with a project that includes only one or two of these factors.

FIGURE 5.2
Project Opportunities

Sweet Fruit
Design for Manufacturability

Bulk of Fruit
Process Characterization & Optimization

Low-Hanging Fruit: easily obtainable results
Basic TQM methods (cause & effect, Pareto charts, process mapping, etc.)

Rotted Fruit
Observations, Logic, and Intuition

Initial Six Sigma projects come from the bulk of fruit. Design for Six Sigma harvests the sweetest fruit.

Adapted from: The Vision of Six Sigma: A Roadmap for Breakthrough, Mikel J. Harry, © 1994 Sigma Publishing Company

DOING SIX SIGMA: Project Selection

Sometimes the site Controllers become a barrier to the success of Six Sigma, fearing that if they report the money that was saved by the projects, they will have a budget cut the next year. For instance, if you saved $10 million in a $100 million budget, some companies take it away and you have to now operate on $90 million. The Executive Champion has to say to everyone, "We're DOING SIX SIGMA to save x amount of dollars in this area." It has to be a directive from the top to save money. The ideal is when the Six Sigma projects ARE the cost improvement projects for the business. Then you have everyone's cooperation and attention. The controller wants it to happen as much as the Black Belts and there is an incentive to roll out real dollar savings.

Rewarding the efforts is the best way to remove this barrier. The business unit gets to keep the money it saved from Six Sigma projects but they have to show what they are going to do with it that is different from the past.

Max Gordon
Champion

SOURCES OF PROJECT IDEAS

Project ideas can come from many sources. Looking at Cost-of-Poor-Quality factors often yields a gold mine of projects. First of all, there are many recognizable "work-arounds" that were created to overcome barriers or to put a band-aid on a production problem. Work-arounds include:

- Excess inventory
- Inspection
- Expediting
- Rework and repair
- Excess approvals

- Replanning and overstaffing
- Duplicate and triplicate paperwork

All these examples are used to temporarily fix something that a problem in your process has caused. Excess inventory is maintained because you can't count on the production capability of your line. We inspect because we don't trust the capability of our process to produce defect-free products. We rework and repair the products found defective so we save something out of the initial effort. ***Work-arounds do not fix the root cause of the problem.***

DOING SIX SIGMA: Project Selection

The best projects you can choose are ones that have a clear line-of-sight to the strategic objectives of the corporation. If you get buy-in to clear line-of-sight objectives, everyone is working to achieve the same goals. The CEO says, "This is what we are going to focus on this year and these Black Belt projects will help get us there." Everyone in the company understands why you are doing these things.

A project also has to have a significant impact to the business. It can't be a two or three percent improvement; it needs to achieve a minimum of 50 percent improvement in what you are measuring. A home run, or at least a double. The project has to have money in it and has to relate to where the company is going to be in two or three years. It can't be something that works with old technology or no one will care about it. It must be a strategic, future-oriented project with money written all over it.

Ray Everhart
Master Black Belt

Project ideas can also come from a review of non-value-added activities that do NOT add form, fit, or function to a product. Non-value-added factors include:

- Setup time and shift changeover
- Downtime (machine utilization)
- System utilization
- Material handling
- Inspection and rework
- Sorting and stacking
- Tool changes
- Order entry rework
- Re-quoting
- Delivery expediting

Getting at the root cause of the need for any of these non-value-added activities and improving the process to eliminate them can be good Six Sigma projects.

Projects can be derived from the value-added activities that your company is involved in — those that make up the core of your business. Value-added activities are critical to the customer. Value-added activities include:

- Machining
- Assembly
- Plating
- Order entry
- Billing
- Processing transactions
- Painting
- Stamping
- Welding
- On-time fill rate
- Material receipts

DOING SIX SIGMA: Project Selection

A good example of finding a gold mine in value-added processes, happened when I went to the production site of a potential new client for an assessment visit. They made a control cable for cruise control, which is made up of a half-dozen or so individual cables. I looked around and saw money all over the floor; four to six inch pieces of cable lying there which had been trimmed because their process was not precise enough to get the correct length on the first pass.

As I laid these pieces out end to end, I asked the plant manager, "What do you see?" He had no answer until the lengths approached the full measure of the final cable, when he finally realized that the waste on the floor represented a whole lot of complete cruise control cables! At six cents per foot, each six-inch wasted piece was worth about three cents. When you add that up over time it amounted to a considerable waste of money.

This was lower than low-hanging fruit! I refer to this type of cost savings as rotted fruit. Your normal quality and cost control system should address rotted fruit.

Environmental Impact Projects

Projects that have an environmental impact are good examples of cost avoidance. If a company does something wrong to the environment, that company is a bad corporate citizen, and you can't put a value or a cost on that. Environmental projects are often not obvious in their cost savings, but the cost of **not** doing them is huge. The controller may say, "We can't tell you what it's worth to the bottom line, but we can tell you what it'll cost if we DON'T do it." I worked on a project with an environmental focus for General Electric, and it was a good management decision because of the dollar savings and what it meant to the environment.

PROJECT RESOURCES REQUIRED

To successfully complete a Six Sigma project, your Black Belts must have all the needed resources at their disposal. Any resource limitation must be identified early in the planning process. If resources are not readily available, the project should be rejected until the necessary resources **are** available, or until a Champion helps get the resources.

Are the necessary data available to facilitate initial measurement and analysis? Your Master Black Belt and Champion should review the availability and adequacy of the data before proceeding with the selection of any project.

Data are the driving force behind the success of Six Sigma: Without data you are wasting your time. Once a company has a Six Sigma infrastructure of Black Belts and Master Black Belts, data development and collection can actually be a project in and of itself, a mini-project that precedes the launch of a more critical project. Remember, data collection can be as simple as a checklist requiring only a piece of paper and a pencil.

With $1.5 billion in estimated savings already achieved, Six Sigma is one of the most ambitious projects ever undertaken. The scope of Six Sigma has now been broadened to include all of AlliedSignal's quality and productivity efforts, and to extend them from manufacturing to all processes, including back-office operations.

AlliedSignal 1997
Annual Report

PROJECT SCOPE

The scope of a project is an important step in selecting a project. If you are training a new Black Belt, the project should be completed within the training period of four months. Existing full-time Black Belts may take on projects that could be completed within four to six months, and usually begin a new project as the ownership of the "old" project is transferred to others on the team (see Figure 4.2). Large projects that are more strategic and take longer to complete can be broken into smaller projects in order to show more immediate benefits.

FIGURE 5.3

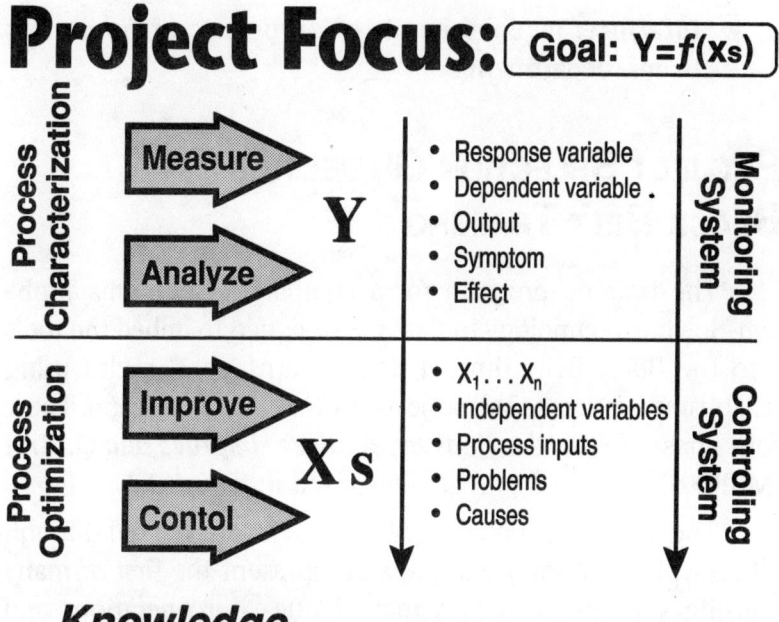

Project Focus: [Goal: Y=*f*(xs)]

Process Characterization

> Measure
> Analyze

Y

- Response variable
- Dependent variable .
- Output
- Symptom
- Effect

Monitoring System

Process Optimization

> Improve
> Contol

X s

- $X_1 \ldots X_n$
- Independent variables
- Process inputs
- Problems
- Causes

Controling System

Knowledge

Process Characterization is concerned with the identification and benchmarking of key product characteristics, and with determining improvement opportunities and goals.

Process Optimization is aimed at the identification, containment and control of those process variables which exert undesirable influence over the key product characteristics.

Adapted from: The Vision of Six Sigma: A Roadmap for Breakthrough, Mikel J. Harry, © 1994 Sigma Publishing Company

Project scope includes:

- **Process boundaries**: the start and finish of the project process flow map;

- **Process constraints**: limitations of data availability, data collection, resources;

- **Outside affecting issues**: suppliers, customer issues, regulatory requirements;

- **Interface**: required inputs or outputs to or from other teams, departments.

PROJECT SELECTION GUIDELINES FOR BLACK BELT TRAINING

The training program for a company's Six Sigma Problem-Solving Technology Initiative is designed to imbed the tools into the Black Belts through four "learn/apply" cycles using real business issues as the projects for training application. These four phases follow the **Measure, Analyze, Improve and Control** (MAIC) of Chapter 3 and are illustrated in Figure 3.1.

The business issues, scoped as projects, are worked through all four phases during training and represent the first of many real-life solutions to issues that plague your operations and impede your ability to satisfy customers and shareholders.

A Project Selection Guide (Figure 5.7) is a useful tool for scoping projects. These guidelines can be used by the new Black Belt candidates and their Champions to select the initial projects for the training program. *When selecting an initial training project, it is important to look for high-leverage projects where the return justifies the investment in time and effort, and where the need for improvement is substantial.*

Please keep in mind that decisions based on factual data are always better that those based upon intuition, hearsay or folklore. Also, be sure to consider each problem or opportunity possibility in its relationship to the product family or group as a whole. For instance, something that is a large problem to one person may have a small impact on the performance of the product line overall.

It's always best to use the magic of data in selecting projects. Your opinion, hearsay and folklore are not data!

The first projects will be those which jump out at you because they have been chronic and painful. The temptation to fix these will usually create a project too large to solve in the four months of training and application. Be prepared to back the project down once the first phase, measure, is completed. Unbundling a large project into four or five parts will allow the Black Belt to have success on the first one and then he or she can attack the others. Typical projects are easily identified within their categories of poor quality characteristics (see Figure 5.7).

Digging for Chronic, High-Impact Projects

An excellent tool to use that creates a more focused and therefore successful first project is the Pareto analysis. Pareto analysis is named after Wufredo Pareto, a European economist whose "Pareto Principle" is well known — 80 percent of the trouble comes from 20 percent of the problems. A Pareto analysis unbundles the data and shows it in descending order form most to least.

**Pareto Principle:
80 percent of the trouble comes from
20 percent of the problems.**

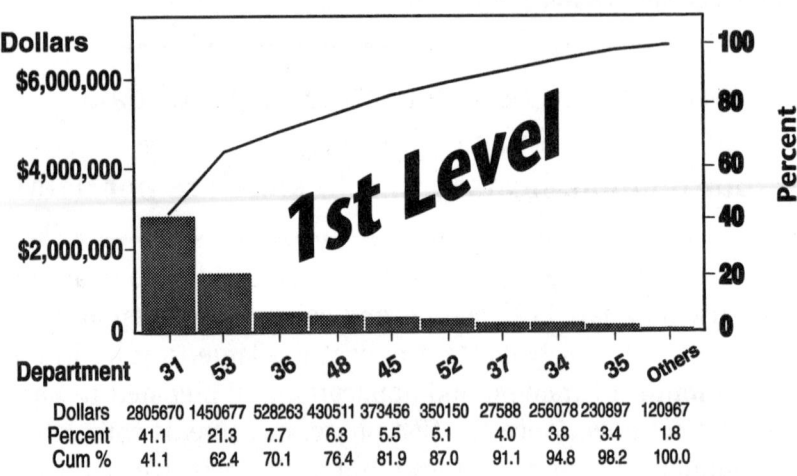

FIGURE 5.4

Pareto Chart for Departments

Department	31	53	36	48	45	52	37	34	35	Others
Dollars	2805670	1450677	528263	430511	373456	350150	27588	256078	230897	120967
Percent	41.1	21.3	7.7	6.3	5.5	5.1	4.0	3.8	3.4	1.8
Cum %	41.1	62.4	70.1	76.4	81.9	87.0	91.1	94.8	98.2	100.0

The examples demonstrate how you can use three ever-narrowing Pareto analyses to identify the *Vital Few.* This is where to put your money for improvement. The first level Pareto chart breaks down the problem by departments. It is obvious from the chart where to focus additional analysis. Department 31 has the highest costs, so it's a good bet to look for projects there first.

The second level Pareto chart focuses just on Department 31 and identifies the process that will give you the most savings (Op-40). Finally, the third level Pareto chart breaks down the individual steps of the process identified by the second level analysis. This level of analysis shows that the extrusion process of Op-40 was the most costly. In this way, you identify the *Vital Few,* and are better able to focus your first Six Sigma efforts.

FIGURE 5.5

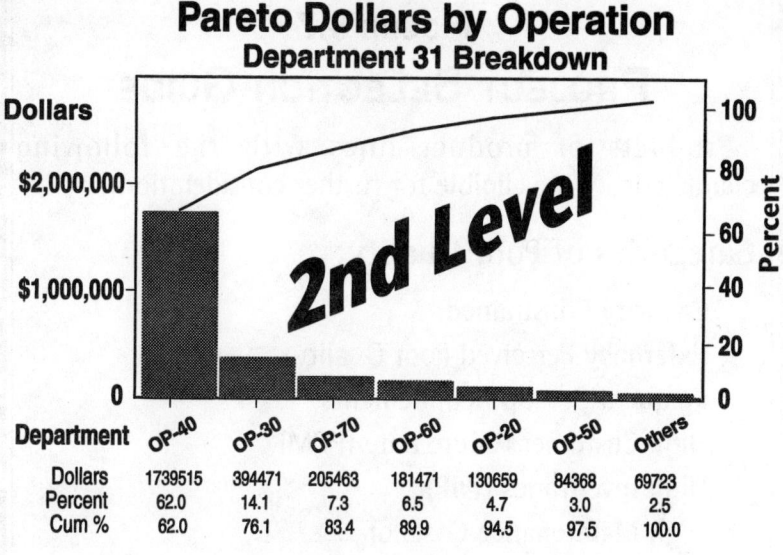

Pareto Dollars by Operation
Department 31 Breakdown

Department	OP-40	OP-30	OP-70	OP-60	OP-20	OP-50	Others
Dollars	1739515	394471	205463	181471	130659	84368	69723
Percent	62.0	14.1	7.3	6.5	4.7	3.0	2.5
Cum %	62.0	76.1	83.4	89.9	94.5	97.5	100.0

FIGURE 5.6

Pareto Chart for OP-40 by Step

Process Step	Extrusion	Cut	Form	Heat	Flux	Others
Dollars	890500	478321	135900	125875	74902	34017
Percent	51.2	27.5	7.8	7.2	4.3	2.0
Cum %	51.2	78.7	86.5	93.7	98.0	100.0

The result of this Black Belt project was a 50 percent reduction in the cost of the extrusion process, a savings of $445,000, and a similar reduction in the cut-to-length process, the second most-costly step in Op-40 identified by the Pareto chart.

FIGURE 5.7
PROJECT SELECTION GUIDE

Products or product lines with the following characteristics are eligible for further consideration:

Categories of Poor Quality:

Capacity Constrained
Externally Perceived Poor Quality
Frequent Set-Up Requirements
High Customer Failure Rate (PPM)
High Inventories (WIP)
High Maintenance Costs or
  Low Machine Utilization
High Operating Costs
High Set-Up Costs
Frequent Past Due Orders to Customers
High Product Volume
High Quality Costs
High Scrap or Rework Costs
Incoming Product Quality Problems
Internally Perceived Poor Quality
Low Yield Rate
Long Cycle Times
Measured with Variable Data vs. Attribute Data
Poor Process Capability (Cp, Cpk)
Unpredictable Quality
Unpredictable Product Performance

GLOSSARY OF PROJECT SELECTION TERMS

*Many of the categories or definitions overlap and are similar.
These definitions are intended to be classifiers and
descriptors of various poor quality or sub-par performance
situations that exist within your plants and offices. Use them
to make sure all definitions are the same in your world.*

Capacity Constrained: Processes where limited or unpredictable capacity shortfall consistently or frequently causes shortages of products or components for the customer or for the next step in the product chain.

Externally Perceived Poor Quality: Like Internal Perceived Poor Quality, there is a documented history of continual or recurring quality issues from the external customers with no supporting data or evidence through tests or engineering evaluation to substantiate the claims.

Frequent or Costly Set-Ups: When compared to other products or similar processes, set-up costs are inexplicably high. Set-ups are called for more frequently than the volumes and order frequency would seem to demand. Constant adjustment or machine resetting is required during production runs and changeovers.

Frequent Past-Due Orders to Customers: Continual or recurring issues with past-due or undelivered orders to customers, whether the customers are external or internal customers.

High Customer Failure Rate (PPM): Usually measured by the customer in parts per million (PPM). Product has a history of failure either at the customers' factories or in the field.

High Inventories (WIP): Process maintains a high level of work-in-process (WIP) inventories, including inventories of unfinished components that are not planned to be finished or consumed within one week's time.

High Maintenance Costs or Low Machine Utilization: Experiencing frequent unplanned machine or process downtime, or higher-than-budgeted maintenance costs associated with critical machines or bottlenecks.

GLOSSARY OF PROJECT SELECTION TERMS

High Operating Costs: Direct costs associated with the product family or production line which appear to be out of line with other similar processes or production lines.

High Product Volume: Product in question is high volume (compared to other product lines) in sales and/or quality. These product lines which have substantial quality, cycle-time or other throughput issues, usually (although not without exception) offer higher potential payback for the investment than lower volume products.

High Quality Costs: Products or processes which require continual, unusually high levels of inspection or other quality related intervention from operators or members of the quality department in order to provide products in necessary volumes to satisfy all customers.

High Scrap/Rework Costs: Processes which continually or unpredictably produce higher than expected scrap or product that requires reworking.

Incoming Product Quality: Raw material, parts or components coming in from suppliers or other in-house operations usually have an unusually high level of quality issues or reject rates. Also, these quality issues can cause production issues or quality problems when attempts are made to run the faulty material.

Internally Perceived Poor Quality: Processes or products which everyone knows are a pain, but unfortunately, there are no facts or data to support the folklore.

Long Cycle Times: The total manufacturing cycle time for a particular product or process is longer than is normal for similar or benchmark processes.

Low Yield Rate: Processes produce low yields on a continual or unpredictable basis. This can be characterized by lower than expected output numbers or slower than planned for line speeds or production rates.

GLOSSARY OF PROJECT SELECTION TERMS

Measured with Variable vs. Attribute Data: Processes whereby data is acquired through the use of variable gauging is more helpful in determining variation root causes through statistical analysis, than with data acquired through attribute means, i.e. go, no-go gauges, visual yes-no inspection. Therefore, it is easier to solve problems when variable data is available.

Poor Process Capability (Cp, Cpk): Processes in which the capability analysis has consistently produced results at levels below those required by the process or quality specifications.

Unpredictable Quality: The quality of the final product (or components within) varies in an unpredictable and seemingly inexplicable fashion when circumstances or production conditions are normal.

Unpredictable Product Performance: Products often fail final test or inspection, are returned from the customer, or fail while in service in such a way that finding the root cause of the failure has escaped the investigations.

> REMINDER: Your accounting system measures cost-of-goods or services sold (COGS/COSS).
> Look for projects in these areas.

It is important to engage your immediate managers as well as plant or departmental managers in the project selection process. Like any new skill learned, proficiency comes with practice. Selection of the initial training project is preliminary to selection of ongoing projects that Certified Black Belts will lead after the training process has been successfully completed.

It is always best to use the "magic" of data during project selection. Do not rely on hearsay or folklore for this process. Use data to verify your selection.

KEY PROJECT
SUCCESS FACTORS

How do you determine if a Black Belt project was successful? The following checklist can be used to evaluate a project.

- Did the project save the company significant money?

- Is the process operating at the improved, targeted level?

- Are the customers, both internal and external, satisfied with the results?

- Was data collected in advance?

- Were there minimum scope changes after project launch?

- Is long-term process performance being sustained?

- Did the project's cost remain within budget?

- Was the project completed on schedule?

- Were you able to keep work disruptions to a minimum?

If the answers to these questions are YES, congratulations on completing a successful Six Sigma project.

Figure 5.8

Checklist for
Project Selection:

Six Sigma
Project
Check List

- ✔ Project will increase sales, either unit volume or net price.
- ✔ Project will reduce accounts receivable, reduce net inventory, or increase accounts payable.
- ✔ Project will reduce actual spending.
- ✔ Project will avoid a cost not currently being incurred, but which otherwise would be with high probability.
- ✔ Project will reduce the cycle time on critical path steps in a bottleneck operation. It is one which sets the pace for all other operations in its supply chain.
- ✔ Project will improve quality, as measured by the customer.
- ✔ Project will improve service level, as measured by the customer.
- ✔ Recommendations can be determined, implemented, and show results within three months.
- ✔ Potential recommendations are unlikely to be thwarted by management.
- ✔ Historical data on process performance are readily available.
- ✔ Potential recommendations are unlikely to require a large investment in either capital or expense.
- ✔ Project solution is not already known. Project must serve as a learning experience.
- ✔ Project will help you achieve the objectives you set.
- ✔ Project will help your manager achieve his/her objectives.
- ✔ Project will focus on a problem that has been resistant to previous lower-intensity efforts to resolve it.
- ✔ Required team members are able, willing, and available to support you.
- ✔ You have personal knowledge of the process.

EXAMPLES OF BAD PROJECTS

"Bad" projects rate poorly on one or more of the three attribute scales:

• *Little or no business impact*: Creating or revising a report, quantifying the performance of a process, improving a supplier's performance *without* any arrangement to share the benefits, reducing cycle-time of a non-bottleneck operation. Improving the efficiency or quality of an obsolete product or service are examples of projects with little or no business impact.

• *Effort required*: Installing a new computer system, improving profitability of an entire product line or channel, "fixing" the annual planning process.

• *Probability of success*: Improving a process which won't show the benefits for several months, depends upon the completion of other risky projects, requires help from extremely busy people, or is not aligned with management objectives.

To summarize, Six Sigma projects are the vehicles for radical and continuous improvement in *Quality, Cost,* and *Delivery* of a product or service. A good Six Sigma project is one which offers the greatest financial or customer satisfaction leverage. These projects address at least one element of the organization's key business objectives, make good business sense, and address key customers' needs, both internal and external. Six Sigma projects result in customer satisfaction and substantial financial returns to the company.

APPLYING
PROBLEM-SOLVING TECHNOLOGY
TO YOUR COMPANY

Questions to Ask Yourself

Where can possible Six Sigma projects come
from in our company that address customer
satisfaction and financial goals?

What are the "work-arounds" we have created?

What problems are they "fixing"?

What non-value-added activities do we do?

What value-added processes might be a source of projects?

What priorities can come from our strategic operating plan?

What are my company's Cost of Goods and Services Sold?

What is the breakdown of Cost of Goods and Services Sold?

What are my major cost drivers?

Do we have any of the project selection terms listed in
Figure 5.7?

There is one rule
for industrialists
and that is:
Make the best quality
of goods possible
at the lowest cost possible,
paying the highest wages possible.

Henry Ford

CHAPTER 6

Implementing
Six Sigma:
Problem-Solving Technology in Action

The ultimate goal is to produce Six Sigma results, not Six Sigma statistics, producing processes that are as close to perfection as possible.

Discussions in prior chapters are compressed into this chapter to provide a consise description of a Six Sigma implementation.

The first principle of the **Seven Principles of Problem-Solving Technology is Compelling Leadership** with the **vision** to Do Six Sigma. Six Sigma is not a walk in the park. It requires total commitment from the highest levels of management.

Six Sigma implementation is a culture change, requiring mental tenacity and a dedication to the pursuit of breakthrough targets. Implementing Six Sigma is not to be taken lightly. It requires careful planning, visionary leadership, experienced guides, and a tolerance for constant questioning about the truth of sacred beliefs. This is extremely hard work, and has been called "anal-retentive" by many Black Belts!

The **Seven Principles** can be used as a framework for successful implementation of Six Sigma in your company.

Principle #1:

Compelling Leaders The Vision to Do Six Sigma

Senior management – the President, CEO and top executives –***must own*** the Six Sigma vision and link it to the strategy of their business. The strategy for implementation has its beginnings in the ranks of senior management and is linked to the highest priorities and goals of the business.

It is imperative that company leaders create **stretch** goals that force people to rethink how the work is done and not just "tweak" the existing process.

Principle #2:

Embracing Customers Delivering and Anticipating What the Customer Wants

The customer's expectations and satisfaction with your product and service must be the driving force behind Six Sigma implementation. Your knowledge of those expectations and the level of customer satisfaction must be based on hard data, not your opinion or best guesses.

The reason to improve a process or a product must be linked to things that are critical to the satisfaction of your customers, both internal and external, which results in a financial benefit.

Principle #3:
Discovering The $tealth Factory
The Real Cost of Doing it Wrong

How big is **your** stealth factory? How much does it cost your company to "do it wrong?" Have you ever added up all the nonproductive, non-value-added activities that have come into being as a band-aid solution to deeper problems? Have you ever calculated the true cost in time and money for all the rework, scrap, continuous inspection and testing, warranty claims, lost customers, and all the other things that you can't sell? Now is the time to get a benchmark before you implement Six Sigma. You see, an obvious, tangible defect in a product or service only represents about five to eight percent of the total cost of poor quality. The less obvious factors of lost opportunity account for another 15 to 25 percent.

Principle #4:
Exposing the "Vital Few" $Y = f(x)$

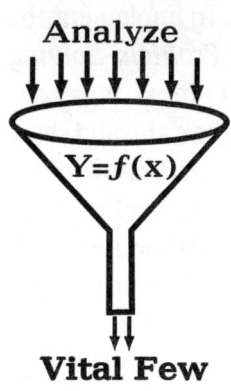

Prior to Six Sigma implementation, you must complete a thorough benchmarking exercise to discover where you stand. Where are you in comparison to your competitors? What is "best in class" for what you do? When you have some idea of where you are, you can apply Six Sigma metrics to expose the **Vital Few** factors that give you the most leverage to improve quality to Six Sigma levels while reducing your costs. Then you can select the projects to address them. Once the projects are selected, you need to find the **Vital Few** in each project, which will yield defect reduction and cost savings.

Principle #5:
Empowering People "The Best of the Best"

People are your greatest resource. It's up to you to give them the tools that empower them to find the best ways to improve your business and reduce costs. A Six Sigma company needs common approaches and processes to guide training and people selection. You want to create clarity and consistency, as well as clearly defined roles when implementing Six Sigma in your company.

Principle #6:
Harnessing The Magic of Data

The Method (MAGIC) without the "G" for Guesswork

The method is **Measure, Analyze, Improve and Control.** To implement the **Seven Principles of Problem-Solving Technology,** we must know what we want to know, capture the data, and share that knowledge with others. Standardized business metrics provide the set of tools we need to establish a common language to communicate the philosophy of Six Sigma.

Principle #7:
Relentless, Constant Journey The "Will"

How do we build and maintain momentum over the long run of three to five years? To build momentum, Six Sigma is best implemented in waves. These waves could flow from department to department, as well as flow within a given business group, from site-to-site, function-to-function, product line-to-product line, from process-to-process, or some combination. When the company's leadership visibly celebrates "wins," and rewards and empowers the people doing the work, this leads to greater momentum. Reaching a critical mass of trained employees and implementing the **Seven Principles** allows a company to integrate Six Sigma into the daily best practices of the business.

With each new client, I use certain best practices or standards that I have learned from data. Individual implementation plans can be benchmarked against these best practices. However, each company is different and implementation may differ from standard practice. Sometimes a company might need to change certain practices to align itself with the benchmark.

In other cases, we may need to modify the implementation of Six Sigma in a given area to reflect important differences in the organization, its industry, and its level of capability. There is a highly predictable method to use for implementation, and there **are** good practices to refer to as benchmarks. Most of the time before we do the analysis, "we don't know — what we don't know," about a specific company.

Lessons learned at other companies are valuable teachers and keep us from reinventing the wheel. Your experienced **Six Sigma training partner** has learned these lessons by being on the front lines of many companies and can assist you in creating your company's implementation manual.

COMPELLING LEADERS FOR SIX SIGMA IMPLEMENTATION

Training for Six Sigma must flow down from the top of the company, starting with corporate leadership. Only the leaders of a company can begin the process by linking Six Sigma to the strategy of the business. These individuals must totally understand the philosophy, concepts, and methodology before any action is taken. With this knowledge, they can begin to wisely identify the high level focus of Six Sigma, to establish broad goals and assign the right people resources to the planning and implementation.

It is vital that a senior manager (or managers) — a Six Sigma Champion — be designated to lead the implementation of Six Sigma, providing day-to-day leadership and support of the effort.

Don't assume that by applying Black Belts to a problem you will automatically achieve financial results. You have to have a budget, you have to know your chronic, high-impact issues, you must identify and quantify cost drivers, those factors that cause rework. "Line-of-site" goals must be identified.

Six Sigma **Problem-Solving Technology** requires that people throughout your company understand and become committed to the vision of Six Sigma quality before you begin to implement changes. Supervisory-level managers must know how to support the project work, and understand the implications of Six Sigma in their areas. These supervisory managers are the main communicators of the Six Sigma concept to employees. They must understand the vision for Six Sigma and how it works so that they can confidently answer the questions their people will inevitably have about *change.*

As with any large change endeavor, the effort and energy invested up front in planning and involvement saves at least ten times the effort that would be expended later by avoiding confusion, rework, and duplication of effort. A lead time of about two months prior to the launch of Black Belt training is needed. During this time period, three main things happen:

- **First,** senior managers are briefed on Six Sigma in order to help them establish the "case for change" and the overall goals and objectives of the effort. During this briefing, management leaders are encouraged to select the initial Master Black Belts who will be responsible for training Black Belts. These Master Black Belts often initially come from your training partner "team," as he or she must be experienced and thoroughly grounded in the methodology. Senior managers who will spearhead the implementation of Six Sigma are also selected. These senior managers become "Champions" for Six Sigma, and are critical to the success of the program. (The specific roles of the Champion, Master Black Belts and Black Belts were described in Chapter 4.)

- **Second,** the senior management Champion(s) of Six Sigma, along with the Master Black Belts and the "guiding coalition," develop a detailed implementation plan. The experience of other companies can be used as a benchmark for this process, and the plan individualized to meet the specific needs of the company. ***Your experienced Six Sigma training partner is critical to mastering this phase of implementation planning.***

[See Figure 6.11 Choosing Your Six Sigma Partner)

• **Third,** senior management Champions and Master Black Belts conduct top-down product benchmarking and process base lining. This exercise is used to establish an initial business-level estimate of quality performance and to guide the identification, prioritization, and coordination of Six Sigma projects. Management also identifies and selects candidates for Black Belt training during this phase.

These management training sessions ignite company leadership to recognize the urgency for change, and to recognize and quantify the **enormous** business opportunities that arise with improved quality and customer satisfaction. Management will also begin to recognize the threats to their business inherent in preserving the status quo or doing "business as usual."

FIGURE 6.1

IMPLEMENTATION PLANNING QUESTIONS

1) What are your top five chronic high-impact problems?

2) How do these compare to your competitors?

3) What do you know about the problems in data terms?

4) Where is, or who has the best data available to establish a baseline?

5) What has been your approach in the past to solve these problems?

6) How will Six Sigma be different in its approach?

FIGURE 6.2

Where to Apply Six Sigma?

Does your company have waste or defects in these areas?
What are these defects and waste costing you?

We have taken the difficult but basic Six Sigma skill of reducing defects and applied it to every business process, from inventing and commercializing a new product all the way to billing and collections after the product is delivered. Just as we think we've generated the last dollar of profit out of a business, we uncover new ways to harvest cash as we reduce cycle times, lower inventories, increase output, and reduce scrap. The results are better and more competitively priced products, more satisfied customers who give us more business, and improved cash flow.

Lawrence A. Bossidy, CEO, AlliedSignal
1998 Annual Report

Figure 6.3: Six Sigma Implementation Road Map

	Task List	Action Owner
1	Executive presentation / review	Six Sigma Partner
2	Decision made to go forward	Company
3	Contract with Six Sigma Partner	Company
4	Approval received from legal for contract or certain portions rewritten	Company
5	Leadership training & concurrent deployment plan	Six Sigma Partner
6	Champion leadership roles formulated, assigned, and communicated	Six Sigma Partner
7	Training material ordered ASAP for quantity discount	Company
8	Notebooks selected to use, and spec on SW needed	Company
9	Six Sigma Partner linked to internal e-mail to open communications to all BB's	Company
10	First Leadership core team meeting	Both
11	Basic selection criteria BB-attribute	Six Sigma Partner
12	Job description to HR	Six Sigma Partner
13	HR start benchmarking compensation plan for BB	Company
14	Timeline established	Six Sigma Partner
15	Job description sent out	Company
16	Resources backfilled (optional)	Company
17	Job description in hands of key management	Company
18	Six Sigma pre-assessment survey sent to all sites	Company
19	Database installed into company network (both internal resources to coordinate with partner)	Company
20	2 people assigned full-time to coordinate the day-to-day activities (the gate-keepers)	Company
21	Six Sigma Partner supplies temporary coordination to train internal assets to accelerate learning curve	Six Sigma Partner
22	Project Selection Guide given prior to Company Champion training	Company
23	Champion training dates set up and communicated	Company
24	Communication plan created, share benchmark communications (internal and external/PR)	Company
25	Training site selection	Company
26	Computers & training logistics	Company
27	Calendar of events created and communicated a (coordinate with instructors)	Company

Six Sigma Implementation Road Map

	Task List	Action Owner
28	Required participation dates for top executives inserted on their calendar	Company
29	Key management return BB-list w/backup list	Company
30	Pre-training survey sent	Company
31	Send survey select form (psychological profile optional)	Six Sigma Partner
32	Selection survey form completed and FedEx'd to BB	Company
33	Complete selection report	Company
34	Six Sigma world-wide Champion-network assigned and identified	Company
35	BB-communication sent	Company
36	Pre-training survey	Company
37	Project selection/pre-assessment guide completed	Both
38	Project set and ready for review w/BB	Both
39	Week of projects to be reviewed w/ BB by Six Sigma Partner & Champion	Both
40	Transactional BB –waves scheduled and identified	Both
41	BB Training — Week 1	Both
42	Measure application period — 3 weeks	Both
43	Report-out and BB Training — Week 2	Both
44	Analyze application period — 3 weeks	Both
45	Report-out and BB Training — Week 3	Both
46	Improve application period —3 weeks	Both
47	Report-out and BB Training — Week 4	Both
48	Control application period - 3 weeks	Both
49	BB Training Wave 2	Both
50	Certification event – Wave 1	Company
51	Plan for back fill of BB (optional)	Company
52	Management reviews of BB projects	Company
53	Leadership and staff to BB reviews	Six Sigma Partner
54	Leadership training makeups	Both
55	Core Leadership team Six Sigma monthly reviews (2 hrs)	Both
56	Overall quarterly review (1/2day) top level management	Both
57	Leadership training makeups	Six Sigma Partner
58	Green Belt train-the-trainer roll-out	Six Sigma Partner
59	Green Belt implementation	Six Sigma Partner

Embracing Customers
Delivering and Anticipating What the Customer Wants

How will you focus and apply the resources of Six Sigma so that the expectations of your customers and key business priorities are addressed? The best way to attack the *root causes* of defects and customer dissatisfaction is to look at *process quality.* Use Six Sigma to identify the processes that are critical to customer satisfaction and that are operating at a low Sigma level. You can also identify the product family or system that contributes the most to poor customer satisfaction and is also a strategically important product or service. This approach requires looking at a number of processes that feed into that product or service.

Projects selected based on the amount management thinks it will save in costs is a more limited approach because it rarely establishes a new mindset about fact- and data-driven decisions. Such approaches don't get into affecting the root causes of process capability. Similarly, focusing on the biggest problem or "fire" is short-sighted and it is usually not clear what process should be addressed. I don't usually recommend using this approach.

Black Belts don't firefight!

There are four additional ways to focus the implementation of Six Sigma. Although customer satisfaction factors should be your priority, it has been my experience that projects often can combine more than one approach successfully.

- **Geography:** Six Sigma may be deployed in stages based partly on geography.

- **Design for Six Sigma:** First focus on evolutionary design, then revolutionary design later on. Initial efforts focus on design improvement of key products, systems, or components. Then the processes linked to the redesigned parts can become the focus of implementation.

- **Internal Processes:** A company might decide to focus initial efforts on optimizing internal processes.

- **Supplier Processes:** It's always best to improve your own internal processes before trying to get your suppliers to improve their processes. If supplier processes are an early focus, you'll need to devote considerable resources to the effort and manage supplier relationships carefully. Get them engaged by training them concurrently, and share in the benefit of the projects.

DISCOVERING YOUR $TEALTH FACTORY

The existing paradigm of inspection, testing, and reworking simply doesn't address the "stealth factory" costs of rework, scrap, inspection, and testing. Six Sigma *does* take these costs into account. The traditional business belief is that the increasing cost of reducing defects makes reaching Six Sigma quality impractical. However, those companies who are striving for Six Sigma have realized that the net "cost" to reduce defects actually lowers as one approaches Six Sigma. They can also dramatically redirect the human resources they currently tie up in looking for and fixing defects, and other "containment" issues.

If you are a billion dollar company using just basic management decision-making processes, no statistical measurement tools whatsoever, you'll probably realize one percent of that one billion dollars as profit. That's your bottom line savings. With the **Seven Principles of Problem-Solving Technology,** using process characterization and optimization, you will begin to understand your processes and the real cost of poor quality. By identifying and eliminating the defects, you can realize between 15 and 25 percent of that revenue stream. That is between $150 million and $250 million added to your bottom line of a $1 billion company (see Figure 6.4 below).

Figure 6.4

Methods vs. the $avings

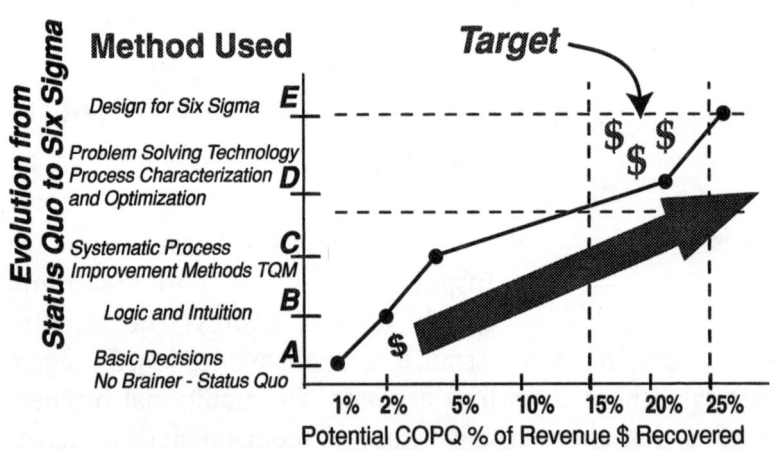

What methods do you deploy now? Where do you want to be?

Six Sigma results are found in the target zone of 15 to 25 percent COPQ.

The key concept of Six Sigma is that variation within a process is the main reason for poor performance. Defects arise from variation and variation occurs from either process, material or design inadequacies. A defect results when a characteristic doesn't conform to a standard and can be uniformly or randomly distributed in a process.

Variation is the creator of defects and waste in your world. This enemy must be destroyed.

Variation is the enemy of certainty and therefore is also the enemy of customer satisfaction. Variation drives the unknown, it adds to customer (and employee) disbelief and lack of confidence in the ability of processes to deliver customer satisfaction. Variation increases risk — the risk that a result will not meet expectations.

Variation has a direct impact on business results in terms of cost, cycle time, and the frequency of defects that affect customer satisfaction. The greater the variation, the less the certainty, belief, confidence, and yield. In short, the more variation in our business processes, and hence in our business itself, then the less we know about how well we are doing.

Six Sigma methodology and training focuses on the drastic reduction of process variation and the virtual elimination of product defects while getting financial results. The purpose is to stop quality variation at the earliest possible point, by attacking variation during the design of the product and process. The result is processes which are very robust, which make very efficient use of resources and assets, and which result in highly efficient organizations.

Figure 6.5

Major Sources of Variation

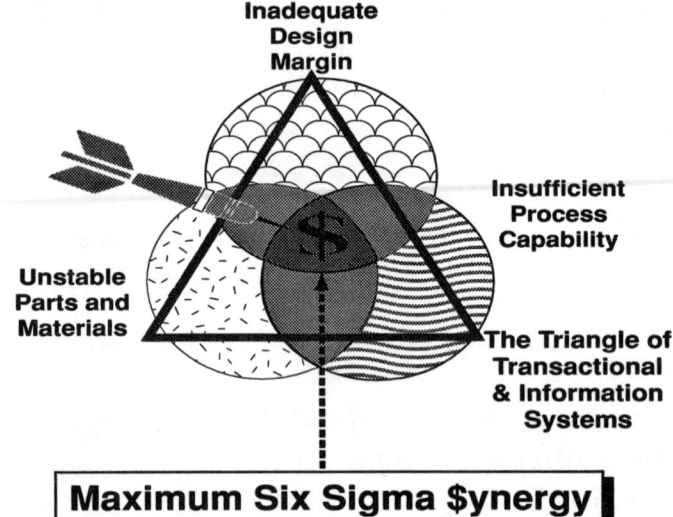

Inadequate
Design
Margin

Insufficient
Process
Capability

Unstable
Parts and
Materials

The Triangle of
Transactional
& Information
Systems

Maximum Six Sigma $ynergy

*When all three areas overlap in a particular project, you have
located the greatest potential for maximum Six Sigma results.*

Adapted from: The Vision of Six Sigma: A Roadmap for Breakthrough by
Mikel J. Harry, © 1994 Sigma Publishing Co.

DOING SIX SIGMA: Asking The Right Questions

*Black Belts must be allowed and required to question
specification limits. For example, a Black Belt demonstrated clearly
that a process step — dipping a part in a de-ox solution — was
not providing any quality benefit. During the project review, the
process owner defended the step as the way it had always been
done, even though the metrics showed clearly that it didn't add
value to the product and cost time and money! At that point,
the company Champion stepped in to intervene to support the
Black Belt and remove the roadblock to accomplishing his goal.
The Black Belt had the data — the process owner did not!*

Major Sources of Variation

There are three main causes of process variation.

Insufficient process capability
caused by processes that produce relatively high numbers of defective units.

Inadequate design margin
resulting in unnecessarily and unreasonably tight process specifications, sometimes tighter than the customer requires.

The use of unstable parts and materials
usually caused by vendors who are unable to control their own processes and end up shipping materials which in turn yield variation in YOUR processes.

The inevitable result of excessive process variation is the production of defective units which are outside the required specifications. Defects cost money in terms of scrap, rework time, waste of human resources, inspection costs, etc. Even if you have a quality-control inspection process in place and you are catching your defects and reworking them,

experience shows that the chance of defects occurring in the field where the customer is affected is substantially higher in reworked products!

If you could prevent defects from occurring in the first place — and you *can* by controlling the sources of variation that *cause* the defect — *why wouldn't you?* The money saved from inspection, rework, and lost customers is substantial! Achieving Six Sigma quality corrects the costly problem of variation by attacking the problem at the source, using statistical tools to identify and select the best candidates to reduce variation and improve the bottom line.

Specification Limits

Defects occur when a process varies from specified limits. Therefore, specification limits **must** be an expression of **customer expectations,** based on hard data regarding what those expectations are. They are the "goal posts" by which defects are determined, and setting them too high or too low is equally negative to the bottom line.

DOING SIX SIGMA: **Fix First Problems First**

I don't want you to think you should stop all variation in all your processes. You want to reduce and control the variation that results in a negative cash flow. There are a lot of people in corporate America spending a lot of time and effort working on the wrong stuff because they don't know what it is costing them.

For example, I worked with a company in Batesville, Arkansas that said they had an extrusion problem. They make the rubber seal around doors. For years they talked about the lumps in the extrusion as the problem. They were devoted to spending their resources to solve that problem. They had to fix it. They had been talking about it and work on it — and they did so for ten years! However, the problem wasn't the lumps in the extrusion process!

*As their consultant, when I looked at the whole process, the lump problem was about the **fifth** problem on the list. I created a 3-level Pareto chart (see Figures 5.4 - 5.6 on pages 152 and 153) that showed the impact of process variation problems and asked them why we were talking about lumps! Show me the data that says we should work on lumps at all. It may be fun to talk about it, but talking costs you money. There are other processes here that account for more than half your problems — the problem of lumps is nothing by comparison. **Let's fix the first problems first!***

Specification limits can be applied to administration or transactions, as well as manufacturing. For example, if the goal of a marketing department is to have requested information in the hands of a prospect or customer in 48 hours, that becomes an Upper Specification Limit (there is no lower limit: this is a one-sided specification typical of cycle-time processes). A defect has occurred if the information does not reach the customer within 48 hours of the request. Unfortunately, specifications are relatively rare in administration or transactions in comparison to manufacturing. A major change in mindset is required to implement Six Sigma in this environment, as it requires the institution of process specifications where none have existed before.

EXPOSING THE "VITAL FEW"

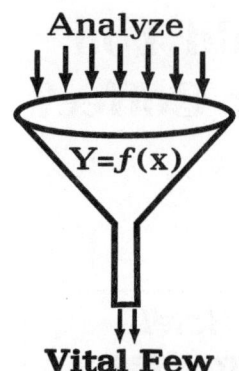

Analyze

$Y=f(x)$

Vital Few

There are three categories of requirements that represent a customer's expectations for purchasing your product: **Quality, Cost and Delivery.** Have you taken the time to survey your customers to find out what is important to them? When you have that information, you can translate the characteristics important to your customer into **Critical-to-Quality** (CTQ) factors. Having established the "Critical-to" factors, it is then possible to prioritize improvement opportunities and select these as Six Sigma projects.

How do you determine critical-to-quality factors for **your** business? First of all, avoid the common pitfall of selecting factors that you THINK matter without checking with your customer first! They may have no interest in what **you** think is important! That's why Six Sigma is based on verifiable FACTS, not "I think," "I feel," or "I believe" statements that are not grounded in reality.

A classic example of selecting the wrong CTQ comes from a survey taken at a conference held at a hotel by a Six Sigma trainee. The Black Belt asked the hotel what they thought constituted good coffee service, then asked the conference attendees the same question. The coffee service example below shows the large *gap* in the perspective of the customer vs. the supplier.

FIGURE 6.6

How Would You Like Your Coffee?

Conference Attendee Expectations	Hotel Provides
• Good Hot Coffee • Fast Line, especially for refills • Close to High-capacity restrooms • Close to Telephones • Room to Chat	• Good Hot Coffee • Clean China • Clean Linen • Attractive Display • Extras - Snacks

Does the Hotel know the expectations of its customers?

> Six Sigma training by qualified,
> experienced experts is insurance that misreading
> your customer won't happen, as customer-focused
> data-gathering is emphasized as
> "Critical to Success."

EMPOWERING PEOPLE
Creating Black Belts for Quality Improvement

Achieving Six Sigma performance across an organization is an enormous challenge. Going from Four to Six Sigma is almost a 2,000 percent improvement! No one person and no one area can accomplish this alone. The challenge to leadership is to harness the ideas and energy of many people across functions, sites, and even business groups. Implementing the **Seven Principles of Problem-Solving Technology** requires you to mobilize your people resources and arm them with the tools they need to accomplish the goal of quality improvement and impressive financial results. Training these individuals to become Black Belts and "change agents" is critical to successful implementation of Six Sigma **Problem-Solving Technology.**

To become a Six Sigma company, it takes more than technology, knowledge, and organization. This quantum leap in quality needs **people** to make it happen. While all employees need to understand the vision of Six Sigma and use some of its tools to improve their work, there are six distinctive roles in the implementation process. More detailed descriptions of these roles are found in Chapter 4.

Six Sigma Champions: As a group, executive managers provide overall leadership and must *own* and *drive* Six Sigma. From within this group, a senior management leader or leaders is assigned to provide day-to-day top management leadership during implementation. We refer to these individuals as *Champions.*

Supervisory-Level Management: These managers play a pivotal role because they own the processes of the business and must ensure that improvements to the process are captured and sustained. They typically also manage the individuals who are selected for Black Belt training, and must understand the challenges facing them, as well as be willing and empowered to remove any roadblocks to progress.

Master Black Belts: These are the full-time trainers for a company's Six Sigma efforts. They act as coaches and mentors for Black Belts. You will grow them from the ranks of your Black Belts with the help of your Six Sigma partner's team of experts. To sustain a program, your best Black Belts become your Master Black Belts and the program becomes totally your own.

Black Belts: Full-time employees who are 100 percent focused on identifying, leading, and facilitating the completion of Six Sigma projects.

Green Belts: As part-time resources, they help Black Belts complete projects and extend the reach of Black Belts. When a Black Belt has access to the time and expertise of Green Belts, it allows the Black Belt to work on overlapping projects, thus completing more projects in a given period of time. Green Belts also work on smaller projects inside their functional areas.

Project Team Members: These are the project-specific, part-time people resources − the "team" − who provide process and cross-functional knowledge. They help sustain the gains achieved by Six Sigma projects, and eventually take 100 percent ownership of a Black Belt project.

FIGURE 6.7

Training "Kick Starts" Implementation

 Training is one of the key success factors in achieving Six Sigma. Careful selection of an experienced Six Sigma training partner is critical to the creation of empowered, educated people armed with the tools and knowledge to implement Six Sigma.

- ***Champion Training*** (Presidents, Executive Vice Presidents) This briefing takes a minimum of three days.

- ***Master Black Belts*** Master Black Belts, in addition to completing Black Belt Training, attend an extra two-week session.

- ***Black Belts*** The mandatory Black Belt training takes four weeks over four months. Weeks 1 through 4 are the one-week sessions of Measure, Analyze, Improve and Control phases. Between the training weeks is a three-week application phase, followed by a one-day project review.

- ***Six Sigma Green Belts*** Green Belt training, usally taught by Black Belts, takes 8 to 10 days. Four two-day sessions are spread over three to four months as part of completing a project.

- ***Supervisory-Level Managers*** Supervisory-level managers should receive a basic one-day Six Sigma introduction. Those who are managing projects attend a more detailed three-day session that covers more background on Six Sigma tools, concepts, and implementation.

The focus of Six Sigma training is to arm your human capital assets with tools to deliver financial results. This quantum leap in quality requires people to make it happen!

PTAR: Plan – Train – Apply — Review

Six Sigma training for Master Black Belts, Black Belts, and Green Belts is based on the Plan-Train-Apply-Review (PTAR) model. It is a closed feedback system where students are able to immediately apply the concepts they have learned and receive real-time coaching and review.

Senior managers in your company are involved in **planning** to ensure that each phase of a Six Sigma project is based on the lessons learned during training sessions. These managers also coordinate activity between projects and departments.

Training happens in a classroom setting where Black Belt candidates learn Six Sigma methods. They then **apply** the tools they learn in class to their assigned project. A formal **review** is held at the  beginning of each training phase with the participation of the supervisory management "owners" of the process and the Champion. A formal project report and review at the beginning of each training session and a final review at project completion also contributes to the learning process. (See Appendix B & C for an example of a completed project report.)

FIGURE 6.8

Black Belt Training Cycle

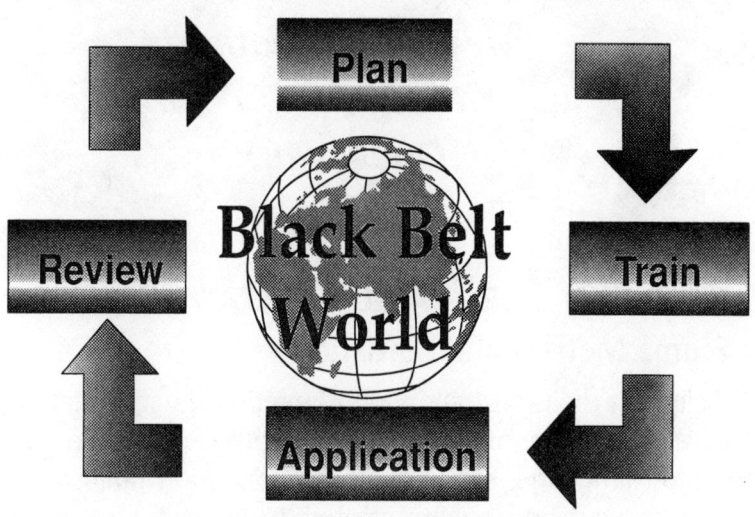

Black Belt Training Cycle:

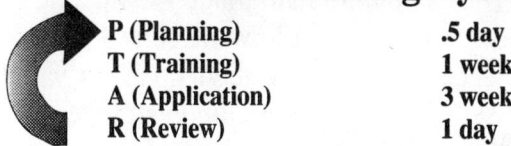

P (Planning)	.5 day
T (Training)	1 week
A (Application)	3 weeks
R (Review)	1 day

The Black Belt training cycle follows the Problem-Solving Technology implementation model titled The Plan-Train-Application-Review (PTAR)

Almost one-third of General Electric's employees have been trained to lead projects and spread Six Sigma tools to co-workers, resulting in more than $70 million in productivity gains in 1997. Six Sigma, even at this early stage, delivered more than $300 million to General Electric's 1997 operating income. In 1998 returns will more than double this operating profit impact.

General Electric 1997 Annual Report

$Y=f(x)$

MA~~G~~IC = Methods Without the "G" for Guesswork!

Harnessing The Magic Of Data
Six Sigma Metrics and Statistics

Selecting the right tools and interpreting the information uncovered is the core of successful Six Sigma implementation. A common language, set of tools, and common philosophy must be created and communicated to achieve successful implementation. With a common language we are able talk to anyone else in the company about how we solved problems or implemented projects. We're able to benchmark a variety of processes using a set of tools everyone understands.

How do we accomplish this objective? **With consistency.** You need a consistent set of training materials and programs which have been thoroughly tested in Fortune 500 companies, and which are tailored for your specific needs. Your Six Sigma training partner will provide a consistent format for project reports so everyone understands them and can find the information he or she wants. Consistent definitions of metrics (e.g. how we calculate Sigma), and consistent statistical software designed for Six Sigma metrics are also needed.

There are three types of metrics (strategic/business, technical/process, and Six Sigma activities) that are used to implement the *Seven Principles of Problem-Solving Technology*.

Strategic/Business: These are the Group- and Division-level measures that will measure and drive Six Sigma implementation. One of the key metrics is the Six Sigma Improvement Curve (see Figure 6.9). It measures progress, at a business unit level, of the reduction of defects over time.

To drive implementation, senior management must establish the goal line that represents the year-over-year reduction in defects expected in each area of the business. The approximate starting defect level (baseline) and the selected percent improvement target determines how long it will take to reach Six Sigma performance levels.

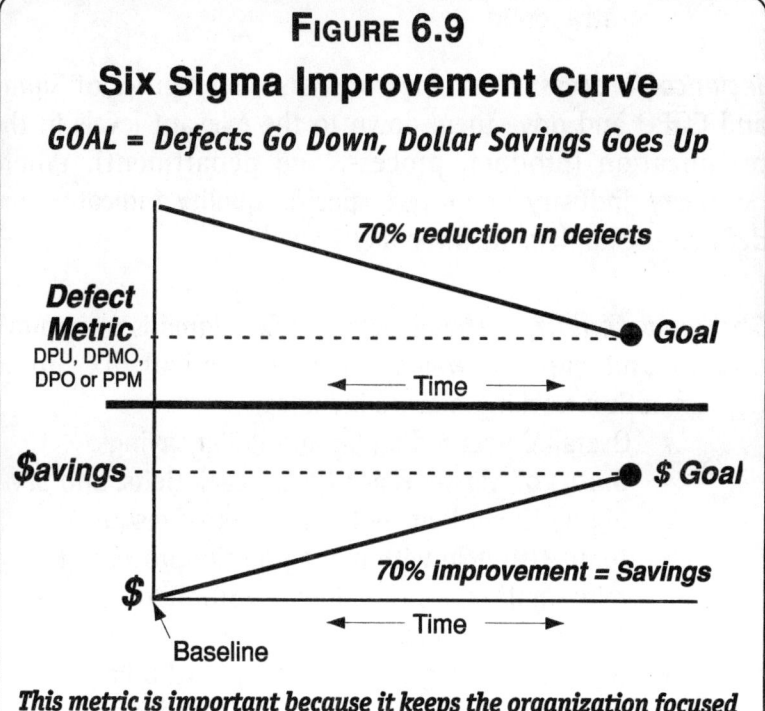

FIGURE 6.9
Six Sigma Improvement Curve
GOAL = Defects Go Down, Dollar Savings Goes Up

70% reduction in defects

Defect Metric
DPU, DPMO, DPO or PPM

●━ **Goal**

◄━━━ Time ━━━►

$avings ┄┄┄┄┄┄┄┄┄┄┄┄┄┄┄┄┄┄● **$ Goal**

70% improvement = Savings

◄━━━ Time ━━━►

$

Baseline

This metric is important because it keeps the organization focused on defect reduction over a number of time periods, not just a one-time improvement. Because the percent improvement level (typically 60 to 70 percent defect reduction each year) is so high, it precludes minor improvement and "tweaking" of the process. It produces a breakthrough target for improvement.

Other strategic metrics include:

- Business-level estimates of Sigma related to the improvement goal [Six Sigma Improvement Curve as defects per million opportunities (DPMO)].

- Where appropriate, performance against key strategic cycle time targets.

- High-level estimate and rate of improvement on Cost of Poor Quality (COPQ).

- Key measures (tailored by business) of customer satisfaction.

Technical/Process: These measures take the metrics of Sigma and COPQ and drive them down to the relevant levels in the organization (product, process, and department). Where necessary, industry or process-specific quality indicators are defined to supplement these metrics.

Six Sigma Activities: The objective of Six Sigma is to improve quality and capture wasted dollars. Typical Six Sigma implemetation tracking metrics include:
- Overall defect reduction and dollar savings.
- Status of Master Black Belts, Black Belts, and Six Sigma Green Belts — the number of resources, tenure (to help with managing the process of reintegration into line jobs), performance, attrition rates, etc.
- Status of management training — who has received various types of training and when.
- Status of projects — track projects against key milestones and reviews, as well as follow up on process improvements and the capture of benefits (savings and customer satisfaction).

Implementing Six Sigma in a Transactional Environment

Some companies overlook the incredible costs that can translate into incredible gains in their transaction-type processes. The simple way to approach this is to agree that all work is a transaction, whether it is a fastening step on the assembly line or entering 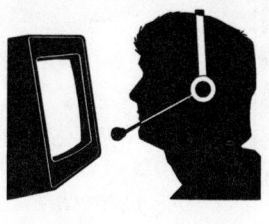 data into a field on a form. All work is really transactions between two or more entities with the opportunity to do it right or wrong. Thus, the potential for costly defects.

Clearly, a Six Sigma program offers tremendous value to your manufacturing processes. These are more easily seen because of their three-dimensional quality. Consider your transaction processes which, although less easily seen, are your volume processes. How many supplier invoices do you process every month? One hundred thousand, two hundred thousand? What is the error rate? What is the cost of rework?

Additionally, how much time do your Materials, Human Resource or Finance Departments spend correcting problems created by "the system" instead of adding value with effective forecasts or business analyses? Just imagine the cash flow improvements you could make if you could eliminate billing errors! These are just a few of the "transactional" opportunities for improvement that can use the Six Sigma approach.

> If you think of "standardization" as
> the best that you know today,
> but which is to be improved tomorrow,
> you get somewhere.
>
> Henry Ford

DOING SIX SIGMA: GE Capital

Our Six Sigma initiative continues to produce significant benefits in the form of increased revenues and lower costs. Our basic approach is to reduce "defects" by focusing on customer needs, improving processes and involving all employees.

Commercial Finance, for example, used Six Sigma tools to win more deals by better understanding customer requirements. It developed a Customer Expectations Pact that has contributed to a 160 percent increase in new transactions won.

Mortgage Insurance developed a flexible new billing system that contributed not only to customer retention but also was instrumental in winning $60 million in new insurance written from one customer.

In Japan, Global Consumer Finance helped customers overcome payment difficulties associated with limited banking hours and saved money by establishing an alternative payment method through a network of 25,000 convenience stores, now used by 40 percent of its customers.

While our employee commitment to Six Sigma is substantial — more than 16,000 associates involved and more than 2,000 projects under way — the benefits to our competitive position are tremendous. Customers are enjoying the results of Six Sigma as our overall responsiveness to their business needs improves dramatically.

Gary C. Wendt
Chairman, President, and CEO
GE Capital Services, Inc.
GE 1997 Annual Report on Six Sigma

FIGURE 6.10
Six Sigma in a Transactional Environment: Where to Look for Cost Savings

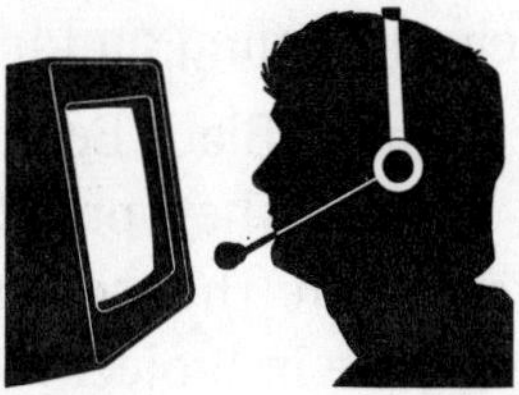

Process Cycle Time Reduction:
Engineering change notices
Cash receipts
Computer installations
Pension estimates
Inventory reclassifications
AS400 query responses
Design disclosure updates
Financial month-end closures
Non-production material purchases
Shop floor planning procedures

Cost Reduction:
Non-value-added work
Development cost
Expedite cost
Material recertification
Unnecessary preventive maintenance
Cutting tools
Inventory

Defect Reduction:
Invoices
Purchase orders
Overhead forecasts

Other Applications:
Capacity utilization
Purchase order reduction
Reusable engineering

RELENTLESS, CONSTANT JOURNEY

The journey to Six Sigma quality requires a long-term commitment. In order to build and maintain momentum that propels us toward our goal, we need a **critical mass of people** in the organization who have received training and have applied the training to projects.

Master Black Belts are critical to the long-term success of Six Sigma. They provide leadership, training, and coaching throughout the company. Master Black Belts must have experience in project implementation, and are grown from the ranks of your Black Belts. You need one Master Black Belt for every seven to ten Black Belts.

The need for Master Black Belts never goes away — they will always be training and coaching new Black Belts and Green Belts. A typical assignment is at least two years long. As some Master Black Belts return to line jobs, new Master Black Belts replace them. Some may decide to remain as Six Sigma trainers indefinitely. If they are good trainers and coaches, and if there is a need, this is a viable career path option for a few people.

You can expect to train roughly one percent of your total employee population as Six Sigma Black Belts. A company needs enough full-time Black Belts to complete a sufficient number of projects to move the many critical processes towards Six Sigma. Their assignment is also a minimum of two years.

Once an infrastructure of Master Black Belts and Black Belts is established, you can begin to train Six Sigma Green Belts. Green Belts are available to work part-time on projects and their presence helps to extend the number of trained personnel available to sustain the gains. The number of projects launched directly determines the number of employees touched by Six Sigma through their participation on project teams. As the number of Black Belts grow, so does the number of projects and project team members.

In summary, experience has shown that the following principles are essential to successful Six Sigma implementation:

- Visible leadership commitment to the initiative. Your employees must see **leadership involvement** from the beginning of the Six Sigma implementation.
- A measurement system to track progress, providing accountability for the initiative.
- Internal and external benchmarking of the organization's products, services, and processes. You must find out where you **really** are in comparison to best practices in order to gain the sense of urgency to implement Six Sigma.
- Setting challenging "stretch" goals that focus your employees on **changing the process,** not just "tweaking" the existing process.
- Educating all levels of your company about Six Sigma philosophy and tools.
- Communication of success stories that demonstrate results and show how the tools can be applied to your specific challenges.
- The infrastructure to support change, including senior management Champions, Master Black Belts, and Black Belts to provide the necessary planning, teaching, coaching, and consulting at all levels in the company.

The only way to get anywhere is to start from where you are.

William Lee

Figure 6.11

A Checklist for Choosing Your Six Sigma Training Partner

Circle the qualifications of your Six Sigma Training Partner Candidate. Six Sigma Consultants and Six Sigma Academy are the only ones to meet all these criteria.

- ✔ Fortune 100 officer experience?
- ✔ Senior executive experience?
- ✔ First-line management experience?
- ✔ Manufacturing plant/business changeover?
- ✔ Successful company-wide Six Sigma implementation experience?
- ✔ Federal government consulting experience?
- ✔ Experience in facilitating/implementing corporate strategic direction?
- ✔ Published writings – technical?
- ✔ Published writings – scientific?
- ✔ Published writings – management?
- ✔ Intellectual property in a software learning tool?
- ✔ Outstanding reputation and proven track record?
- ✔ High return on investment to clients?
- ✔ Market leadership?
- ✔ Blue chip client base?
- ✔ Strong, experienced management team?
- ✔ Excellent resource integration?
- ✔ Highly capable, repeatable process?
- ✔ Capability to deliver Six Sigma Champions?
- ✔ Capability to deliver Master Black Belts?
- ✔ Wall Street recognition?
- ✔ Repository/library of Six Sigma resource material?
- ✔ Video learning tools?

FIGURE 6.12

WHAT YOU CAN EXPECT FROM YOUR SIX SIGMA TRAINING PARTNER

1) Identify customer needs.
2) Establish implementation team.
3) Deliver executive training.
4) Establish executive-level ownership.
5) Select and execute broad-level projects.
6) Develop implementation plan.
7) Select Black Belt candidates.
8) Select detailed Black Belt projects.
9) Define instructional curriculum.
10) Organize instructional material.
11) Transfer Six Sigma knowledge.
12) Design project strategy.
13) Execute project plan.
14) Document and capture results.
15) Measure project outcomes.
16) Analyze project outcomes.
17) Improve implementation plan.
18) Establish infrastructure for self-sufficiency.

What's Next After Implementation:
Six Sigma Problem-Solving Technology Lessons Learned

Six Sigma is a methodology which provides breakthrough results for your company. However, for the breakthroughs and results to continue, you must constantly break down barriers! Many companies have successfully implemented Six Sigma and have made it a part of their "genetic code." Others have tried to do so and have not been successful. What is the difference? Here are some possible answers, based on data I have collected over the past several years.

Nine months after completing training, 20 to 25 percent of all Black Belts were not working on Six Sigma projects. The reasons vary, but included;

- Black Belts were promoted to better positions;
- Black Belts were enticed away from their jobs with better offers ($$$) from suppliers; and
- Black Belts completed one or two projects, then returned back to their original jobs.

All Black Belt projects were successful, but only 70 percent of the dollars could be tracked to the bottom line. Reasons included;

- many projects were of the "cost avoidance" variety;
- the Finance Department was not involved in project selection/tracking;
- projected savings were used to mask other operating issues;
- projects were too future-based (product line six-to nine-months out); and
- management did not act on breakthrough — people, inventory, bill of materials.

The majority of suppliers are not at a Five Sigma capability nor are they expected to be in the near future. Reasons included;

- lack of financial resources for Six Sigma Black Belt training;
- no incentive to dedicate resources to quality improvement;
- lack the people talent to dedicate as Black Belts; and
- company cannot afford to dedicate their Black Belts to help suppliers achieve Five Sigma capability.

A lot of sites complain that there are too many quality initiatives: TQM, Six Sigma, Materials, Customer Excellence, Technical Excellence, etc. Reasons included;

- the site management teams did not have a clear understanding of how the individual "tools" are used: Six Sigma, Design For Manufacturability, Supplier Partnership, Customer Satisfaction, etc. It was also not clear how each program interacts.

There are five factors which I have identified from these surveys which have proven to be *critical* in order for companies to achieve continued Six Sigma breakthroughs. Reasons included;

- additional Black Belt training every 9 to 10 months is needed to renew the pool of talent in your company;
- senior Management must be involved in the planning and implementation process;
- site leadership training in Six Sigma Problem-Solving Technology is necessary to insure that they align with the vision and philosophy of Six Sigma;
- Black Belts must be dedicated to projects for two years full-time; and
- suppliers must improve to at least Five Sigma.

APPLYING
PROBLEM-SOLVING TECHNOLOGY
TO YOUR COMPANY

Do These Statements
Apply To You?

Our company's leadership is willing to invest in training to understand Six Sigma philosophy, concepts and methodology.

We are willing to calculate the return-on-investment from Doing Six Sigma in our company.

We are able to benchmark our product and processes to estimate our quality performance.

We have already identified potential Black Belt candidates, have recruited a Master Black Belt or have hired or identified an experienced training partner.

Our main source of variation is _____.

Specification limits have been established based on customer needs.

Our costs of poor quality include _____.

Author's Closing Comments

In closing, after reading this book I hope you have a good understanding of both the challenges and the extraordinary rewards directly linked to implementing Six Sigma. While no cookbook is available for the implementation of Six Sigma, the methodology stays the same and is proven to work when implemented with integrity and discipline.

Each organization brings resources and competencies of varying degrees to the task of doing business every day. While there are differences, there is one central truth for all.

All companies have customers. All have products or services for which you bill the customer. All customers have expectations about your product or service that are critical to their decision whether they re-buy or switch to a competitor . You are judged in the marketplace daily by how well you satisfy the customer's expectations of quality, price, and delivery.

Six Sigma is a program to align your company's resources and corporate mind to satisfying and re-satisfying your customer every day. Early on I challenged you as a leader to examine the will required to relentlessly pursue excellence. Just like the scene in <u>Butch Cassidy and the Sundance Kid</u> when Paul Newman asks Robert Redford about the authorities doggedly chasing them day after day, "Who are those guys?" You must let your people know that you will pursue excellence with that same determination. Tireless in your pursuit of excellence, you will wear down your internal detractors and your competitors. You will replace complacency and status quo in your company with achievement. Data rules, not "I think or I feel."

I invite you to join the other excellent companies, whose stories of implementation were mentioned in this book, and Do Six Sigma.

Greg Brue

All this will not be finished
in the first one hundred days. Nor
will it be finished
in the first one thousand days, nor
in the life of
this administration,
nor even perhaps in
our lifetime on this planet.

John. F. Kennedy

CHAPTER 7

Doing Six Sigma
Black Belt Project
Completion Summaries

The following pages are summaries of actual Black Belt projects. The company's name and the Black Belt's name have been pulled to maintain propriety.

The purpose is to demonstrate types of projects and the methodology followed to achieve the results. Unseen in these reports are the countless hours and the countless numbers of people involved to complete the project. Good Black Belts never lose sight of the fact that their team members are the reason projects get accomplished. This is not the work of lone rangers. It is a team effort.

The reports are grouped by category:

 Design

 Manufacturing

 Transaction

Doing Six Sigma

Design Opportunity

Customer required changes on extruding line 13 reduced the line speed and increased the scrap levels. Necessary compound changes and optimization of extruding processing conditions are required to increase extruding line speed and reduce scrap.

Problem-Solving Technology

Measure   Process mapping was performed to accurately show the true steps in the procedure, as well as identify key process input and output variables. Gauge R&R studies on the master batch measured viscosity.

Analyze   During the development of a process Failure Mode Effect Analysis (FMEA) other issues related to the production process came to the forefront, such as cleanliness of the process at critical points.

Improve   A two-factor, two-level Design of Experiments (DOE) was performed, showing a significant relationship between carbon-black weight and polymer weight. Two-way interaction and curvature points were not significant.

Control   A compound and extruding control plan was developed based on the process Failure Mode Effect Analysis (FMEA). This will be made accessible to the shift supervisor to aid in Problem-Solving. Controls were implemented in the process to monitor weighing consistency.

Results   More than one option was found to reduce viscosity, therefor reducing the amount of carbon-black and extending the scorch time. The extruding barrel temperature was optimized with the 12 other lines in the plant, immediately reducing scrap.

Savings $120,000 in Cost of Poor Quality from scrap.

Doing Six Sigma

Design Opportunity

A standard high-pressure gas valve was experiencing a low first yield rate and high scrap rate. Management set goals of improving yield from 47 percent to 70 percent and another issue was identifying the main causes for body, cover, and gas cock casting scraping.

Problem-Solving Technology

Measure   The first steps were creating a process map and a characterization selection matrix to evaluate which actions are value-added or non-value-added. A 3-level Pareto chart also helped identify the top three defects on which to focus. By performing a process FMEA, the need to eliminate as many sources of contamination possible became evident.

Analyze   An attribute Gauge R&R showed the test fixtures and operators were capable. A cause-and-effect diagram was generated to identify Key Process Input Variables (KPIVs that need attention in accomplishing the goals. Also, a variable Gauge R&R study on gauges for the body resulted in removal of one gauge from the production floor.

Improve   A hypothesis study focusing on leakage in the body caused by burrs indicated the problem was internal, and raised the possible need for additional training on the second shift. When a DOE with five variables was performed, it verified that the current process and procedure provide the minimum leakage. A hypothesis test based on contamination from cardboard shipping containers, revealed the need to use plastic, reusable containers.

Control   Gauges that are not capable are replaced or modified to bring them back to acceptable levels. The enforcement of mandatory training and the discipline to keep contamination from creating defects will sustain the gains.

Results   High-quality castings will limit defects at the supplier or front of the line.

Savings $16,680 in scrap and rework, plus an additional $62,000 per year obtained from the use of reusable shipping containers.

Doing Six Sigma

Design Opportunity

Electronics Module Assembly involves the installation of the circuit card assembly into a metal housing and filling the housing with a compound. The operation involves 3.4 hours of touch labor and 25 steps. The objective was to remove or improve several of these operations.

Problem-Solving Technology

Measure   A process map was developed, identifying the 25 steps in the procedure. Significant key process inputs and outputs were incorporated into a Characteristic Selection Matrix.

Analyze   During development of the Failure Mode Effect Analysis (FMEA), additional factors became evident and were included in process steps. Nitrogen gas, resin leakage, and improper mixing were the most important steps. Gauge R&R studies were performed on Balance and Shore Durometers.

Improve　　A hypothesis test concluded that the hardness produced by an 11-hour room temperature cure was the same as the presently used 16 hours. These results served as parameters for the Design of Experiments (DOE). The objective was to ascertain whether curing times and/or temperatures could be reduced.

Control　　The process specification that details the step-by-step processes for the module was modified to incorporate changes. As part of new requirements, measurements will be made and records kept on the weights of all modules.

Results　　Throughput time was reduced from 21.4 hours to 12.9 hours. Several process steps were eliminated or improved.

Savings　　$138,100 from reduction in touch-labor hours.

Doing Six Sigma

Design Opportunity

Noise and dirt accumulated in the bottom of automobile doors. One part (called a sill plate) needed to be developed to seal out noise and dirt along the entire door and at the same time replaced 20 other parts that required difficult assembly. A new semi-rigid compound needed to be developed and manufactured.

Problem-Solving Technology

Measure   A process map revealed the key output and input variables for the sill plate that could cause shrinkage. The Gauge R&R study showed the measurement system was adequate.

Analyze   A Taguchi Design of Experiment (DOE) with five factors and two interactions was designed to evaluate which factors had an impact on part shrinkage. The results showed a strong effect of vacuum, cooling #1, and infrared heaters and no significant interaction. Production parameters were modified with dramatic results. A full factorial DOE with three factors was performed to optimize process parameters.

Improve   Results of a study on infrared heater settings were analyzed with one-way ANOVA and found to have significant differences. Alternate compounds were evaluated for processing effects, attribute of appearance and surface, and shrinkage of the final part and punchouts.

Control   Extrusion operators continued to follow the Control Plan. Productivity measured with output per shift increased. A punch-out sample is collected periodically. These samples are measured several days later to record the amount of shrinkage that occurs.

Results   Specific results include providing continuous, on-time supply to the customer, establishing optimum process conditions, and increased output per shift of over 20 percent.

Savings   Scrap recovered saved $23,000. Improved compounds will save $8,070 per month. Improved operations meant avoidance of an appropriation for a $45,000 piece of equipment.

Doing Six Sigma

Design Opportunity

The transfer molding operation historically has created a high amount of defective product requiring rework. Since rework has only recently been tracked, it became obvious to management that significant throughput improvement opportunity existed.

Problem-Solving Technology

Measure   Defects were put into a Pareto chart by shift, cause, day of week, part numbers, and mold setup. A detailed process map with tally points was created and initial process capability of key process inputs like mold temperature were determined. Gauge R&R studies were also performed.

Analyze   A process FMEA was developed. As an output of the FMEA, the team used hypothesis tests to narrow the number of significant contributors.

Improve   Design of Experiments was undertaken on several factors. Mold temperature, coating, and cut method were chosen. The design was a full factorial, 3-factor, 2-levels, with four center points on mold temperature. The DOE pointed that the use of attribute data was then the only available option, which required use of larger sample sizes.

Control

Evolutionary Operation of Process (EVOP) was an obvious tool in the solution to further optimize the mold temperature and injection pressure. An EVOP study was designed and implemented which introduced relatively small, five-degree, changes in temperature and five-PSI changes in pressure. The team was able to optimize at 370 degrees and 60 PSI.

Results

Equipment settings section of Standard Operating Procedure has been modified and all operators were trained on new changes. RTY improved from 82 percent to 95 percent.

Savings

$200,000 in capital avoidance.

Doing Six Sigma

Design Opportunity

Capacity problems on Type One presses is a key issue, and any improvements will have the greatest impact to the plant. The inability to perform fast, efficient mold changes were impacting delivery schedules and customer satisfaction.

Problem-Solving Technology

Measure   The first step was the creation of a Process Map. A FMEA was also performed to measure the effects of each key process input and output variable. Finally, a Gauge R&R was performed on the measurement equipment. It was determined that tolerance limits used were too tight, as the process proved to be more robust than originally thought.

Analyze   Brainstorming of problems and solutions occurred. Analysis of Variance on pre-heater capacity resulted in a redesign of the pre-heater.

Improve   The Design of Experiment (DOE) focused on the redesigned pre-heater. Objectives were to establish optimum settings and ascertain heater capability. Controls were then set to achieve optimum settings, and a "recipe" master disk was created for use during mold changing.

Control   Structured training of press operators on mold setup was initiated. Another step was the simplification of the measurement system. Preventative maintenance will impact mold change times as mechanical/electrical problems disappear.

Results   Mold change time reduced from 3.6 hours to 1.7 hours.

Savings $525,000 in sales capacity created.

Doing Six Sigma

Design Opportunity

A sensor assembly has a net negative material and labor variance over an equivalent product of $86/unit. The line COPQ drives this loss to nearly $100/unit. These losses, at current line ship rate of 1,200/week, result in $500,000 lost profit per year.

Problem-Solving Technology

Measure   Significant cost drivers for the line were documented. The amount of field returns were investigated as an indicator of customer satisfaction.

Analyze   A cost analysis for the product was completed and studied. Sales order data for this product was utilized to cross correlate with overall sensor sales to determine any leverage. A matrix plot showed the only sales leverage could be found in a different product.

Improve   Complete throughput costing analysis was completed to assure that the losses in manufacturing were not compensated for by profitability in sales. The configuration for the sensor line was evaluated to have approximately $30 profit at sale. A recommendation was made to senior management to retire the product.

Control   A focus on Champion involvement is necessary. The prevention of "end runs" and the attempts to propagate misinformation is also critical.

Results   Retiring a product line that was causing a net loss in sales would save overall profit for the company. The recommended action had yet to be taken, but senior management was reviewing.

Savings $500,000 in profit before tax. This represents the loss in sales due to returns and defects.

Doing Six Sigma

Manufacturing Opportunity

The rejection of an acceptable batch of rocket motor propellant, due to an inaccurate test, results in $40,000 loss of propellant. The acceptance of nonconforming batches of propellant and subsequent casting of rocket motors eventually results in a $700,000 recovery effort when the motors are rejected during lot acceptance testing.

Problem-Solving Technology

Measure   Process mapping identified the process input and output variables. The process inputs were further characterized as critical parameters, process parameters, standard operating procedures, tribal knowledge, and noise. A Cause-and-Effect Matrix and a Failure Mode Effect Analysis (FMEA) were used to define the relationship between key process input variables (KPIVs) and key process output variables (KPOVs).

Analyze   Hypothesis testing was done in an effort to further characterize the effect of KPIVs on the KPOVs. Gauge studies were also performed to quantify the uncertainty of the process output (burn rate test data).

Improve   The primary tool used was the Design of Experiments (DOE) to determine a mathematical expression describing the burn rate test as a function of pressure and temperature. Another DOE was designed to determine if delay time between propellant mixing and strand casting is a significant factor affecting burn rate results.

Control   The short-term control approach involves procedural modifications establishing tolerances for controlling KPIVs and the addition of pressure and propellant temperature measurement and recording. The long-term action plan is to provide a PC-based data and control system that has the capability to sequence the process, initiating testing only when the specified test conditions are met.

Results   Traditional testing method was an inadequate tool for accurate test results for higher burning propellants. Increased burn rate test sizes are now utilized.

Savings $740,000 in lost propellant and engine recovery.

Doing Six Sigma

Manufacturing Opportunity

The electric power bill for this facility was $1.4 million. Senior Management considered that the facility should be more effective in its use of power, and approved power usage reduction as a Six-Sigma project. A reduction target of $125,000 was established.

Problem-Solving Technology

Measure   Other than very basic utility metering on the incoming supply, no system existed for any detailed analysis of consumption patterns or sources. In addition, when power was consumed above a level set (Peak) by the utility company (5500KVA), additional costs were incurred. Drawings for the power distribution system were updated together with a process map of consumption. A monitoring system was then installed on all key points in the system.

Analyze   A Pareto chart and Regression Analysis was done of collected data. This showed that one work section alone contributed to 70 percent of the variation in the facilities' power consumption while a second contributes to the largest total. A time series study of the first work section showed uneven demand across the three production shifts. Hypothesis tests were conducted that showed with better than 92 percent confidence that changing production schedules and labor start-ups within this work section could make a statistically significant change in the peak power consumption. Opportunities were identified in the second work section related to radiant heating on a painting line.

Improve   A Designed Experiment was conducted on the radiant heating portions of the painting line in the second work section which indicated a significant number of the heaters could be turned off. Changes were made to the production schedule and labor start-ups to reduce the daily variation in power consumption in the first section.

Control   A Control Plan was established and a Failure Mode Effect Analysis (FMEA) published.

Results   Peak power demand and charges were significantly down.

Savings $82,000 plus an additional $48,000 per year after the installation of additional power factor correction.

Doing Six Sigma

Manufacturing Opportunity

On a high-speed rotating component, an oil drain slot, by its location and size, determines the service life of the component, due to the stresses induced. Current annual known costs of scrap due to inadequate manufacturing of this slot equals $170,000.

Problem-Solving Technology

Measure   A Gauge Repeatability and Reproducibility (Gauge R&R) study was conducted that showed that the measuring system variation contributed to 17.5 percent of the total variation being measured on the smallest dimension. While greater than the preferred 10 percent, it was still less than the recommended maximum of 30 percent. Measurements of the slot dimensions indicated a low Sigma value ranging from 0.6 (Forward Slot Axial Position) to 0.7 (Aft Slot Parallelism). Work commenced on identifying reasons for the low sigma values.

Analyze   A tooling pin that establishes the alignment of the component in the machining fixture was identified as having significant run-out (taper) that allowed out-of-specification location of the component in the fixture. Additionally, the pin holder was identified as being damaged. This was replaced immediately, with the axial location Sigma Values rising to 4.3 from 0.6 and 0.7 respectively. Tool deflection and tool wear was also identified using hypothesis testing as a major cause of deviation from requirements.

Improve A stiffer tool holder was then introduced, together with a program of changing the mill tool more frequently. A proposal was developed for enlarging and changing the slot profile so that a larger milling tool could be introduced that would deflect less during use. A study was commenced on the impact of the life cycle of the component with this enlarged slot using Monte Carlo Simulation.

Control A new slot design was trialed and analyzed, together with a complete three-dimensional stress analysis to determine the impact of the change. Changes were made to setups and manufacturing, and a risk analysis on the new slot design introduction was performed.

Results Final throughput yield increased from 28 percent to 94 percent for the finished component with the existing slot design.

Savings $309,000 annually.

Doing Six Sigma

Manufacturing Opportunity

The present fabrication methods for the electronics module assembly require excessive touch labor and long cycle times to assemble the module through testing. The current contract called for a lower cost per unit.

Problem-Solving Technology

Measure   The process flow map revealed an area where "cosmetic" rework was performed without having its time captured in the system. Once the Characteristics Selection Matrix was prepared, several inputs became the focus of the project.

Analyze   The Process FMEA was prepared using the top five highest categories from the CSM. Many of the parameters that were critical to quality actually have controls in place that eliminate the possibility of bad hardware being processed on to the next operation. Two Gauge R and R's were performed, one on connector bonding and the other on test fixtures.

Improve   A DOE was performed on the bonding process, which proved to have the highest RPN value in the PFMEA. The results demonstrated that the wrong variables were considered noise. In reality, the application method proved to be more of a contributor to the bonding process than the fixture pressure and cure temperature.

Control   Changes to the existing criteria in the application and inspection of the bond line were relaxed. The adhesive application method was modified to eliminate the continuous wiping of the surface to remove the excess. A reduction made in cure time reduced cycle time and freed up floor space.

Results   Design of Experiments done on adhesive cure time and bonding pressure revealed the real problem as application method and adhesive location. Assembly instructions were modified to eliminate rework and to correct inspection procedures.

Savings   Total cost avoidance of $105,408 due to reduction in application rework.

Doing Six Sigma

Manufacturing Opportunity

Current contracts with major government customers are on a "cost plus" basis, but there is significant pressure from these government customers to reduce costs. One of the substantial costs relates to the use of Micro-focus X-Ray Inspection of critical components. If this inspection can be reduced or eliminated, savings are estimated by management to be at least $300,000 annually in labor and consumables. Additionally, a one time expense of $300,000 can be avoided by not purchasing planned replacement equipment. Additionally, Ultrasonic Inspection is currently conducted prior to Micro-focus X-Ray Inspection, but is not considered capable of detecting all types of flaws.

Problem-Solving Technology

Measure   Measurement of data from the Micro-focus X-Ray Inspection process showed that 4.75 parts per hundred were rejected by inspection process. Over 98 percent of these rejected parts were either one or two types from a testing pool of 11 item types.

Analyze   Detailed analysis of all results showed that all indications of failure revealed by the X-Ray inspection were related to one specific failure type at a certain location on these two product types.

Improve   Twelve Variables were identified as contributing to the most common failure mode. Designed Experiments were conducted on a controllable subset of these variables, and process changes made. Changes were also made to the Ultrasonic test set up in relation to testing frequency and tooling so that these failure modes could be detected by Ultrasonic Inspection, in lieu of Micro-focus X-Ray Inspection.

Control   Work Instructions were revised to reflect the changes made to the process. Because of the nature of this product being supplied, change approvals had to be obtained from the Government Customer.

Results   Reduction of Defects, together with the development of a technology break-through in Ultrasonic Inspection, and subsequent elimination of Microfocus X-Ray Inspection.

Savings $443,000 annual savings. One time cost avoidance of $610,000 for the purchase of replacement Micro-focus X-Ray Equipment.

Doing Six Sigma

Manufacturing Opportunity

Cycle time for a flow tube was seven weeks, with an additional seven-week lead time. Competitors selling similar tubes were benchmarked to deliver in four weeks. A two-week cycle time goal was set.

Problem-Solving Technology

Measure
The first step was developing a process flow chart. The cycle time of each operation was measured for its contribution. Then inventory requirements were defined to meet a four-week delivery with the existing process.

Analyze
A Pareto analysis identified the subcontract operations, painting and lining, as accounting for 74 percent of cycle time. Second-level Paretos compared actual required process time with queue time. Excess queue time was identified as the primary opportunity for improvement.

Improve   Excess queue time between operations
               was the greatest contributor to cycle time
               in the lining process, while material
               handling, travel, and queue time were
               identified as major contributors in the
               painting process. A new layout was
               designed in the plant for a dedicated
               final assembly area.

Control   Black Belt has responsibility to institute
               the new layout. Management must imple-
               ment changes to quoted delivery (recom-
               mendation is to 4 weeks). The buyer/plan-
               ner initiates the start of the build cycle
               with due dates for sales orders.

Results   Subcontractor issues, new plant layout
               and tooling, and accurate schedules all
               contributed to improved cycle time. Sub-
               contracting continues to be a constant
               constraint to reducing cycle time below
               two weeks.

Savings $55,000 in inventory carrying costs; an
               initial impact of $500,000 resulted from
               freeing up working capital.

Doing Six Sigma

Manufacturing Opportunity

Re-blend of latex is created in small amounts each day. It is worked away in small amounts in selected products. The creation and work-away of re-blend are affected by both technical and management factors.

Problem-Solving Technology

Measure   The first step was to create a process map featuring key process input and output variables (KPIVs & KPOVs). A cause-and-effect matrix and a fishbone diagram were also created. Hypothesis testing focused on the #4 Blowdown Tank.

Analyze   The FMEA was conducted on the process. A total of five Gauge R&R tests were conducted. For each, samples of three base latexes were prepared and formed to optimize process parameters.

Improve　　A single DOE (three factor, full factorial, single replicate) was conducted. It was designed around the initial findings that Blowdown Tank #4 caused less dilution. Since this tank had been installed two years later than the others, consensus was the mechanical condition of the steam inlet nozzles was better. Source reduction is one key. The other key is dilution prevention.

Control　　Purging water flow into filter end bearing seals reduced dilution flow by 1,000 pounds per day. Installation of better rinse hose nozzles continued in several areas. Changes to batch recipes were also made.

Results　　Recipe changes affecting selected latexes, along with recommended changes to operational/maintenance which affect production processes, were made. Technologies to remove water from diluted material are being evaluated for risk.

Savings　　$48,000 in recovered raw materials, along with $46,000 in cost reduction.

Doing Six Sigma

Transaction Opportunity

A large government customer issues a significant number of un-priced orders for specialized products from this supplier. Because of the supplier's long administrative time frames, these products are often shipped to this customer before the price has been agreed to for the products. This has led to a constant level of $13 million in nominal receivables for these orders, which is reducing cash flow and directly costing up to $400,000 in tied-up capital. The goal of this project was to reduce the total receivables trapped due to un-priced orders by 85 percent.

Problem-Solving Technology

Measure   Measures were introduced into the order issue, entry, schedule, proposal, and negotiation phases of the existing process, with the existing MIS system being used to flag out-of-control phases against time specifications.

Analyze   Targets were set for the processing time for orders in each phase of the order process. "C" Charts were used to monitor performance at each stage with out-of-control exceptions noted and investigated.

Improve   Negotiation with the Customer resulted in the ability of the supplier to bill for 75 percent of the supplier's proposed value of the order at the time of shipment. A Tracking report for un-priced orders was introduced, with a policy change to first-in-first-out (FIFO) order processing.

Control   Permanent changes were introduced into the MIS System for handling and monitoring un-priced orders. Further work, as a result of this project, is anticipated on the overall order-entry process. Additionally, the customer and supplier are working to reduce the use of the un-priced order process.

Results   Reduced the amount of receivables trapped by un-priced orders by 96 percent, in excess of the 85 percent target, resulting in $12.5 million being freed up in the four months of the project's duration.

Savings $300,000 to $400,000 per year in financing charges.

Doing Six Sigma

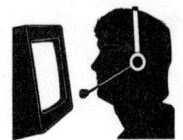

Transaction Opportunity

Customized options available for the company's standard range of products are underpriced in the marketplace and are poorly related to the cost of manufacture. Initial estimates put this cost in the millions of dollars. The customized options can be either automatically priced by the sales software, or manually priced by a range of staff, both domestic and international.

Problem-Solving Technology

Measure   Existing MIS Reports related to options pricing were reviewed. Extensive interviews were conducted, and a detailed process map developed for the existing options pricing process. After mapping the process, it became clear that the existing MIS reports would not be able to provide data on key aspects in the process or to identify relationships within the process. A new reporting system was developed to use available data.

Analyze   The new reporting system was able to sort the measurement data by distribution channel, order frequency, and dollar impact by product line. In doing so, and distributing the information, each area of the business was able to see, and take immediate corrective action as necessary.

Improve   A management process was set in place
for managing price changes throughout
the system in a structured way on an ongoing basis.

Control   Monthly and quarterly margin reporting
was established, and the project was
handed over to line management within
the product lines and distribution
channels.

Results   Permanent changes were made to the
process with respect to the highest
frequency and largest dollar impact items.

Savings $810,000 per annum based on list price
increases achieved in the marketplace,
with an additional $540,000 per annum
estimated to be available if the second
phase of this project is completed.

Doing Six Sigma

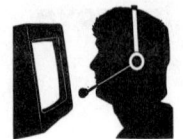

Transaction Opportunity

The purchase order placement cycle is too lengthy and will not effectively support a high volume and repetitive manufacturing program. Current purchase order (PO) placement cycle times often result in inefficient purchasing manpower allocations as well as material deliveries not supporting planned stock dates.

Problem-Solving Technology

Measure   Since an effective data collection system did not exist, the first step was to collect detailed historic records on POs from the previous business year. PO placement cycle time specs were created. Process capability indicated material was late 23 percent of the time.

Analyze   Pareto charts by dollar threshold values were created. A common problem area amongst all four categories was the process span time from supplier selection to actual entry of the PO. A hypothesis test was performed to alleviate concern that dollar value thresholds had an impact on PO placement cycle time drivers.

Improve   Review of data and brainstorming pointed
to three problems causing long cycle times:
buyer work-load distribution, lack of a
preferred supplier base, and inadequate
purchasing software. Work teams were
organized to manage buyer work-load issues. A preferred/certified supplier program
was started, and on-line procurement forms
have been made available.

Control   A management report series has been
developed to report monthly on
departmental and individual metrics.
Performance goals were introduced to buyer
annual performance plans.

Results   Overall process capability improved.
Average cycle time dropped from 17 days
to 11 days. Material deliveries improved from
and average of 23 percent late to 16 percent late.

Savings $105,000 annually in decreased buyer
manpower requirements.

Doing Six Sigma

Transaction Opportunity

The company's domestic delinquent accounts receivable greater than 30 days overdue has averaged $7 million per month for the last financial year. Approximately 65 percent of these overdues result from commercial issues or administrative problems. At current commercial interest rates, this represents a $325,000 annual expense.

Problem-Solving Technology

Measure   Primary and secondary metrics were developed to track progress on the Project: Monthly Delinquent Accounts Receivable Dollars > 30 Days overdue (Baseline $7 million) and Monthly Delinquent Accounts Receivable Dollars / Total Month End Accounts (Baseline 15 percent Defective [Delinquent]). Process Maps and Interviews were conducted with all functional areas. A new measuring system was installed to assign category and causes to receivable disputes, together with a two-level Pareto analysis of 12 months prior disputes. Four issues were identified as contributing to 80 percent of the commercial disputes, which contribute to 65 percent of all delinquent accounts.

Analyze   Additional order data (salesperson, district, region, order type, etc.) was obtained. Hypothesis tests showed no significant difference between each group. A list of five key factors (Xs) were found to be drivingthe four issues contributing to the commercial disputes. All of these five factors (Xs) resulted in the sales order information being inconsistent with the purchase order / contract information.

Improve   A Designed Experiment was conducted at the point of ordering to validate these five key factors. A New Corporate Policy, MIS procedures and Training Program was initiated.

Control   Both a time series and X-Bar R Chart were established for monitoring purposes.

Results   Improvements to cash flow and financing charges.

Savings   Up to $325,000.

Doing Six Sigma

Transaction Opportunity

Errors are being made in the ordering process with the customer receiving the wrong product or too many products. Administrative Processing Errors represent 50 percent of the non-defective product returns.

Problem-Solving Technology

Measure   Members of each functional area were interviewed to understand the ordering process. An Attribute Gauge R&R was conducted at the Call Center point were a customer requests a return authorization. Among other things, Credit Return Error Codes are allocated to Customer Returns. The system of allocating codes was found to be deficient. New Defect Data Collection Sheets were introduced and the Data collected and categorized into 1st and 2nd levels of reasons for return.

Analyze   The Categorized data was subject to Chi-Squared Tests to validate data concerning differences by Sales Region, Representatives and Ordering System. Differences were found to be significant by Ordering System.

Improve   Changes were made to the processing of customer orders to check for a range of conditions that resulted in too many products being provided, which was the main supplier-controllable error.

Control   A simple control system was introduced to review all orders received the previous day. New Procedures were introduced for the assignment of Credit Return Error Codes at the Call Center.

Results   In the first 12 weeks after implementation in one sales region, 32 Sales Orders were identified as duplicates for a total of 139 line items.

Savings $308,000 for one sales region on an annual basis representing the value of stock that was produced but not required by customers.

Doing Six Sigma

Transaction Opportunity

Deliveries from the Central Receiving Dock to anywhere in the plant must be made in a quick and efficient manner. For this particular defense contracting industry, the average dock-to-stock time is 5.8 days with a range of 2 to 14 days. Management wanted the current dock-to-stock cycle time for source or certified supplier material reduced from its current 7.3 days to 1.5 days. In addition, receipt documentation errors had to be reduced to 5 percent.

Problem-Solving Technology

Measure   Historical Electronic and Manual records for a six-month period were reviewed to break down the errors being experienced. A 2-level Pareto showed that all these errors started with the assignment of the Inspection code on the Purchase requisition. A detailed process flow map was then developed which involved nine different functional groups and a total of 33 process steps. A Cause-and-Effect Matrix was also constructed.

Analyze   For each step in the Process Flow map, a FMEA was conducted. Seven Failure Modes were identified, and four significant causal factors assigned.

Improve   An improvement plan for individuals in the organization covering communication, written procedures, software changes, and vendors was put in place and completed.

Control   A control process was established to standardize error identification and tracking and to monitor the process. The revisions were handed over to a newly established team charged with the introduction of a bar code tracking system.

Results   The average days were reduced to 2.3 days, a reduction of over 68 percent.

Savings $13,000 annually in direct labor savings.

Doing Six Sigma

Transaction Opportunity

On average, every order delivered to customers had one component missing (short-shipped). Management has directed that the incidence of such short shipments be reduced by 50 percent and thus lessen the administrative burden of coordinating such shipments, increase customer satisfaction, and reduce the risk of loosing future sales.

Problem-Solving Technology

Measure

Over 80 percent of the short-shipments were due to one section, the Industrial Division. Of these, only half were "Approved Short-Shipments." In other words, the other half of the short-shipments was only detected by customers upon unpacking or installation. A total of 838 Parts or kits had to be shipped later to enable the customer to complete the installation. There was no formal process in place for managing short shipments.

Analyze

Process Maps and Cause-and-Effect Matrices were developed to identify the key variables (Xs) driving the short-shipping results. Chi Squared tests where conducted to test peoples' beliefs that differences by product groups existed within the Industrial Division. No differences were detected.

Improve   A new Short-Ship Process was designed since no formal one existed. An FMEA was conducted to identify those factors that could cause this new process to fail. These factors were either fool-proofed or controlled.

Control   System Controls were put in place that did not exist before, including a more effective checklist, tagging of the location on the product where missing parts were required, and utilization of the corporate information system to track the short shipments effectively. Further opportunities were identified in reducing some of the causes of the short shipments that fell outside the scope of this project, e.g. Order Entry and Production Scheduling.

Results   A 52 percent reduction in additional shipments required to complete an order.

Savings $116,000 in direct cost savings in the Shipping function, not including soft savings in the retention of customers.

Appendix A

Deming's 14 Points

1. Constancy of Purpose: Create constancy of purpose toward improvement of product and service, with the aim to become competitive and to stay in business and to provide jobs.

2. Everybody Wins: Adopt the new philosophy. We are in a new economic age. Western management must awaken to the challenge, must learn their responsibilities, and take on leadership for change.

3. Design Quality In: Cease dependence on inspection to achieve quality. Eliminate the need for inspection on a mass basis by building quality into the product in the first place.

4. Don't Buy on Price Tag Alone: End the practice of awarding business on the basis of price tag. Instead, minimize the total cost. Move toward a single supplier for any one item, for a long-term relationship of loyalty and trust.

5. Continuous Improvement: Improve constantly and forever the system of production and service, to improve quality and productivity, and thus constantly decrease costs.

6. Training for Skills: Institute training on the job. People are the only ones who can create continuous improvement.

7. Institute Leadership: The aim of leadership should be to help people, machines, and gadgets do a better job. Leadership of management is in need of overhaul, as well as leadership of production workers.

8. *Drive out fear*: Build trust, so that everyone may work effectively for the company. The idea of strict control is the opposite of cooperation.

9. *Break down barriers*: Abolish competition within the company, between departments. People in research, design, sales, and production must work as a team to foresee problems in production and in use that may be encountered with the product or service.

10. *Eliminate slogans*: Slogans, exhortations, and targets for the work force asking for zero defects and new levels of productivity are meaningless and divert attention from the goal. Such exhortations only create adversary relationships, as the bulk of the causes of low quality and low productivity belong to the system and thus lie beyond the power of the work force.

11. *Method*: Eliminate work standards (quotas) on the factory floor. Eliminate management by objective. Eliminate management by numbers, numerical goals. Substitute leadership.

12. *Joy in Work*: Remove barriers that rob the hourly worker(s) of their right to pride of workmanship. The responsibility of supervisors must be changed from sheer numbers to quality. Remove barriers that rob people in management and in engineering of their right to pride of workmanship. This means, the abolishment of the annual or merit rating, and management by objective.

13. *Continuing Education*: Institute a vigorous program of education and self-improvement.

14. *Accomplish the Transformation*: Put everybody in the company to work to accomplish the transformation. The transformation is everybody's job.

Appendix B

Sigma

Manufacturing Plant
Hometown, USA

MASTER BLACK BELT FINAL REPORT:

Six Sigma Tools
Integrated With Lean Implementation

PROJECT NO. :   MBB-0012

CHAMPION :   John Doe
BLACK BELT :   Brue Lee
TEAM MEMBERS :

S.G., H.H., E.W., D.B., J.P., P.G.,
R.F., R.S., J.S.

START DATE: 3/09/XX
END DATE: 11/10/XX

Contents

1.0   Executive Summary

This project deals with improving the Processes and implementing Lean Principles in Department X Line X. At project startup the production schedule (98-02) equaled 155 units per shift. The department's manpower roll had 117 total workers with 39 assigned stations per shift. On-floor inventory levels averaged 46.4 days.

The team's goal was to evaluate the current processes and inventory levels, identify any inefficiencies or poor methods, improve processes, and implement Lean Principles wherever possible to help eliminate waste, reduce cost, and improve quality.

As a result of the team's effort, five sub-assembly stations were relocated line-side to their component's point-of-use, reducing total travel distances by 91 percent. Two sub-assembly operations were eliminated. 9,000 square feet of line-side space was better utilized. Drop zone delivery distances of transmissions and clutches were reduced by 93 percent & 86 percent respectively. On-floor inventory levels fell 28 percent to an average of 33.3 days. Six fewer men were required on the manpower roll at a higher production level of 163 units. Identified Cost Saving: $392,296.

2.0   Problem Statement

2.1   Process Description / Background

Line X in Department X has two engine types trimmed out on this line, the XYZ Model 1 and the XYZ Model 2. The engines are transported through the department on an overhead hanging conveyor in an elongated U shape configuration (see Area Layout Attachment 1). The length of the conveyor is 636 feet and has 52 engines spaced an average of 12.24 feet apart.

Engines are delivered to the engine line by forklift in transport racks. The XYZ model 1 racks are designed to hold 2 engines, the XYZ model 2 racks will hold three engines. The engines are then moved through the stations at a preset speed that is determined by the build schedule. When this study began the production schedule was 155 units per shift, causing the line to move at 4.27 feet-per-minute, creating a station cycle time of 2.86 minutes.

As the engines travel through the various stations major components and minor attachments are assembled to the engine for major component assemblies. The engines are then transported to the main assembly line for installation into the truck frame.

The material for the stations is delivered from the warehouse to 14 drop zones to be distributed by stores personnel to the appropriate stations.

Prior to X date, assemblers were classified as piece workers. Each assembly operation had an established time standard associated with it. The scheduled quantity for this feature / variation was multiplied by this standard and a daily total time was established for this particular operation. All operations assigned to a worker in a station were totaled to yield his daily work minutes. Under contract agreement no assembler's daily workload was permitted to exceed 444 minutes per shift. The supervisors would try to load a worker as close to this limit as possible without going over. As product mix and quantities fluctuated over time operations would have to be moved and re-balanced in order not to violate the 444 minute constraint. Using this method of man-assigning many inefficiencies began to occur. Work became fragmented, discontinuous, and had poor flow. Sub-assemblies were established to get work off the line and redistribute workloads, resulting in a buildup of buffer-stock. Turnover of supervision and workers caused this practice to grandfather-in over time and became the accepted method of assembling components to the engines.

Under the new agreement assemblers are classified as day workers and can perform group assigned work, the 444-minute rule is no longer the primary factor for balancing work. This project was assigned in an attempt to re-introduce good workflow, efficient methods, and lean principles.

2.2 Project Objectives

- Map & evaluate the current processes and inventory levels on the line.
- Identify inefficiencies and poor methods.
- Improve processes and establish Lean Principles to help eliminate waste, reduce cost, and improve quality.

2.3 Project Strategy

The primary focus of the project was to improve processes and implement Lean Principles. In order to achieve this goal it was necessary to not only examine the production effort for improvement of the assembly methods, but also examine the material levels and their processes, thus providing more available space and more efficient material delivery.

The Team's effort was broken down into three phases: Short, Intermediate, and Long-Term.

1. Short-Term Goal: Preliminary Analysis (Measurement & Analysis)

- **Methods**

  Macro Level
  - Identify Area Layouts & Product Flow
  - Perform Operations Process Mapping

  Micro Level
  - Complete Detail Flow Process Maps
  - Perform Operational Analysis

- **Materials**
  - Identify Stock Locations & Layouts
  - Map Material Process
  - Identify Part Usage

2. Intermediate Goal – Improve Processes & Product Quality

- **Methods**
  - Organize Efficient Layouts & Methods
  - Implement Lean Principles
  - Utilize Efficiencies of Group Assignments
  - Emphasize Complete Installations
  - Improve Standards Accuracy

- **Materials**
  - Improve Flow and Handling Techniques
  - Establish Pull Methods and Improve Existing Kanban System

3. Long-Term Goal
  - Implement Control Processes
  - Ensure Successful Transition to New Product Processes
  - Extend Lean Principles to Suppliers

Specific Methods used to Measure, Analyze, and Improve:

MATERIALS:

IDENTIFY CURRENT STOCK LOCATIONS

Drop Zones

  Where located

  Delivers to what location

Line-side

  Station stock

  Pockets of excess

MAP

Material process

Line stock process

IDENTIFY

Excess inventory

Opportunity for order pick / low usage

Parts with no requirements

Part nos. that shouldn't be on mechanical
  ordering

WALK-THROUGH

Team Leaders / Resource Leaders

Thin-out excess / open space

Move excess from line to drop zone (Kanban
  etc.)

Send back to warehouse

CLEAN UP PAPER

Mechanical Order Adjust

Mechanical Order Delete

MOVE DROP ZONES TO MORE APPROPRIATE LOCATIONS

MOVE KANBAN ORDERING TO 1ST SHIFT ONLY

CONTINUOUS IMPROVEMENT ON DAYS SUPPLY REDUCTION

Adjust station queue factors

MP7 order frequency

IDENTIFY/IMPROVE CONTAINER SIZE/PACK/QUANTITY

SET UP EXISTING KANBAN PROPERLY

Set Up stocking properly

Proper work benches

Eliminate dumping

ESTABLISH VISUAL SIGNALS

Stock on-floor

ASSEMBLY METHODS

IDENTIFY STATION LOCATIONS ON-LINE

MAP PRODUCT FLOW THROUGHOUT AREA

List major components and high user attachments

PERFORM PRELIMINARY SURVEY CHECK SHEET ON STATIONS

(99 QUESTIONS)

PROCESS MAP STATIONS

IDENTIFY VALUE-ADDED, NON-VALUE-ADDED WORK

Distance, Quantity, Time,

What, Where, When, Who, How, Why

Possible Action — eliminate, combine, sequence, place, person, improve

PERFORM DETAILED OPERATIONAL ANALYSIS

3.0   Manufacturing Implementation

3.1 Sub-assembly Relocation

During our baseline measurement and discussion of lean principles it became apparent that five sub-assembly stations across the H gangway were displaying excess distances for delivery, safety issues, and extensive non-value added work. Our effort focused on relocating these stations to point-of-use on the line and examining if the worker performing the assembly could absorb the work.

The five stations investigated involved nine sub-assembly operations — Line-setting of Battery Cables, Sub-assembly of XYZ model 1 Power Steering Pumps, Sub-Assembly of XYZ model 1 / XYZ model 2 Air Conditioner and Freon Compressors, Engine Hose Cutting, Sub-Assembly of Air compressors, Engine Governors, and Sub-assembly of CAC pipe.

The line-setting of the Engine Harnesses and Battery Cables went away and the work was absorbed line-side by the operators. The XYZ model 1 Power Steering work was moved to point-of-use, eliminating delivery travel of 880 feet, sub-assembly is still done but is on a pull-type system, allowing the sub-assembler to pick up additional work. Engine hose cutting was moved to line-side eliminating delivery travel by 200 feet. It is still being addressed by the Lean Continuous Improvement effort to establish a flow-through rack for a more appropriate pull situation. The XYZ model 2/XYZ model 1 Air Conditioner Freon Compressors were in the same situation. They were moved line-side thus eliminating 868 feet of delivery distance. However, they could not be established in a direct pull situation due to an area restriction caused by XYZ model 2 starters needing relocation and awaiting appropriation for a hoist. The hoist is projected to be installed in the December 98 shutdown and should allow the compressors to be moved to point-of-use with a direct pull and visual controls.

The XYZ model 1 Air Compressor was moved closer to point-of-use by 502 feet, however, available line space would not allow the team to get it line-side and is still being delivered by cart 12 at a time a distance of 70 feet. A special flow cart is being built of Creform to reduce handling effort by 60 percent.

On original analysis it was felt by the team that the CAC sub-work could be moved to point-of-use and absorbed by the installation worker. An ergonomic decision restricted the amount of work performed over the 54-inch guideline and the work remained a sub-assembly, with the completed assembly being installed by another worker. The sub-assembly work was still moved line-side reducing delivery distance 1,320 feet. The sub-assembler uses visual controls and can now do additional work that was not previously done.

Due to the relocation of the sub-assemblies over July Shutdown, two men were immediately removed from the man assignment. Due to refining these stations on a continuous improvement effort a two-man increase due to schedule increase was offset in September. The remaining two men were removed at the end of October.

3.2 Material Relocation

In the preliminary phase of our measurement the team was challenged to make room available line-side in order to move the sub-assemblies up closer to point-of-use. It was therefore necessary to investigate our on-floor inventory levels in order to determine what material needed to be in the stations.

Upon mapping the area it was identified that not only was there too much stock in the stations and drop zones, there were small pockets around the engine line being used for mini stock-piles of material. Approximately 9,000 square feet of valuable floor space around the line was being utilized as storage space.

Using the procedure previously mentioned for our materials strategy we began to thin out unnecessary stock, determine appropriate station levels, then developed more efficient procedures and controls. Mapping and Pareto charts provided the appropriate focusing to identify our big hitters. Several sweeps were done through the area to return excess or obsolete material back to the warehouse and then correct the material ordering process.

As available space began to appear around the engine line, it was used by our sub-assemblies coming line-side. The moving of the drop zones west of the H Gangway appeared to make good sense also. Material could now be consolidated and monitored more easily. No more mini storage spots around the line also allowed for fewer bulk Kanban racks, better visual controls, and more efficient layout of our drop zones. The round-trip delivery distance per shift for our transmissions was reduced by 20,150 feet (a 93 percent improvement). The round-trip delivery distance per shift for our clutches was reduced by 86 percent or 1,500 feet.

Other material accomplishments included:

- Deleted 372 part numbers from Mechanical Ordering

- 50 percent of Parts now on Order-Pick

- S.E. Crib eliminated (of 400+ S.E. parts, 300+ deleted from Mechanical Ordering)

- Kanban ordering now on 1st shift only, for better control

- A total of 79 part numbers were reviewed and excess returned to warehouse
- Reduced top 10 part numbers from Eby report from Ave. on-floor of 1,510 days to 161 days, representing 89 percent reduction of top 10
- Identified all Kanban part numbers used in Dept 62, their daily requirement, the proper on-hand levels, and their excess inventory on the floor
- Now Current Day plus one on open order fill
- Adjusted queue factor of stock stations for better fit (after sub-assembly stations eliminated).

All of the above-mentioned efforts combined with the drive of supervision to incorporate discipline, the heightened awareness of the operators, visual signals, refined reports, and enforced control plan all contributed to On-floor inventory levels going from an average 46.4 days to 33.3 days.

3.3 Process Controls
Materials:

- Establish and maintain visual controls for pallet stock located in the production stations (ex. Battery cable, Alternators) by taping off with blue tape the area in which the part number will physically be presented to the production operator.
- Establish and maintain proper "pull" procedures on Kanban parts by acquiring proper flow racks capable of holding a two-day supply or minimum of two containers of each part number required on that work station.

- Consolidate and properly identify material drop zones to allow for easy visual monitoring of inventory levels on a daily basis. Linestocking has also begun a monthly evaluation held with the linestocking Team Leader and each stockman.

- Perform quarterly checks on stock station Queue Factors and adjust when necessary if any production work is moved to another location.

- Adjust and maintain MP7 order frequencies at five days.

- Establish and maintain "Excess Inventory" tagging procedure as another visual inventory monitor.

- Establish three-week rotation of Days Supply Monitor in which the stockmen are given a report showing any part number with greater than five days supply of inventory. This will provide them the opportunity to identify container quantity and size problems, spec issues and other streams of excess material.

Methods / Process / Layout

- Any movement of operations from point-of-use to off-line/remote locations need to be evaluated by Industrial Engineering.

- Industrial Engineering needs to utilize process mapping operations analysis forms, and Lean Principles as approval criteria.

- Industrial Engineering supervisor needs to be informed, and, after review of the supporting data, approve any such request.

4.0 Experimentation

4.1 Pareto

In order to determine what the big hitters were in our materials effort, Pareto Charts were utilized. When examining our parts reports it was determined that Stock Stations 6208, 6215, 6201 had the biggest supply of on-floor parts greater than 10 days. Within these stations, MP 7ß parts displayed the largest on-floor count.

4.2 Trendline

As a metric in how well we were cleaning up the material on-floor, we monitored the Daily On-Floor reports generated by our material group. When the project started the Daily On-Floor equaled 46.4 days, 75 data points were collected throughout the project with our latest average equaling 33.3 days. Except for two spikes which occurred during our two plant shutdowns (where inventory levels are built up) there was a definite trend downward with a linear equation $Yt = 47.1353 - 0.14260*t$.

4.3 Hypothesis Test

One of our goals on this project was to reduce the on-floor inventory by 50 percent. With a baseline of 46.4 days this equates to a target of 23.2 days (delta =23.2). Analyzing with descriptive statistic on our weekly averages it was determined our StDEV = 5.6423. Our delta/sigma = 23.2 / 5.6523 = 4.1045. Using a sample size sheet with the delta/sigma value 4.1045 indicated four samples were necessary from each sample population, in order to test if they were equal.

The results:
Normal Probablity Plot
P-Value: 0.072   Data Normal

Null Hypothesis (Two Sample T)
              Mean1=Mean2
P-Value: 0.0007   Difference is Signicant

This supports our downward trend on the Trendline chart showing that there was indeed an improvement in our on-floor inventory levels.

5.0   Conclusions / Recommendations

Due to past contract guidelines and poor practices in the way we used to man-assign, the manufacturing environment on Line 1, X line was not structured for optimal efficiency of resources, materials or high quality output. The project's main emphasis was Methods Improvement and Lean Implementation. Analysis of the Materials Processes and Inventory Levels took an early lead in our effort due to the crowded conditions when the project was first started, and the need to make room more available.

The concept of Lean Principles is very counter-intuitive in nature and was met with some resistance from the outset. To ask a production supervisor to reduce or eliminate his safety stock and produce a quality vehicle with fewer people was a challenge from the beginning. The initial effort was to educate all team members in the principles of Lean and to coach them in thinking of their processes differently, not from the traditional push system but one built around a pull concept with smooth flow and little or no buffer stock.

During the measuring and analysis phase getting people involved in the process was difficult. We had been doing things a certain way for so long that the idea of changing was looked at with reservation.

After the data started to develop, the materials group was the first to come on board. They had nowhere to go but up. The options presented tremendous possibilities for their situation in the department to improve. Production saw this as fewer men doing the same work and making their jobs more difficult.

Due to the in-depth measurement and analysis done up front, and the limited resources, the project began to slip to the right. However, due to a walk-through visit by our Division President and his show of support, the project was revitalized. He did state that he would like to see it accelerated. This had some risks associated with it; some moves would be done before the complete concept was thoroughly thought-out. Making moves that had some gaps in it would give fuel to the critics. It was noted to all involved that this was just a starting point and the need for continuous improvement was critical and the process was never ending.

As stated in the report, the project was successful. Even though our production schedule went from 155 units per shift to 163 units per shift:

- On-floor Material Levels were reduced from 46.4 days to 33.3 days, a 28.2 percent improvement.

- Assigned manpower was reduced by six men, a 7.6 percent improvement.

Jobs are operating more efficiently and delivery of materials to the line is more controlled and accurate. Lean has been introduced to the Manufacturing Plant and several jobs have been picked up as continuous improvement efforts. The project has saved the company $392,296 and because of its success, multiple projects in eight areas of the plant have now been initiated using the same approach

6.0 Team Members

S G – Resource Leader Line 1
H H – Engine Line Supervisor
E W – Engine Line Industrial Engineer
D B – Industrial Engineering Consultant
J P – Black Belt Material Rep.
P G – Resource Leader Materials
R F – Engine Line Supervisor 2nd Shift
R S – Engine Line Union Steward
J S – Plant Engineering

7.0 Acknowledgments

M A – Material Handling
J S – Advanced Manufacturing Engineering
P G – Planning
D W – Black Belt
J V – New Product Development
S G – Materials Team Leader

Appendix C

Company A

Transactional Quality Final Report

Plant/Bus. Unit   Company A
                         West Coast Operations

Project: Reduce Errors on Manual
                         Requisitions

Project Number: JH97

TQ Candidate: J.H.

Project Sponsor: W. A.

Start Date: September 12, 19XX

Report Date: January 23, 19XX

Contents

1.0 Executive Summary

2.0 Problem Description
    2.1 Problem Statement
    2.2 Objective
    2.3 Original Estimate of Savings
        Estimate of Savings

3.0 Process Description
    3.1 Primary Metric
    3.2 Secondary Metric
    3.3 Process Map
    3.4 Capability Analysis

4.0 Analysis
    4.1 Measurement System Analysis
    4.2 Fishbone
    4.3 Characteristic Selection Matrix
    4.4 Pareto Chart
    4.5 Hypothesis Testing
        Homogeneity of Variance Test for Response
        Mood Median Test for Response

        4.5.1 Auditing/Review Instructions

    4.6 Confidence Interval for Population Mean
        Descriptive Statistics
        Normal Probability Plot

5.0 Improvement Actions
    5.1 Implemented
    5.2 Planned

Contents (continued)

1.0 EXECUTIVE SUMMARY:

Company A currently spends approximately $85,820 per year correcting incomplete or erroneous data on requisitions received into the Procurement Services Department. Data accumulated since August 19XX, indicated that the average error rate was 1.62 errors per requisition. A Six Sigma team was formed composed of five procurement professionals, two material planners, and one Quality Assurance Engineer. The team goal was to reduce the error rate by 50 percent, to .81 errors per requisition, by January 31, 19XX. This task was to be completed without impacting the historical average of 2.12 days processing time for each requisition.

The team employed the Six Sigma methodology and tools to understand the causes for the errors and to execute a corrective action plan. Process improvements included the review and implementation of improved auditing criteria for the Procurement Personnel. The team also revised, updated, and corrected erroneous data codes contained in the Procurement Requisition Form Instructions located on the company intranet.

As of January 13, 19XX, the team exceeded our goal of .81 errors by achieving an average error rate of .03 errors per requisition, which equals a 98 percent reduction of errors. The annual projected savings has been updated to $84,100. The average elapsed days from requisition date to accepted date was improved from 2.12 days to 1.05 days.

2.0 PROBLEM DESCRIPTION

2.1 Problem Statement:
Manual requisitions received into Procurement are incomplete or contain erroneous data. The average error rate is 1.62 errors per requisition.

2.2 Objective:
The goal of this Six Sigma project team was to identify, through the application of several Six Sigma tools, data-driven conclusions and solutions for process improvements to reduce the error rate on incoming manual requisitions by 50 percent, from 1.62 to .81 errors per requisition.

2.3 Business Impact:
2.3.1: Fiscal year, 19XX: $0.00
2.3.2: Year-to-date, 19XX $16,316
2.3.3: Estimated 19XX Impact: $82,897
2.3.4: Estimated Annual Impact: $84,100

ORIGINAL ESTIMATE OF SAVINGS

Days per year	260.0	Requisitions	230
Est. Hours per day	_7.5_	Effort related to errors	_692_
Hours per year	1950.0		922

Errors	346	% of time errors= 692/922	75 %
Additional effort	346	% of time requisitions= 230/922	_25_ %
Effort related to errors	692		100 %

Unproductive time procurement	1950 hours times 75 %	1,464
Unproductive time originators	1950 hours times 25 %	_486_
		1,950

Savings for 50 percent reduction	**1,950** hours times 50 %	975

Estimated savings @ 44.01 per hour

975 hours times $44.01 $ 42,910

LOGIC: PROCUREMENT REQUISITIONS WITH ERRORS REQUIRE ADDITIONAL EFFORT. (1 Unit for Original Effort, 1 Unit to Leave System to Obtain Required Data, and Another Unit to Re-enter Data into the System.)

LOGIC: ORIGINATOR REQUISITIONS WITH ERRORS REQUIRE ADDITIONAL EFFORT TO OBTAIN DATA FOR PROCUREMENT (Assumes Effort Would Equal 1 Unit of Procurement Effort.)

UPDATED ESTIMATE OF SAVINGS:

Savings for 98 percent reduction =
1,950 hours times 98 percent = 1,911 hours

Estimated savings at $44.01 per hour: 1,911 X $44.01 = $84,103

3.0   PROCESS DESCRIPTION

3.1   Primary Metric

The primary metric is used to measure the team success, and includes three series, plotted as a function of time: Baseline performance, actual performance, and objective. The metric established for this project was the ratio of errors to requisitions per month. We added the total number of errors for the three month period from August through October, and divided by the total number of requisitions for this same time period to establish our baseline metric of 1.62 errors per requisition. Our goal was to improve by 50 percent to .81 errors per requisition. Our ratio of errors to requisitions as of January 13, 19XX was **.03** errors per requisition.

RATIO OF ERRORS TO REQUISITIONS

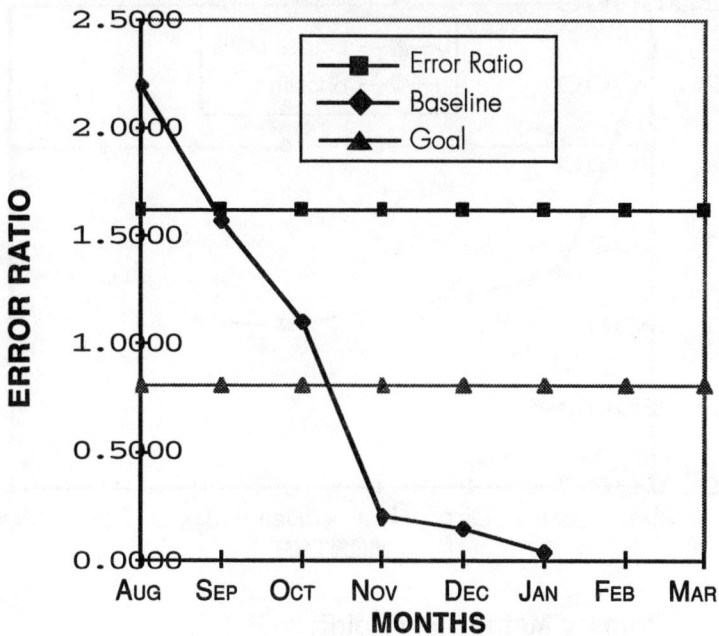

3.2 Secondary Metric

The secondary metric was used to track the potential negative consequences of our project. The data from August through October indicated that the cycle time from requisition date to accepted date on incoming requisitions was 2.12 days. We did not want any process changes to increase this cycle time. As of January 13, 19XX, the actual cycle time had improved from 2.12 days to **1.05** days. (Note: Although many requisitions are processed in hours or even minutes, we do not track the process cycle time in less than 1-day increments.

3.3 Process Map

By creating a process map (see page 275) the team was able to understand each key process input and output, and established two tally points for collecting data:

Cycle Time in Days

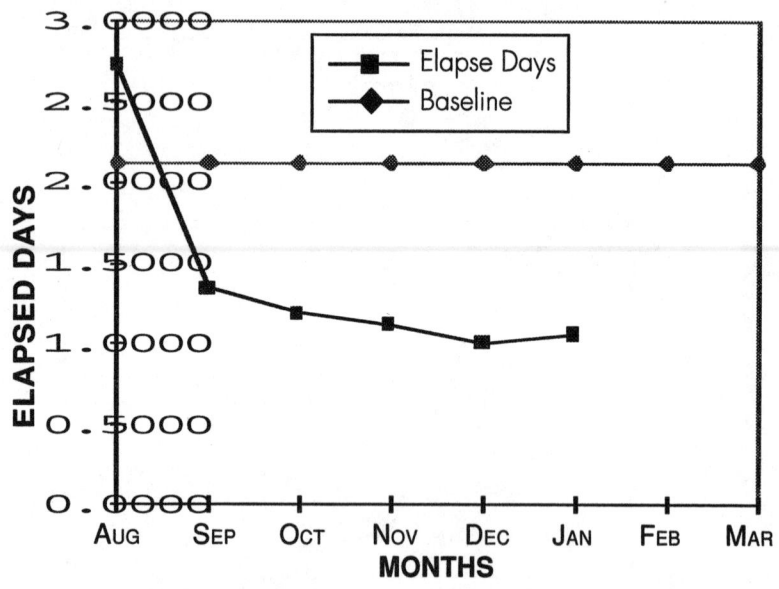

Primary Metric Tally Point:
(1) Procurement Services receives the written requisition and audits the (19) required data field blocks and highlights each error made on every requisition. Since August 19XX, a photocopy of every requisition including error data was provided to the team and the data was entered into an Excel spreadsheet and MINITAB for analysis.

Secondary Metric Tally Point:
(2) Procurement Services manually dates the requisition when received into Services. When all data in the (19) blocks has been accepted, the requisition is formally date-stamped. Since August 19XX, a photocopy of every manual requisition with the cycle time has been collected on a daily basis by the Six Sigma Candidate and entered into an Excel spreadsheet for analysis. The elapsed cycle time between the two dates supports the secondary metric.

PROCESS FLOW

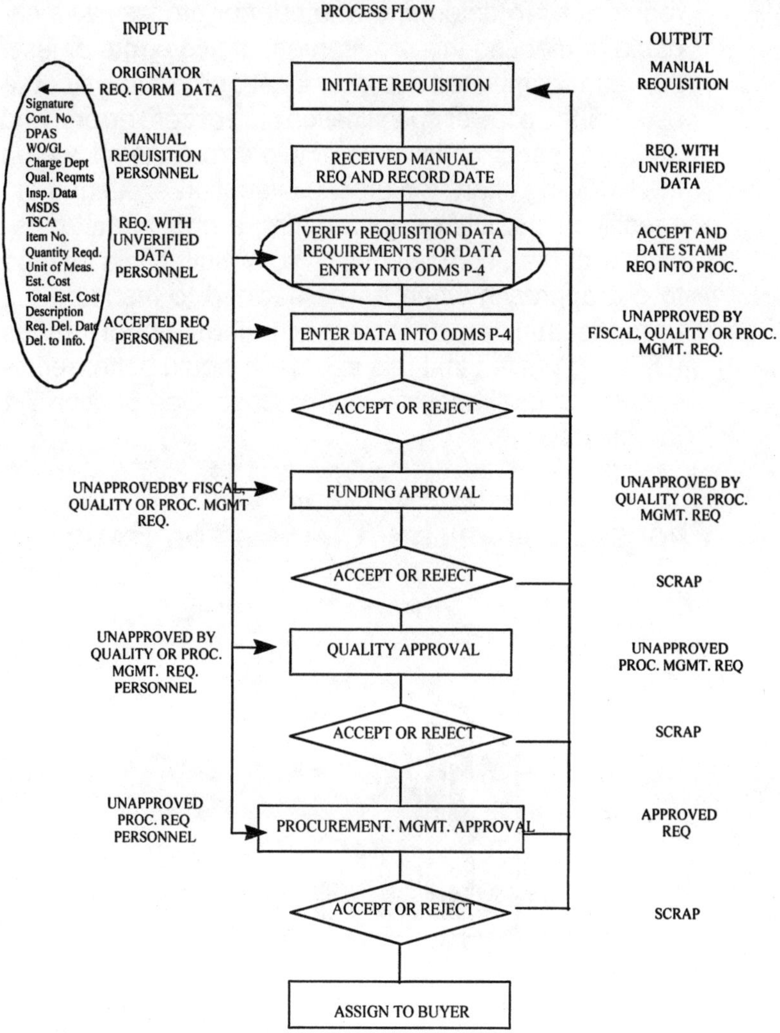

PROCESS FLOW
INPUT
OUTPUT
ORIGINATOR
REQ. FORM DATA
Signature
Cont. No.
DPAS
WO/GL
Charge Dept
Qual. Reqmts
Insp. Data
MSDS
TSCA
Item No.
Quantity Reqd.
Unit of Meas.
Est. Cost
Total Est. Cost
Description
Req. Del. Date
Del. to Info.
MANUAL
REQUISITION
PERSONNEL
REQ. WITH
UNVERIFIED
DATA
PERSONNEL
ACCEPTED REQ
PERSONNEL
UNAPPROVEDBY FISCAL,
QUALITY OR PROC. MGMT
REQ.
UNAPPROVED BY
QUALITY OR PROC.
MGMT. REQ.
PERSONNEL
UNAPPROVED
PROC. REQ
PERSONNEL
INITIATE REQUISITION
RECEIVED MANUAL
REQ AND RECORD DATE
VERIFY REQUISITION DATA
REQUIREMENTS FOR DATA
ENTRY INTO ODMS P-4
ENTER DATA INTO ODMS P-4
ACCEPT OR REJECT
FUNDING APPROVAL
ACCEPT OR REJECT
QUALITY APPROVAL
ACCEPT OR REJECT
PROCUREMENT. MGMT. APPROVAL
ACCEPT OR REJECT
ASSIGN TO BUYER
MANUAL
REQUISITION
REQ. WITH
UNVERIFIED
DATA
ACCEPT AND
DATE STAMP
REQ INTO PROC.
UNAPPROVED BY
FISCAL, QUALITY OR PROC.
MGMT. REQ.
UNAPPROVED BY
QUALITY OR PROC.
MGMT. REQ
SCRAP
UNAPPROVED
PROC. MGMT. REQ
SCRAP
APPROVED
REQ
SCRAP

3.4   Capability Analysis

Two representatives on our team determined the customer requirement of two errors or less per requisition. To determine whether our process was capable of meeting this requirement of two errors or less, the team completed a process capability analysis. We established a lower specification limit of zero errors, and an upper specification limit of two errors. As shown on the following chart, the process variation exceeded the specifications. Discussions during a project status review with the Six Sigma Instructor resulted in a change to our approach when it was decided to measure the process utilizing defects per million opportunities (DPMO). We felt that this approach would better represent the overall health of our process. See Section 7.1 for this data.

PROCESS CAPABILITY ANALYSIS FOR RATIO

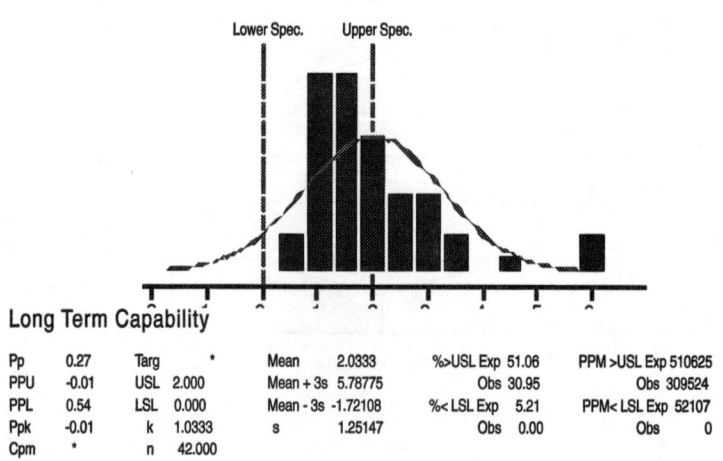

Long Term Capability

Pp	0.27	Targ	*	Mean	2.0333	%>USL Exp	51.06	PPM >USL Exp	510625
PPU	-0.01	USL	2.000	Mean + 3s	5.78775		Obs 30.95		Obs 309524
PPL	0.54	LSL	0.000	Mean - 3s	-1.72108	%< LSL Exp	5.21	PPM< LSL Exp	52107
Ppk	-0.01	k	1.0333	s	1.25147		Obs 0.00		Obs 0
Cpm	*	n	42.000						

4.0 ANALYSIS:

4.1 Measurement System Analysis

On October 19XX, a Gauge R & R was completed to assure the team that the Procurement Personnel reviewing the incoming requisitions for errors were using the same criteria consistently. Operator #1 received a 100 percent score, and Operator #2 had a 86.67 percent score. The team immediately held a training session with

ATTRIBUTE GAUGE R & R EFFECTIVENESS

SCORING REPORT

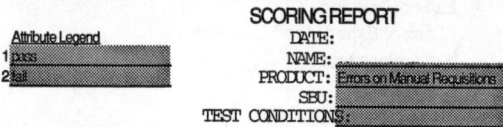

Attribute Legend
1 pass
2 fail

DATE:
NAME:
PRODUCT: Errors on Manual Requisitions
SBU:
TEST CONDITIONS:

Known Population		Operator #1		Operator #2		Operator #3		Y/N	Y/N
Sample #	Attribute	Try #1	Try #2	Try #1	Try #2	Try #1	Try #2	Agree	Agree
1	Pass	Pass	Pass	Fail	Pass			N	N
2	Pass	Pass	Pass	Pass	Pass			Y	Y
3	Pass	Pass	Pass	Pass	Pass			Y	Y
4	Pass	Pass	Pass	Pass	Pass			Y	Y
5	Pass	Pass	Pass	Pass	Pass			Y	Y
6	Pass	Pass	Pass	Pass	Pass			Y	Y
7	Pass	Pass	Pass	Pass	Pass			Y	Y
8	Pass	Pass	Pass	Pass	Pass			Y	Y
9	Pass	Pass	Pass	Fail	Pass			N	N
10	Pass	Pass	Pass	Pass	Pass			Y	Y
11	Pass	Pass	Pass	Pass	Pass			Y	Y
12	Pass	Pass	Pass	Pass	Pass			Y	Y
13	Pass	Pass	Pass	Pass	Pass			Y	Y
14	Pass	Pass	Pass	Pass	Pass			Y	Y
15	Pass	Pass	Pass	Pass	Pass			Y	Y
16									
17									
18									
19									
20									
21									
22									
23									
24									
25									
26									
27									
28									
29									
30									
% APPRAISER SCORE [1] ->		100.00%		86.67%		0%			
% SCORE VS. ATTRIBUTE [2] ->		100.00%		86.67%		0.00%			

SCREEN % EFFECTIVE SCORE [3] ->	86.67%
SCREEN % EFFECTIVE SCORE vs. ATTRIBUTE [4] ->	86.67%

Note:

(1) If % Appraiser Score is less than 100% training needs to occur, focus on specific areas
(2) % Score vs. Attribute is an error against known population as deemed by experts
(3) 100% is the target for Screen % Effectiveness Score
(4) Screen % Effective vs. Attribute is an error against a known population as deemed by the experts
(5) Attribute legend can be what defect codes are needing a score

both operators to ensure they both understood the audit criteria. In October, a second Gauge R&R was completed, both operators received a 100 percent score.

CAUSE AND EFFECT FISHBONE CHART

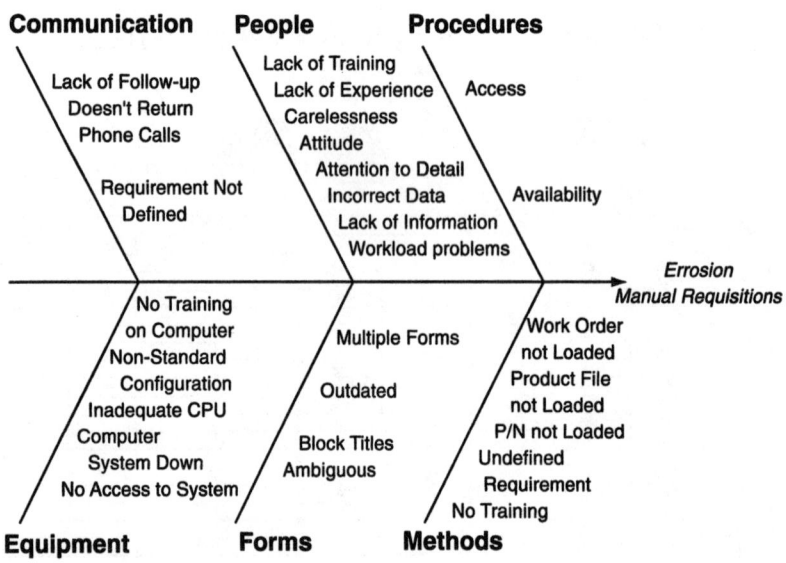

4.2   Fishbone

The above fishbone chart allowed our team to identify and graphically display all of the possible root causes for the errors found on requisitions. The information initially gathered was confirmed by the characteristic selection matrix as shown in Section 4.3.

4.3 Characteristic Selection Matrix

Characteristic Selection Matrix

Rating of Importance to Customer	10	4	10	10	3	4	7	7	10	
	1	2	3	4	5	6	7	8	9	
Process Inputs	Manual Req.	Unverified data Req.	Accepted Data	Electronic Req.	Audit Trail	Routing for Approval	Funding Auth.	Quality Requirements	Authority to procure	Total
1 Originator	10	0	8	5	2	0	1	6	10	385
2 Requirement	10	3	3	3	3	3	10	10	10	433
3 Req. Forms	10	5	10	0	0	0	0	0	0	220
4 Signatuare	10	0	10	0	0	0	0	0	0	200
5 Contract No.	10	0	10	0	0	0	0	0	0	200
6 DPAS Rating	10	0	10	0	0	0	0	0	0	200
7 W/O - G/L	10	0	10	0	0	0	0	0	0	200
8 Charge Dept.	10	0	10	0	0	0	0	0	0	200
9 Quality Req.	10	0	10	0	0	0	0	0	0	200
10 Insp. Data	10	0	10	0	0	0	0	10	0	270
11 MSDS	10	0	10	0	0	0	0	0	0	200
12 TSCA	10	0	10	0	0	0	0	0	0	200
13 Item No.	10	0	10	0	3	0	0	0	0	209
14 Quantity Reqd	10	0	10	0	6	0	9	0	0	281
15 Unit of Meas.	10	0	10	9	3	0	4	0	0	327
16 Est. Cost	10	0	10	0	0	0	8	0	10	356
17 Total Est Cost	10	0	10	0	0	0	8	0	10	356
18 Description	10	0	10	9	0	0	8	10	7	486
19 Req. Del. Date	10	0	10	10	10	0	0	0	9	420
20 Deliver to Info	10	0	10	7	0	0	0	5	0	305
21 Dwgs/Specs	0	0	0	0	0	0	0	10	0	70
Total	2000	32	1910	430	81	12	336	287	560	

The Characteristic Selection Matrix, or "Cause-and-Effect Matrix" was used by the team to analyze the relationship between the key input and output variables using a scale of importance of 1 to 10. The totals in the right hand column are designed to direct the team to focus and analyze the most important "input" variables. However, in our case, the process "inputs" all had approximately the same rating. However, two process "outputs," the manual requisition (2,000 points) and the Accepted Data (1,910 points) resulted in the team focusing on the requisition and the data fields contained therein.

4.4   Pareto Chart

A Pareto Chart allows the team to focus on the causes that will have the greatest impact if solved. Each requisition form contains (19) separate blocks of required data. The team needed to know which data blocks were most frequently filled out incorrectly, and the results are shown on the following chart:

PARETO CHART OF DEFECTS THROUGH OCTOBER

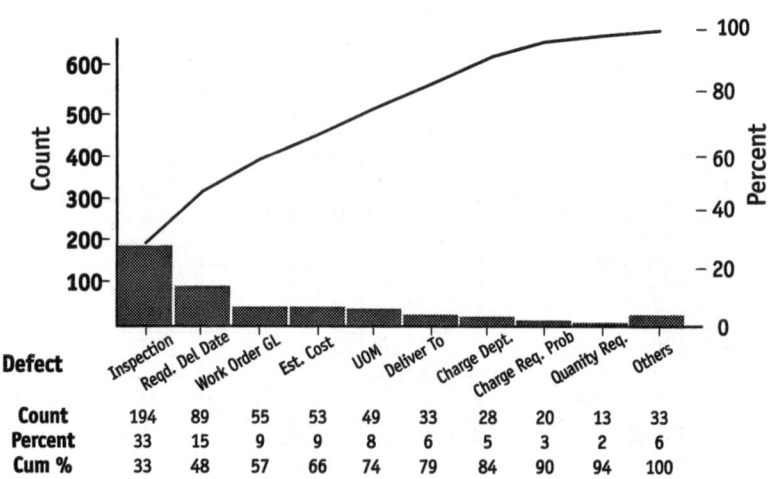

Defect	Inspection	Reqd. Del Date	Work Order GL	Est. Cost	UOM	Deliver To	Charge Dept.	Charge Req. Prob	Quantity Req.	Others
Count	194	89	55	53	49	33	28	20	13	33
Percent	33	15	9	9	8	6	5	3	2	6
Cum %	33	48	57	66	74	79	84	90	94	100

The Pareto Chart shows that 74 percent of the problems were contained in (5) blocks of data: Inspection (33 percent), Required Delivery Date (15 percent), Work Order/GL (9 percent), Estimated Cost (9 percent), and Unit of Measure (8 percent). The team decided to focus on why there were so many errors in these five blocks of data. See Section 4.5, Hypothesis Testing and Section 4.5.1 Auditing/Review Instructions for more information. The team then attempted to determine what individual requisitioners might be making most of the mistakes in filling out the requisition. Our intent was to isolate these individuals, and focus on a training program for them. The following Pareto Chart and Scatter Chart display the results of our analysis:

We discovered that during the three-month period from August 19XX, through October 19XX, 151 different people had written requisitions. Further analysis showed that 137 different people wrote six requisitions or less. We had no focus group! We decided to focus on our policies, procedures, and written instructions for use by all company employees, in order to eliminate errors on future requisitions.

NUMBER OF ORIGINATORS VS NUMBER OF REQUISITIONS

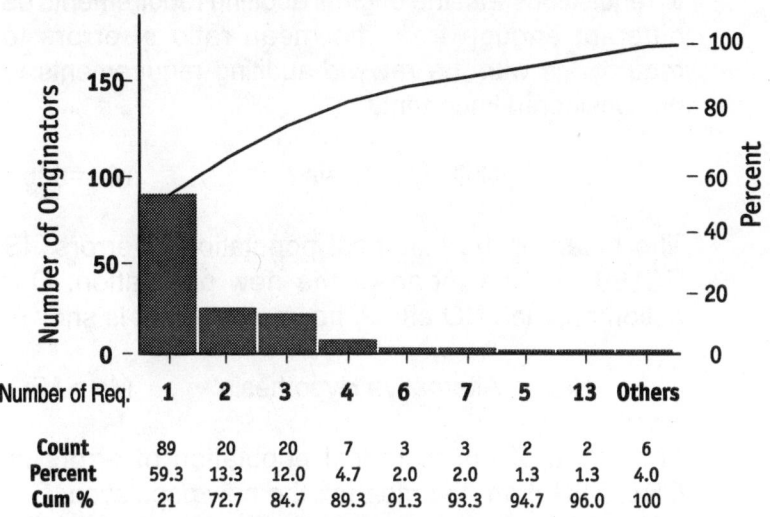

Number of Req.	1	2	3	4	6	7	5	13	Others
Count	89	20	20	7	3	3	2	2	6
Percent	59.3	13.3	12.0	4.7	2.0	2.0	1.3	1.3	4.0
Cum %	21	72.7	84.7	89.3	91.3	93.3	94.7	96.0	100

SCATTER CHART OF REQUISITIONS AND PEOPLE

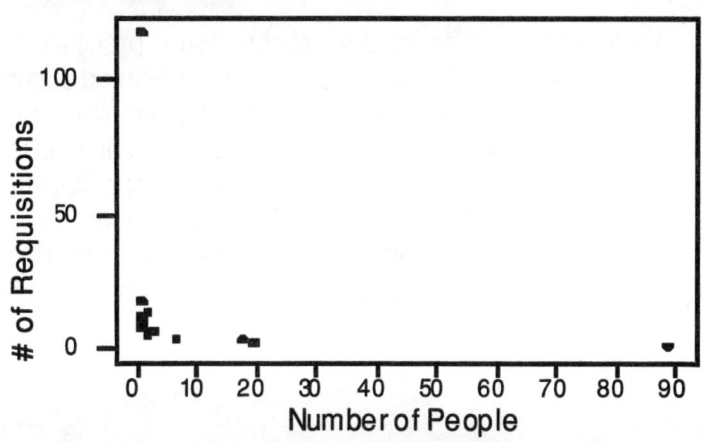

4.5   HYPOTHESIS TESTING

Business Question: Will revising the Procurement Services audit criteria for reviewing and approving input data on the requisition form reduce the number of errors per requisition? (See 4.5.1 for list of actual changes made)

Statistical Question: The statistical question we attempted to answer was, "Will the mean ratio of errors to requisitions with the *original* auditing requirements be different enough from the mean ratio of errors to requisitions with the *revised* auditing requirements to be considered important?"

> Ho: Null Hypothesis   Ma = Mb

The mean of the historical population of errors IS EQUAL to the mean of the new population. Our action has had NO effect, no improvement is shown.

> Ha: Alternative Hypothesis   Ma > Mb

The mean of the historical population of errors IS GREATER than the mean of the new population. Our action DID cause an improvement and did reduce the mean.

Due to the nature of this transactional process, the hypothesis test data was not normally distributed according to the Anderson-Darling Normality Test (See Section 4.7, Confidence Interval for Population Mean). This situation resulted in the use of nonparametric statistical testing to evaluate the hypothesis results. Our P value was .000. Per the hypothesis testing selection chart, if P is less than .05, you need to complete a Homogeneity of Variance test.

Homogeneity of Variance Test for Response

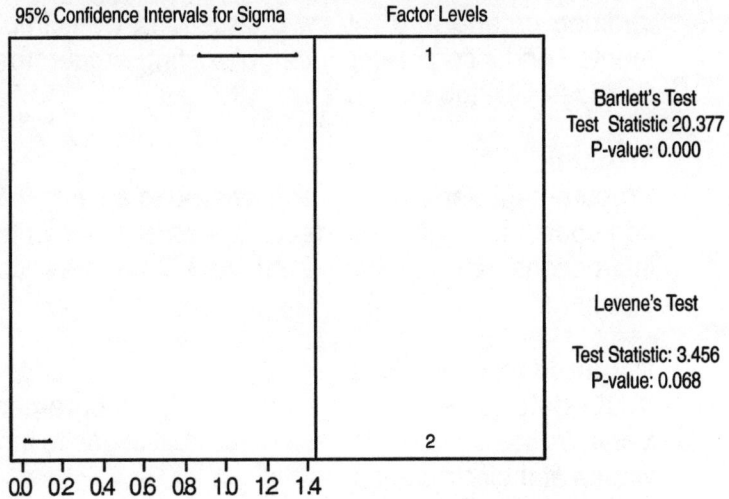

95% Confidence Intervals for Sigma   Factor Levels

1

Bartlett's Test
Test Statistic 20.377
P-value: 0.000

Levene's Test

Test Statistic: 3.456
P-value: 0.068

2

0.0 0.2 0.4 0.6 0.8 1.0 1.2 1.4

Levene's test told us that our P value was .068, which is greater than .05. The hypothesis test road map then directed us to complete a Mood Median Test:

Mood Median Test for Response

Chi-Square = 5.10   DF = 1   P = 0.024

Factors	N<=	N>	Median	Q3-01	
1	27	30	1.36	1.00	
1	5	0	0.05	0.08	

Overall median = 1.25
NOTE Levels with < 6 observations have confidence < 95%
A 95.0% CI for median (1): - median (2): (1.17, 1.54)

RESULTS:
       The median was now .05 and P was equal to 0.024. **If P is less than .05 you must reject the Null Hypothesis (Ho), and accept the Alternative Hypothesis (Ha).** We proved that the mean of the historical population of errors is greater than the mean of the new population. *Our actions did cause an improvement and did reduce the mean.*

4.5.1 AUDITING/REVIEW INSTRUCTIONS

On November 3, 19XX the following changes in our auditing criteria and review instructions were implemented and incorporated into the existing Procurement Services desktop instructions.

Inspection:
Procurement Services was empowered to enter inspection code if missing, or correct if necessary, per written instructions dated 8/18/XX from Pro3 Data Base Management.

Required Delivery Date:
If NO date is listed in this data field, Procurement Services has been empowered to default to one to three weeks at their discretion.

Command Media will be updated on the intranet to advise our customers that if there is no date listed or urgent requirement noted in this data field, the system will default to a maximum of three weeks. The default will depend on the complexity of the purchase.

Work Order / GL:
No change at this time. The end user currently is the only one who can determine the financial account to be charged for the purchase. If this data field is empty, Procurement Services must continue to contact the originator for the required data.

The team intends to work with both Accounting and Information Systems to improve the communication and availability of the required information for this data field and update the Command Media with complete instructions.

Estimated Cost:
If NO cost is stated, Procurement Services has been empowered to estimate the cost at .01 to satisfy the computer system requirements for data entry (Per Procurement Procedures, the Buyer can commit up to $2,500.00 without consulting the originator for approval).

Command Media will be updated on the intranet to advise our customers that if there is NO estimated cost data or budget stated in this data field, the system will default to .01 and the Buyer can commit up to $2,500 without further approval.

Unit of Measure:
Procurement Services empowered to enter the UOM if missing or correct if necessary, per the written instructions from Pro3 Data Base Management. Command Media will be updated on the intranet, with clear instructions given for this data block.

4.6   Confidence Interval for Population Mean

The confidence interval shown below was used by the team to verify that the sample data being evaluated during this project reflected the actual population characteristics, and confirmed the probability that the mean in the sample is the same as the mean in the total population. The descriptive statistics also demonstrated that our sample data was not normally distributed and was skewed as confirmed by the Normal Probability Plot which follows on page 287.

Descriptive Statistics

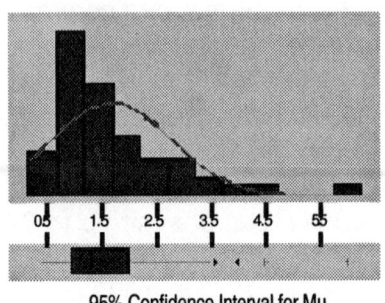

95% Confidence Interval for Mu

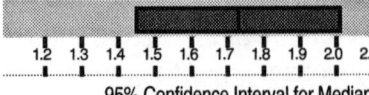

95% Confidence Interval for Median

Variable Ratio or
Anderson-Darling Normality Test

A-squared	2.728
P-value	0.000
Mean	1.73158
SD	1.06649
Variance	1.13740
Skewness	1.68657
Kurtosis	3.28561
N	57
Minimum	0.4700
1st Quartile	1.0000
Median	1.3600
3rd Quartile	2.0000
Maximum	6.0000

95% Confidence Interval for Mu
1.44860   2.01456

95% Confidence Interval for Sigma
0.90000039   1.300831

95% Confidence Interval for Median
1.18659   1.67000

Note: The mean of 1.73158 on the above chart is different from the mean of 1.62 stated in my problem statement, and can be explained as follows: When the team originally started collecting and entering data into our check sheets, we failed to establish a cut-off date for our monthly data. For example, in October we received requisitions dated in August or September, and we went back and entered these requisitions and error data into the appropriate spreadsheets. When the Six Sigma Candidate was taught about confidence interval charts, the back-up data was different from the original data used to establish the original 1.62 primary metric. When this discrepancy was discovered by the Six Sigma Instructor during his project review, we established a cut off date of two (2) days after the end of any one month period.

Normal Probability Plot

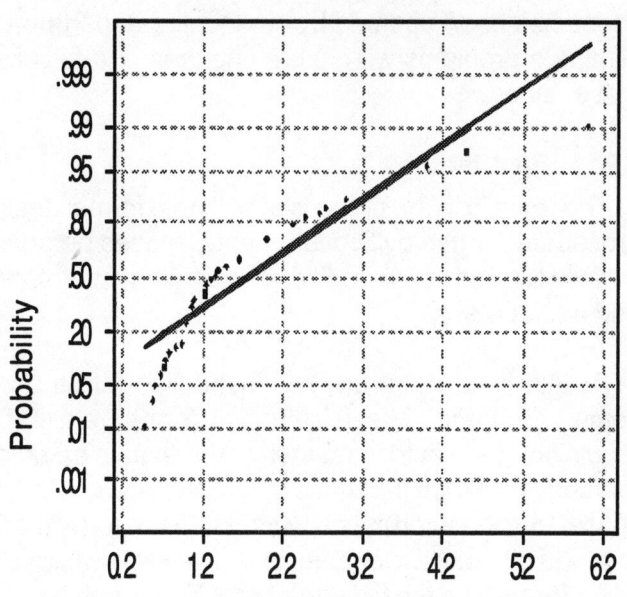

Ratio of Errors to Requisitions

Average: 1.73153
SD: 1.06649
N 57

Anderson-Darling Normality Test
A-squared: 2.728
P-value: 0.000

5.0   IMPROVEMENT ACTIONS

5.1   Implemented:

1) The auditing criteria for reviewing and approving input data on the requisition form was reviewed and revised as outlined in Section 4.5.1. All effected personnel were trained and written desktop instructions provided.

2) The existing internal procedures and guidelines on the company intranet were reviewed and found to contain numerous inspection code and unit of measure code errors. These errors have been corrected. The internal procedure for updating, revising, or correcting these codes has been updated by our Quality Department, to eliminate problems with future changes or additions to these codes.

5.2   Planned:

1) The team is in the process of writing a formal desktop procedure for use by Procurement Services personnel, which will clearly outline all requisition data requirements and audit criteria.

2) At this time, there are two instruction forms on the company intranet. These instruction forms state that the requisition form is the first step in the execution of; a) a material or service purchase or, b) the material plan. It is critical that the information written into the form is accurate and complete. Company A is using two basic requisition forms with these instructions. The Purchase Requisition and (PR) instructions are utilized on "indirect" requirements. The instruction document is fourteen pages long. The Direct Purchase Requisition and (DPR) instructions are used on "direct" requirements in support of a program's time phased net requirements. The instruction document is sixteen pages long. It is obvious to the team that these instruction forms are too long and unwieldy and their length precludes people from reading and understanding all the requirements. At this time, the team is in the process of combining both sets of instructions into one all-inclusive document for ease of use by all company requisitioners.

6.0   CONTROL/MISTAKE-PROOFING

Mistake-proofing is a tool for achieving zero defects by detecting errors at their source. The Six Sigma transactional candidate will continue to collect and analyze all requisition and error data. The candidate intends to contact personnel making errors, and train them as necessary to eliminate repeat or future errors. The process metric established during this project will continue to be generated on a monthly basis by the Six Sigma Candidate and distributed to the process owners.

The team originally planned to implement the use of one electronic requisition form. This form would have electronic links and "pull down menus" for each of the nineteen required data blocks on the requisition. If there were questions regarding how to fill out the form or any one particular block, one "click" and the requisitioner would be linked to the instruction form for clarification. Missing or wrong information would be eliminated and errors would not be passed on to the customer. However, as stated in Section 7.3, Company A is in the process of evaluating a new Enterprise Resource Planning application, so any additional changes to the manual requisition process have been put on hold until the abilities of SAP are known.

7.0   CONCLUSIONS:

7.1   Discussion of Results:
Accurately defining the incoming manual requisition process and defining the data requirements was very important. During discussions supporting the development of the process flow, an error in our existing command media was detected. At that time, we empowered our Procurement Services Personnel to enter missing codes and to correct erroneous data when necessary. The team then corrected much of the command media that was available to requisition writers on the company intranet. Additional changes and corrections are still in process.

The term "sigma" is used to designate the distribution or spread about the mean or average of a process, and indicates how well the process is performing. The common measurement is "defects per unit" and measures the capability of the process to perform defect-free-work. A defect is anything that results in customer dissatisfaction. As sigma increases, cost and cycle time go down, and customer satisfaction goes up. The capability of our existing process was calculated using data collected from August 19XX, through January 19XX. We calculated our DPMO, or Defects Per Million Opportunities, and utilized the following chart to calculate our short term Sigma capability.

Short-Term Sigma Capability

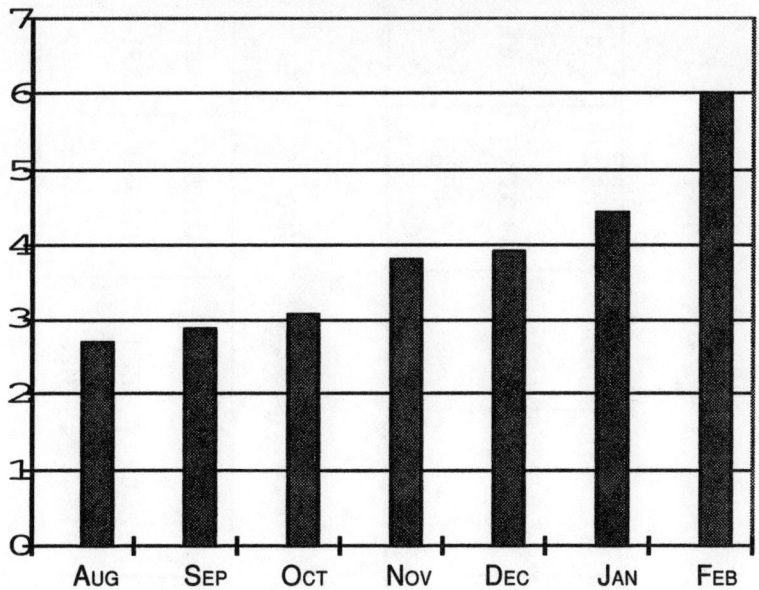

The following process capability analysis was completed for the period of November 19XX, through January 19XX, and clearly shows an improvement from the original analysis shown in Section 3.4. The one data point shown outside the upper specification limit represents two requisitions written on November 19XX, which contained a total of four errors Req. S00452 one error, (Work Order missing) and Req. M42697 three errors, (change Req. Number, Work Order and charge department missing). Both originators were contacted and trained to eliminate data errors on future requisitions.

The original Pareto Chart (See Section 4.4) was completed so the team could focus on which blocks of data were most frequently filled out incorrectly. At that time, 74 percent of the problems were contained in the following five blocks of data: Inspection (33 percent, 194 errors), Required Delivery Date (15 percent, 89 errors), Work Order/GL (9 percent, 55 errors), Estimated Cost

DEFECTS PER MILLION OPPORTUNITIES
PRIOR TO ANY FORMAL PROCESS IMPROVEMENTS

Reqs/m	#of Req Produced	Defects Observed	DPU	Number of Ops	DPMO	Total Ops	DPO	Zst Sigma
Manual req 8/97	41	90	2..195	19	115,533	799	0.115533	2..70
Manual req 9/97	83	130	1.566	19	82,435	1577	0.082435	2.89
Manual req 10/97	342	376	1.099	19	57,864	6498	0.057864	3.07

DEFECTS PER MILLION OPPORTUNITIES
AFTER INITIATING FORMAL PROCESS IMPROVEMENTS

Reqs/m	#of Req Produced	Defects Observed	DPU	Number of Ops	DPMO	Total Ops	DPO	Zst Sigma
Manual req 11/97	195	39	0.2000	19	10,526	3705	0.010526	3.81
Manual req 12/97	104	15	0.1442	19	7,591	1976	0.007591	3.93
Manual req	59	2	0.0339	19	1784	1121	0.001784	4.41

(9 percent, 53 errors), and Unit of Measure (8 percent, 49 errors). The number of errors in each data block ranged from a low of 11 errors (Total Estimated Cost) to a high of 194 errors (Inspection).

On January, 19XX, we completed a follow-up Pareto Chart, utilizing the requisition data from November 19XX, through January 19XX. This chart clearly shows improvement in all data blocks. The number of errors in each data block range from one to twelve errors. The chart does point out the continuing problem with the Work Order/GL block. The team is working with Accounting and Information Systems to improve the communication and availability of the required information for this data field to eliminate errors in the future.

Defects By Data Blocks Nov. - Jan.

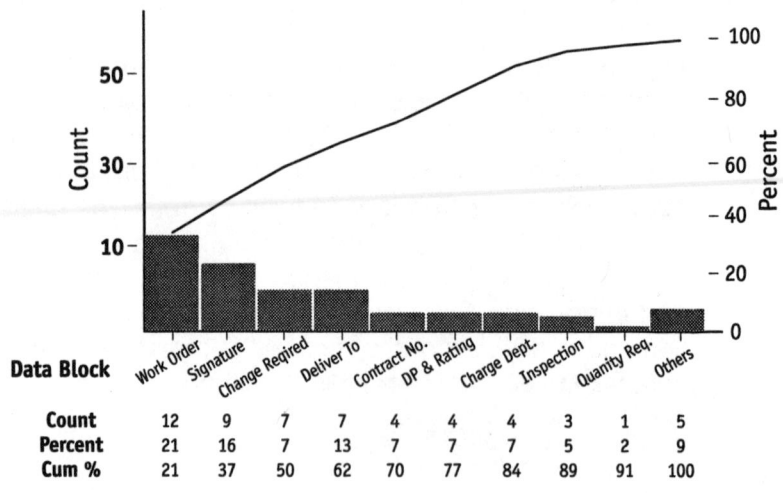

Data Block	Work Order	Signature	Change Reqired	Deliver To	Contract No.	DP & Rating	Charge Dept.	Inspection	Quanity Req.	Others
Count	12	9	7	7	4	4	4	3	1	5
Percent	21	16	7	13	7	7	7	5	2	9
Cum %	21	37	50	62	70	77	84	89	91	100

Process Capability Analysis Nov. - Jan.

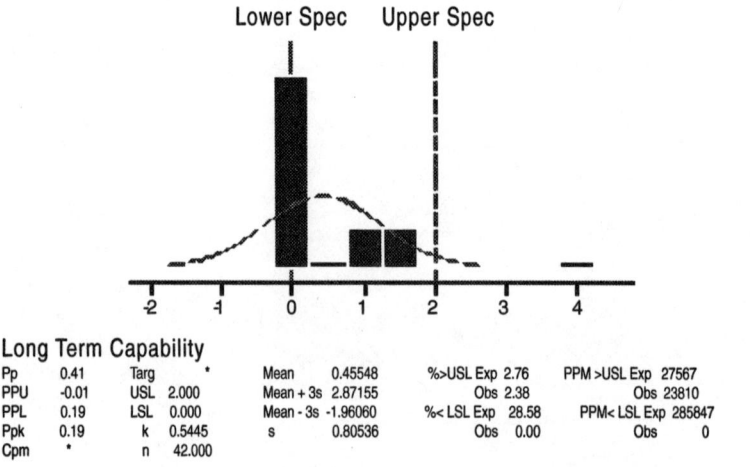

Long Term Capability

Pp	0.41	Targ	*	Mean	0.45548	%>USL Exp	2.76	PPM >USL Exp	27567
PPU	-0.01	USL	2.000	Mean + 3s	2.87155	Obs	2.38	Obs	23810
PPL	0.19	LSL	0.000	Mean - 3s	-1.96060	%< LSL Exp	28.58	PPM< LSL Exp	285847
Ppk	0.19	k	0.5445	s	0.80536	Obs	0.00	Obs	0
Cpm	*	n	42.000						

7.2   Lessons Learned / Recommendations:

1) All Six Sigma Transactional Candidates should have a strong mathematical and statistical analysis background. The candidate should have training on a lap-top computer, and be skilled in the use of various computer programs such as Microsoft Word, Excel, and PowerPoint.

2) While all members of my team were active and supportive, it would have been helpful if they knew more about the Six Sigma methodology and "why" we were doing what we were doing. An all-hands meeting should be held for all employees to outline the Six Sigma philosophy so the roles and expectations of team members are clearly defined to themselves and their management at the start of any project assignment.

3) The Six Sigma process is very demanding and time-consuming. All team members should be allocated adequate hours within their work schedule to support the project in an effective and timely manner.

7.3   Future Plans:

The team would like to see a plan to limit the number of requisition writers and implement the use of ONE intranet electronic requisition form for all purchases. The form would ensure the transfer of complete, valid data from our customer to the buyer. At this time, company A is in the process of evaluating a new Enterprise Resource Planning application, called SAP, for implementation. Accordingly, any additional changes to the manual requisition process have been put on hold until the capabilities of SAP are known.

7.4 Closing Comments:

7.4.1 Team Members

My team was committed to the success of this project, and without their dedication and support, this project would not have been successful. My team included the following individuals:

EB - Procurement Services
VM - Procurement Services
MK - Lead Buyer, Procurement
RP - Buyer, Procurement
JL - Product Planner, Statistical Analyst and Right Hand Man
HM - Procurement Material Planner & Requisition Writer
DV - Quality Assurance, Quality Engineer
JH - Procurement, Six Sigma Candidate

7.4.2 Acknowledgments/Additional Support

Special thanks to the following individuals for their support:

BY - Six Sigma Champion
JM - Six Sigma Black Belt
BH - IS Support
MS, PM and BF (Fellow Transactional Candidates: With their help, support, computer and mathematical skills, I survived the training classes. Thank you!)
BH - for just (and still!) being there

8.0 BIBLIOGRAPHY

Six Sigma Transactional Quality Training Manual
The Memory Jogger II, Michael Brassard & Diane Ritter
Six Sigma Tool Kit, Six Sigma Consultants, Inc.
Business Statistics, Third Edition -Douglas Downing and Jeffrey Clark
The Vision of Six Sigma, Mikel J. Harry Ph.D, 1994

Appendix D & E

Appendix D -See insert in CD packet for explanation of Six Sigma for Leadership presentations.

Appendix E -See insert in CD packet for installation of MINITAB software 60-day trial copy.

www.dosixsigma.com

Bibliography

Abramovitz, M., and I.A. Stegun. Editors. (1964) *Handbook of Mathematical Functions.* National Bureau of Standards Applied Mathematics Series 55, Washington, D.C., p. 955.

Anderson, V.L., and R.A. McLean. (1974) *Design of Experiments.* New York: Marcel Dekker.

Andreasen, M.S. Kahler, and T. Lund. (1983) *Design for Assembly.* IFS Publications, Ltd.

Baldwin, L.V. (1983). "New Modes for Advanced Engineering Study." *Journal of Engineering Education; Vol.* 31, pp. 384-386.

Bancroft, C. (1988) "Overlooked Aspects of Design for Manufacturability." *IEEE Circuits Devices Mag.* USA;Vol. 4, No. 6, Nov. pp. 15-19.

Barker, Paul A. (1989) "Design for Manufacturability." *Printed Circuit Design, Vol.* 6, No. 1, Jan. pp. 37-38.

Battin, L. (1988) "Six Sigma Process by Design." *Design and Dimensions, a Publication of Group Mechanical Technology; Vol.* 1, No. 1, p. 4, Government Electronics Group, Motorola Inc.

Baumeister, T., and L.S. Marks. (1967) *Standard Handbook for Mechanical Engineers.* New York: McGraw-Hill Book Co.

Becker, David. (1988) "Flex Circuitry: Designing for Manufacturability." *Printed Circuit Design; Vol.* 5, No. 8, Aug. pp. 54-57.

Bender, A. (1962) "Benderizing Tolerances - A Simple Practical Probability Method of Handling Tolerances for Limit-Stack-Ups." *Graphic Science.* Dec.

Bender, A. (1968) "Statistical Tolerancing as it Relates to Quality Control and the Designer." *Society of Automotive Engineers;* SAE Paper No. 680490, May.

Billatos, Samir B. (1988) "Guidelines for Productivity and Manufacturability Strategy." *Manufacturing Review,* Univ. of Connecticut, Storrs, CT., Vol. 1, No. 3, Oct. pp. 164-167.

Bohling, D.M., and L.A. O'Neill. (1970) "Interactive Computer Approach to Tolerance Analysis." *IEEE Trans Comput; C*19(1), pp. 10-16.

Boltz, Roger W. (1977) *Production Processes - The Producibility Handbook.* North Carolina: Conquest Publications.

Boothroyd, G., et al. (1982) *Automatic Assembly.* New York: Marcel Decker, Inc.

Boothroyd, G. and P. Dewhurst. (1986) *Product Design for Assembly.* Rhode Island: Boothroyd Dewhurst, Inc.

Boothroyd, G., and P. Dewhurst. (1983) *Design for Assembly: A Designer's Handbook.* Rhode Island: Boothroyd Dewhurst, Inc.

Box, G., and S. Bisgaard. (1988) "Statistical Tools for Improving Designs." *Mechanical Engineering,* Jan.

Box, G.E.P., et al. (1978) *Statistics for Experimenters.* New York: John Wiley and Sons, Inc.

Boyer, David E., and J.W. Nazemetz. (1985) Introducing Statistical Selective Assembly - A Means of Producing High Precision Assemblies from Low Precision Components." *Proceedings, American Institute of Industrial Engineers.* Annual Conference and Convention, pp. 562-570.

Bralla, J.G. (1986) *Handbook of Product Design for Manufacturing.* New York: McGraw-Hill Book Co.

Brayton, R.K., et al. (1980). "Yield Maximization and Worst-Case Design with Arbitrary Statistical Distributions." *IEEE Transactions on Circuits and Systems; Vol.* 27, No. 9, pp. 756-764.

Breyfogle, Forrest W., (1999) *Implementing Six Sigma: Smarter Solutions Using Statistical Methods,* John Wiley and Sons, Inc., New York, NY

Brown, John 0. (1987) "Producibility Problem Solving Or the Supplier Quality Paradox - A Fix?" *Annual Quality Congress Transactions.* (Forty-First Edition). Wisconsin: ASQC.

Bunselmeyer, K. (1987) "Manufacturability Checklist for Printed Wiring Assemblies." *Printed Circuit Des.* Missouri: Manuf. Eng. Srvcs. Vol. 4, No. 6, Jun. pp. 23-4.

Burgess, John A. (1984) *Design Assurance for Engineers and Managers.* New York: Marcel Dekker.

Charbonneau, Harvey C., and G. L. Webster. (1978) *Industrial Quality Control.* New Jersey: Prentice-Hall.

Chase, K.W., and W.H. Greenwood. (1987) "Design Issues in Mechanical Tolerance Analysis." *ASME Conference Paper.* Winter Annual Meeting of the American Society of Mechanical Engineers. Dec. 13-18. pp. 11-26.

Cochran, W., and G. Cox. (1957) *Experimental Designs.* (Second Edition). New York: John Wiley and Sons.

Coffman, Cathy. (1987) "Make Me A Match: Getting Design and Manufacturing Together - Simultaneously." *Automotive Industries; Vol.* 167, No. 12, Dec. pp. 62-64.

Cooke, et. al. (1984) *A Guide to Design for Production.* Institution of Production Engineers.

Cowden, Dudley J. (1957) *Statistical Methods in Quality Control.* New Jersey: Prentice-Hall.

Cramer, H. (1964) *Mathematical Methods of Statistics.* New Jersey: Princeton University Press.

Daetz, D. (1987) "The Effect of Product Design on Product Quality and Product Cost." *Manuf. Res. Center.* California: Hewlett-Packard Labs. Vol. 20, No. 6, 64(7), Jun.

Daniel, C. (1976) *Applications of Statistics To Industrial Experimentation.* New York: John Wiley and Sons.

Dao-Thien, My. (1981) "Approach for Optimum Tolerancing of the Design Components." *CANCAM Proceedings.* Canadian Congress of Applied Mechanics 8th, Vol. 1, pp. 333-334.

DeGarmo, Paul. (1974) *Materials and Processes in Manufacturing.* (Fourth Edition). New York: MacMillan.

Deming, W. Edwards. (1982) *Quality, Productivity and Competitive Position.* Massachusetts Institute of Technology, Center for Advanced Engineering Study. Cambridge, MA.

Deming, W. Edwards. (1986) *Out of the Crisis,* MIT Center for Advanced Engineering Study, Cambridge, MA.

Department of the Navy. (1986) *Best Practices for Transitioning from Development to Production.* NAVSO P-607 1. Washington.

DeVor, R.E. (1987) "Role of Parameter Design in the Simultaneous Engineering of Products and Processes." *American Society of Mechanical Engineers, Production Engineering Division.* New York: Vol. 27. pp 131-135.

Doyle, L.E., et al. (1969) *Manufacturing Processes and Materials for Engineers.* New Jersey: Prentice-Hall, Inc.

Duncan, Acheson, J. (1965) *Quality Control and Industrial Statistics.* (Third Edition). Illinois: Richard D. Irwin, Inc.

Dwivedi, Suren N., and B. R. Klein. (1986) "Design for Manufacturability Makes Dollars and Sense." CIM *Rev; Vol.* 2, No. 3, pp. 53-59.

Evans, David H. (1958) "Optimum Tolerance Assignment to Yield Minimum Manufacturing Cost." *Bell System Technical Journal;* 37(2).

Evans, David H. (1970) "Statistical Tolerancing Formulation." *Journal of Quality and Technology;* 2(4), pp. 226-231.

Evans, David H. (1972) "Application of Numerical Integration Techniques to Statistical Tolerancing - III." *Technometrics;* 14(1), pp. 23-35.

Evans, David H. (1974) "Statistical Tolerancing: The State of the Art, Part 1: Background. "Journal *of Quality and Technology;* 6(4), pp. 188-195.

Evans, David H. (1975) "Statistical Tolerancing: The State of the Art, Part II: Methods for Estimating Moments." *Journal of Quality and Technology;* 7(1), pp. 1- 12.

Farag, M.M. (1979) *Materials and Process Selection in Engineering.* London, England: Applied Science Publishers Ltd.

Feigenbaum, A.V. (1961) *Total Quality Control.* New York: McGraw-Hill Book Co.

Fortini, E.T. (1967) *Dimensioning for Interchangeable Manufacture.* New York: Industrial Press.

Gardiner, Paul. and Roy Rothwell. (1985) 'Tough Customers: Good Designs." *Design Studies; Vol.* 6, No. 1, Jan. pp. 7-17.

Grant, E.L., and R.S. Leavenworth. (1972) *Statistical Quality Control.* (Fourth Edition). New York: McGraw-Hill Book Co.

Greenwood, G. (1986) "Manufacturability and Testability Issues Increase Design Creativity." *Automated Design and Engineering for Electronics West.* Proceedings of the Technical Sessions, 209-11. Illinois: Cahmers Exposition Group.

Greenwood, W.H., and K.W. Chase. (1987) "A New Tolerance Analysis Method for Designers and Manufacturers." *Journal of Engineering for Industry; Vol.* 109, pp. 112-116.

Guenther, W. (1973) *Concepts of Statistical Interference.* New York: McGraw-Hill Book Co.

Hadley, G. (1967) *Introduction to Probability and Statistical Decision Theory.* California: Holden-Day, Inc.

Hahn, G., and S. Shapiro. (1967) *Statistical Models In Engineerings.* New York: John Wiley and Sons.

Hald, A. (1952) *Statistical Theory with Engineering Applications.* New York: John Wiley and Sons.

Harry, Mikel J. (1987) *Electrical Engineering Application of the Taguchi Design Philosophy.* Government Electronics Group, Motorola, Inc.

Harry, Mikel J. (1987). *The Nature of Six Sigma Quality.* Government Electronics Group, Motorola, Inc.

Harry, Mikel J and J. Ronald Lawson. *Six Sigma Producibility Analysis and Process Characterization* 1992, Addison-Wesley Publishing Company.

Harry, Mikel J. (1994a) *The Vision of Six Sigma: A Roadmap for Breakthrough,* Sigma Publishing Co., Phoenix, AZ.

Harry, Mikel J. (1994b) *The Vision of Six Sigma: tools and Methods for Breakthrough,* Sigma Publishing Co., Phoenix, AZ.

Harry, Mikel J. (1998) "Six Sigma: A Breakthrough Strategy for Profitability." *Quality Progress,* May. pp. 60-64.

Harry, Mikel J., and R. Schroeder. (2000) *Six Sigma: The Breakthrough Management Strategy Revolutionizing the World's Top Corporations,* Doubleday/Currency, New York, NY.

Heath, H.H. (1979) "Statistical Tolerancing of Engineering Components: Is It Worth It?" *Precision Engineering;* 1(3), pp. 153-156.

Hennessey, Mike, and G. Krutz. (1986) "Expert CAD System for Statistical Tolerancing Internal Hydraulic Components." *Proceedings of the National Conference on Fluid Power.,* Annual Meeting 41st, pp. 115-120.

Hicks, C.R. (1964) *Fundamental Concepts in the Design of Experiments.* New York: McGraw-Hill Book Co.

Hicks, T.G. (1972) *Standard Handbook of Engineering Calculations.* New York: McGraw-Hill Book Co.

Hunter, J.S. (1985) "Statistical Design Applied to Product Design." *Qual. Technol.; Vol.* 17, No. 4, Oct. 210(21).

Ishikawa, Kaoru. (1976) *Guide to Quality Control.* Asian Productivity Organization, Revised Edition.

John, P.W.M. (1971) *Statistical Design and Analysis of Experiments.* New York: The McMillan Company.

Johnson, L.G. (1964) *Theory and Techniques of Variation Research.* Elsevier Publishing Co.

Jones, S.W. (1973) *Product Design and Process Selection.* London, England: Butterworts.

Joshi, Dileep C. (1985) *Advantages of Simultaneous Design of Product and Processes.* Proceedings of the National Electronics Conference; Vol. 39, Professional Education Int. Inc. pp. 650-657.

Juran, J.M., and Frank M. Gryna Jr. (1970) *Quality Planning and Analysis.* New York: McGraw-Hill Book Co.

Juran, J.M., et. al. (1976) *Juran's Quality Control Handbook,* 4th ed. McGraw-Hill, New York, NY.

Kackar, R.N. (1985) "Off Line Quality Control, Parameter Design, and the Taguchi Method." *Journal of Quality Technology;* 17(4), pp. 176-188.

Kackar, R.N., and A.C. Shoemaker. (1986) *Robust Design: A Cost-effective Method for Improving Manufacturing Processes.* New Jersey: AT&T Bell Labs. Vol. 65, No. 2, Mar.-Apr. pp. 39-50.

Kelly Sines, R. (1988) *Integrating Simultaneous Engineering Into New Product Introduction.* Sponsor: Troy Conferences; Boothroyd & Dewhurst. Proceedings of the 3rd International Conference on Product Design for Manufacture and Assembly. Michigan: Troy Conferences. 10 pp.

Kempthrone, 0. (1952) *The Design and Analysis of Experiments.* New York.

Kendall, M.G., and A. Stuart. (1963) *The Advanced Theory of Statistics.* New York: Hafner Publishing Co.

King, James R. (1971) *Probability Charts for Decision Making.* New York: The Industrial Press.

King, Robert. (1987) "Listening to the Voice of the Customer: Using the Quality Function Deployment System." *National Productivity Review; Vol. 6,* No. 3, pp. 277-281.

Knauer, Karl, and H. J. Pfleiderer. (1982) "Yield Enhancement Realized for Analogue Integrated Filters by Design Techniques." *IEEE Proceedings, Part 1: Solid-State and Electron Devices;* 129(2), pp. 67-7 1.

Kwok-Leung, Tsui. (1988) "Strategies for Planning Experiments Using Orthogonal Arrays and Confounding Tables." *Qual. Reliab: Eng. Int.* AT&T Bell Lab., New Jersey (UK), Vol. 4, No. 2, Apr.-Jun. pp. 113-122.

Langford, T. (1986). "Design for Manufacturability - Cooperation +CAD+CIM." *Automated Design and Engineering for Electronics.* East. Proceedings of the Technical Sessions, NCR, Corp; Illinois: Cahners Exposition Group, Sep.-Oct. pp. 45-54.

Lewis, G.M. (1988) "Design for Manufacturability Applying the Methodology." *Proceedings of the 3rd International Conference on the Product Design for Manufacture and Assembly.* Michigan: Troy Conferences.

Lichtenberg, L.R., M. Sleiman, and M.J. Harry. (1986) "Statistics, Designed Experiments Assembly." *Circuit World, Journal of the Institute of Circuit Technology;* 12(4), pp. 34-39.

Lin, K.M., and R.N. Kacker. (1986) "Optimizing the Wave Soldering Process." *Packaging and Production;* Feb. pp. 108-115.

Lipson, C., and N. Sheth. (1973) *Statistical Design and Analysis of Engineering Experiments.* New York: McGraw Hill Book Co.

Little, R.E. (1980) "Statistical Tolerance Limits for Censored Log-Normal Data (Tolerance Limit Computations: Fatigue Life Applications.)" *Journal of Testing and Evaluation;* 8(2), pp. 80-84.

Lowe, J. (1998) *Jack Welch Speaks,* Wiley, New York, NY

Maddoux, K.C., and S.C. Jain. (1986) "CAE for the Manufacturing Engineer: The Role of Process Simulation In Concurrent Engineering." *American Society of Mechanical Engineers. Production Engineering Division.* New York: ASME, Vol. 20, Dec. pp. 1-15.

Mansoor, E.M. (1963) "The Application of Probability to Tolerances Used in Engineering Design." *Proceedings, Institute of Mechanical Engineering;* 178 1 (1).

McGregory, J., and H. Conklin. (1986) "Analyzing Manufacturability and the Effects of Design Changes." *Printed Circuit Des.;* Vol. 3, No. 5, May pp. 25-27, 3 1.

McFadden, F.R. (1993) Six Sigma Quality Programs, *Quality Progress,* June pp. 37

Melander, W., and K. Mast. (1986) "Design for Manufacturability: It's Not Just Design Rules Anymore." ATE East - E.I. Conference #10327, Hewlett-Packard Co., Massachusetts: MG Expositions Group. June pp. IV 11AV. 21.

Mendenhall, W., and R. Schaeffer. (1973) *Mathematical Statistics With Applications.* Massachusetts: Duxbury Press.

Mercadante, M. (1986) "The Hewlett Packard Company's Approach to Design for Manufacturability." *Automated Design and Engineering for Electronics* - Proceedings of the Technical Sessions. IL: Cahners Exposition Group, Sep.-Oct. pp. 437.

Miller, Irwin, and J. E. Freund. (1965) *Probability and Statistics for Engineers.* New Jersey: Prentice-Hall, Inc.

Montgomery, D.C. (1984) *Design and Analysis of Experiments.* (Second Edition). John Wiley and Sons.

Mood, A. and F. Graybill. (1963) *Introduction To The Theory of Statistics.* (Second Edition). New York: McGraw-Hill Book Co.

Moses, L.E. (1959) *Elementary Decision Theory.* New York: John Wiley and Sons.

Myers, R.H. (1971) *Response Surface Methodology.* Massachussets: Allyn and Bacon, Inc.

Natrella, Mary G. (1963) *Experimental Statistics.* Washington, D.C.: National Bureau of Standards Handbook 9 1, Government Printing Office.

Neville, A.M., and LB. Kennedy. (1964) *Basic Statistical Methods for Engineers and Scientists.* International Textbook Co.

Nie, N.N., et al. (1975) *Statistical Package for the Social Sciences.* (Second Edition). New York: McGraw-Hill Book Co.

Oh, H.L. (1987) 'Variation Tolerant Design." *American Society of Mechanical Engineers - PED,* General Motors. New York: ASME. Vol. 27, pp. 137-146.

Olivera, R. (1988) *Sigma/Fit Tolerance Analysis.* Communications Sector, Motorola, Inc., Illinois.

Osborn, A. (1957) *Applied Imagination.* New York: Charles Scribner's Sons.

Ott, Ellis R. (1975) *Process Quality Control.* New York: McGraw-Hill Book Co.

Parry, G.W., et al. (1981) "Statistical Tolerance in Safety Analysis." *Nuclear Safety;* 22(4), pp. 459-463.

Patel, M.S. (1962) "GroupScreening with More Than Two Stages." *Technometrics;* 4(2), pp. 209-217.

Pearson, C. (1983) *Handbook of applied Mathematics,* (Second Edition). New York: Van Nostrand Reinhold Co.

Pearson, E.S., and H.O. Hartley. (1972) *Biometrika Tables for Statisticians; Vol.* 2. Cambridge, Eng.: Cambridge University Press.

Phadke, M.S., and K. Dehnad. (1988) "Optimization of Product and Process Design for Quality and Cost." *Quality and Reliability Engineering International.* AT&T Bell Lab. New Jersey: Vol. 4, No. 2, Apr-Jun. pp. 105-112.

Phadke, Madhav S. (1986) "Design Optimization Case Studies." *AT&T Tech. J.,* AT&T Bell lab. New Jersey: Vol. 65, No. 2, Mar.-Apr. pp. 51-68.

Pignatiello, J.J., and I.S. Ramberg. (1985) "Discussion." *Journal of Quality Technology;* 17(4) pp. 198-206.

Pike, E.W., and T.R. Silverberg. (1953) "Assigning Tolerances for Maximum Economy." *Machine Design;* Sep. pp. 139-146.

Plackett, R.L., and L.P. Burman. (1946) "The Design of Optimum Multifactorial Experiments." *Biometrika; Vol.* 33, pp. 305-325.

Priest, L.W. (1988) *Engineering Design for Producibility and Reliability.* New York: Marcel Dekker.

Ramalingam, Subbiah. (1985) "Expert Systems for Manufacturing: Examples of Tools to Assess Manufacturability." *SME;* 13th NAMRC Proceedings. Michigan: pp. 411-417.

Russell, G.A. (1985) "Design for Manufacturability of Printed Circuit Board Assemblies." *CIRP Annuals.* Berne, Switzerland: Technische Rundschau, Vol. 34, No. 1, Aug. pp. 37-40.

Ryan, Thomas P. (1988) "Taguchi's Approach to Experimental Design: Some Concerns." *Quality Progress.* ABI/Inform. Vol. 21, No. 5, May pp. 34-36.

Senge, P.M. (1990) *The Fifth Discipline: The Art and Practice of the Learning Organization,* Doubleday/Current, New York, NY.

Shewhart, W.A. (1931) *Economic Control of Manufactured Product.* New Jersey: Van Nostrand Book Co.

Shigley, Joseph E. (1972) *Mechanical Engineering Design.* (Second Edition). New York: McGraw-Hill Book Co.

Shoemaker, Anne C., and R. N. Kacker. (1988) "Methodology for Planning Experiments in Robust Product and Process Design." *Quality and Reliability Engineering Intn'l.* New Jersey: AT&T Bell Lab. Vol. 4, No. 2, Apr.-Jun. pp. 95-103.

Singhal, K., and J.F. Pinel. (1981) "Statistical Design Centering and Tolerancing Using Parametric Sampling." *IEEE Transactions on Circuits and Systems;* 28(7), pp. 692-701.

Slater, Robert. (1999) *The GE Way Field Book: Jack Welch's Plan for Corporate Revolution.* New York: McGraw-Hill.

Snedecor, G.W., and W.G. Cochran (1967) *Statistical Methods.* (Sixth Edition). Iowa State University Press.

Spotts, M.F. (1977) "Running the Risk of Interference Fits." *Machine Design;* 49(17), pp. 106-111.

Spotts, M.F. (1978) "Fast Dimensional Checks With Statistics." *Machine Design;* Oct. pp. 171-173.

Standard IPC-PC-90.(1989) *General Requirements for Implementation of Statistical Process Control.* Illinois: Institute for Interconnecting and Packaging Electronic Circuits.

Starkey, John M., and G. J. Florin. (1986) "Design for Manufacturability." *American Society of Mechanical Engineers (Paper).* New York: ASME. Pap 86-DET-121, 6p.

Tietjen, Gary L., and M. E. Johnson. (1979) "Exact Statistical Tolerance Limits for Sample Variances.--*Technometrics;* 21 (1), pp. 107-110.

Trucks, H.E. (1974) *Designing for Economical Production.* Michigan: Society of Manufacturing Engineers, 1974.

Wade, Oliver R. (1967) *Tolerance Control in Design and Manufacturing.* New York: Industrial Press, Inc.

Wallace, J.R., and L.L. Grant. (1977) "Least Squares Method for Computing Statistical Tolerance Limits." *Water Resources Research;* 13(5), pp. 819-823.

Wallis, W.A., and H.V. Roberts. (1956) *Statistics: A New Approach.* The Free Press.

Ward, L, and E. Jennings. (1973) *Introduction to Linear Models.* New Jersey: Prentice-Hall

Watson, G.S. (1961) "A Study of the Group Screening Method." *Technometrics;* 3(3), pp. 371-388.

Western Electric Company. (1956) *Statistical Quality Control Handbook.* Pennsylvania: Mack Printing Co.

Wheeler, D.J. (1988) *Understanding Industrial Experimentation.* Tennessee: Statistical Process Control Inc.

Index

G

H

I

K

L

M

P

Q

Y

Z

Order More Copies of
Six Sigma for Leadership
The Seven Principles of
Problem-Solving Technology
to Achieve Significant Financial Results

Order Form

Web-Site, Fax, Mail to:
www.dosixsigma.com
(505) 856-6771
Six Sigma, 8619 Tennyson NE, Albuquerque, NM 87122

Company Name:_____

Attention:_____

Address:_____

City:_____**State:**_____**Zip:**_____

Phone:_____**Fax:**_____

Email:_____

Soft Cover $69.95 (includes 2 CDs)

Quantity Ordering Pricing:

2-10 books	10% discount	$62.95 ea
10-100 books	20% discount	$55.95 ea
100+ call for pricing 1-877-587-4872		

Number of books_____x price_____=_____

Add $5 S&H for the first book, $2 each for books 2-25
and $1 for each book thereafter.

Total Amount Enclosed:_____

Visa/MC#_____**Exp:**_____

Signature:_____

VISIT US AT
www.dosixsigma.com

Be among the first to find out about Greg Brue's Leadership Training Seminars, open to corporate executives who want to become Champions of Six Sigma. New products will also be announced on the site.

www.dosixsigma.com

www.dosixsigma.com